DATE DUE

The Wedding

The Wedding

a Family's Coming Out Story

Douglas Wythe and Andrew Merling

Roslyn Merling and Sheldon Merling

AVON BOOKS ◆ NEW YORK

AVON BOOKS, INC.
An Imprint of HarperCollins*Publishers,*
10 East 53rd Street
New York, New York 10022-5299

Library of Congress Cataloging in Publication Data:
The wedding : a family's coming out story / Douglas Wythe . . . [et al.].—1st ed.
p. cm.
1. Wythe, Douglas—Marriage. 2. Merling, Andrew—Marriage. 3. Same-sex marriage.
4. Gay male couples—Attitudes. 5. Parents of gays—Attitudes. I. Wythe, Douglas.
HQ 1033. W43 2000
306.84'8—dc21   99-059512

First Avon Books Printing: March 2000

AVON TRADEMARK REG. U.S. PAT. OFF. AND IN OTHER COUNTRIES,
MARCA REGISTRADA, HECHO EN U.S.A.

Printed in the U.S.A.

FIRST EDITION

QPM   10   9   8   7   6   5   4   3   2   1

www.harpercollins.com

This book is for our beloved grandma,
Esther Briskin,
who gives us all cause for hope.

ACKNOWLEDGMENTS

We are indebted to the many editors, friends, and colleagues who've counseled, coached, and cheered us along the way: Hamilton Cain, Charlotte Abbott, Bret Witter, Jed Mattes, Eric Marcus, Lori Huck, Jacqueline Bolduc, Nancy Distel, Judith Kiersky, Roma Shuker, George Barrett, Geri Wolfsheimer, Nahum Gelber, Rebecca Posner, Mark Mazer, and Lona Lapin.

Our gratitude also goes to Kate Meehan for research and technical support.

Like a team of surgeons (except that they never operated in the same room), these psychologists helped each of us survive a delicate procedure: Dennis Karogeropoulos, Ph.D., April Martin, Ph.D., Lisa Kayata, Ph.D., and Elizabeth Halsted, Ph.D. We offer our heartfelt thanks to all of them.

Finally, our deep appreciation and admiration go to the team from ABC News who made network TV history with their *Turning Point* program "For Better or Worse: Same-Sex Marriage." We owe a particular debt of gratitude to the producer, Denise Schriener, who gave freely of her insight, intuition, time, and much, much more.

CONTENTS

Part Three: The Wedding

INTRODUCTION

Father, mother, son . . . and the man who popped the question. The four of us, Sheldon, Roslyn, Andrew, and I, waded together into treacherous waters at the instant I surprised Andrew with a proposal of marriage. And though we didn't know it at the time, we did the same thing once again when the four of us decided to tell that story here, in print.

Once the very words *gay marriage* were an oxymoron. Now the words—and the deed—seem to be everywhere. More and more gays and lesbians are getting wed. The news media is pushing gay marriage into the limelight. And as politicians debate whether to block recognition of same-sex marriages, the topic has become a lightning rod in "culture wars" across North America.

Our family learned firsthand how gay marriage polarizes society. Even on the very day of the event, we *still* couldn't agree on what to call it. Was it, as Andrew and I said, a "wedding" . . . or the "commitment ceremony" Sheldon and Roslyn described?

It wasn't a question of mere semantics; the disparity in those terms begged some enormous questions. Exactly what separated our union from that of any other couple? Was it simply different, or somehow less important? Was it cause for celebration or shame? Or could it be, incredibly, a reasonable cause for both?

Every wedding is fraught with complications. Through them we all learned how much our experience was both like and unlike that of any other family. Like most large weddings, this one was to be a gathering of three very different entities: family, friends, and community. For ages, interfaith unions have split these groups along a generational and philosophical divide. And although our ceremony brought together two Jewish families, it raised even deeper questions about faith, tradition, and the limits of love and acceptance.

Once we decided to tell this painful, joyful odyssey of discovery in print, our initial problems were twofold: how much would we tell and how would we tell it? We decided there wasn't any point in going through all the work unless we exposed ourselves fully, revealing all our doubts, fears, countless mistakes, and misunderstandings; in short, telling the truth.

Next problem: what, exactly was *that*? We soon discovered that truth was relative; we each recalled even the most unforgettable moments differently. Some discrepancies were staggering. It often seemed we were farther apart than different planets; we weren't even in neighboring galaxies. So the format for the book came naturally. We would tell it all from four separate perspectives, in our individual voices.

Now that we've put it all on paper, I'm personally struck by how many times, at crucial crossroads, I was right on the facts but wrong on the reality. I could see tiny details others seemed to miss, but was often blind to the bigger picture. It's an understatement to say all of us now view ourselves—and each other—with far more clarity and understanding since undertaking this book.

In deciding to expose ourselves, we couldn't help exposing—though to a lesser degree—family, friends, and acquaintances as well. For that reason, some names have been changed. There were other people, like Andrew's siblings and my parents, who, though we respect their very private natures, could not remain anonymous. They are each featured within the text to varying degrees. Certain aspects of the book's narrative might have been explored more fully, but we tried to regard our families' wishes.

So what motivated us to tell this story? First let me say what didn't drive us to write this book: We don't think gay marriage is the only—or necessarily the most significant—issue facing gays, lesbians, and their families. And we certainly don't advocate that every gay and lesbian couple run out and tie the knot. Of course, now that the book is complete, we hope it can help other families embarking on a same-sex wedding. If there had been a book like this when we faced our greatest conflicts, it could have helped us understand we weren't alone in our fear and frustration, and it might have also given all of us hope. Yet it wasn't marriage, per se, that moved us to begin this project. Rather, the inspiration for this book came months after the ceremony was over, when we realized that this story is ultimately about something much more important than a wedding. As our subtitle implies, getting married was another—and perhaps the biggest—step in "coming out."

For the four of us the wedding—like the "coming out" it demanded—was a process, not an event. (The same, it turned out, was true of writing this book.) Every step of the way, since the engagement was announced, each challenge was part of our process. All of the internecine haggling and negotiations, about everything from the location for our reception to the minutiae of the ceremony, turned out to be conduits through which we could channel our real concerns. The subtext that had long lurked beneath our relationships was slowly being forced to surface, with the wedding as a catalyst, driving us to find a new level of communication. At last we were required to reveal the secret fears we each had sought to hide even from ourselves. Confronting these fears, and the private guilt, anxiety, anguish, and shame that touched each of us in different manners, was complex. Each of us needed to "come out" and reveal his or her pain in personal ways. And while we each waged an internal battle to overcome our own demons, we had to negotiate a family struggle as well—endeavoring to gain acceptance from each other. And ultimately, thanks to each hurdle we passed, we came within reach of accepting ourselves as well.

—Doug Wythe
June 1999

PART ONE

Becoming Engaged

It's why things will change, have changed.
As much as laws, it's love that does it.

—ANNA QUINDLEN (1995)

January 1995

SHELDON Roslyn was out that Sunday morning, so when I answered the phone I was the first to hear Andrew's announcement: "Doug proposed. We're engaged."

Honestly, I wasn't exactly sure what he meant. So I asked, "Engaged to be what?"

"Married."

"Oh." I wasn't sure what to say next. "We'll talk about it."

ROSLYN Now, four years later, when we hear those words, "engaged to be what?" we smile. And we're amazed at how differently we all remember this pivotal moment.

ANDREW You see, I remember telling my mother first. And every one of us recalls crucial details differently. You'd expect our *opinions* to conflict. We were each seeing the world through our own filter. It appears those filters have shaped not just how we think, but what we remember.

So, given the wide spectrum of our individual perspectives, it seemed fitting that when we decided to share our journey in print, we chose to relate each of our experiences in our four separate voices.

DOUG Among the many truths that this journey has revealed to us, we now understand that getting married is the ultimate act of coming out. That's not to say it's the end of anything. With no final step, coming out is a ceaseless dance between concealment and disclosure. Yet there is perhaps no expression both so final and so inaugural for a gay couple and their family as pledging troth in a public commitment.

Over the span of almost two years, every comfort zone each of us crossed was a tiny point on an infinite graph, whose perhaps unreachable end is unfettered freedom to love who our hearts choose, wisdom to remain honest in the face of unenlightened judges, and strength to replace shame with unconditional acceptance. As we inched along that graph, each of us came closer to an absolute coming out—finding acceptance for ourselves, and each other, with a new willingness to be truthful about our love with everyone in our lives.

CHAPTER 1

A Risky Proposition

DOUG, ANDREW, SHELDON, AND ROSLYN

January 1995

DOUG I was dead set on finding an engagement ring by Andrew's birthday. It was just a week before we had dinner reservations at Sign of the Dove. You know, the one in the commercials where they served unsuspecting customers Folger's coffee. When you read about it in restaurant reviews, like the Zagat guide, it's invariably called a "favorite place to pop the question." I certainly hope that the genesis of our journey wasn't my reading that line in Zagat and saying to myself, "Gee, why don't we become the first gay couple to get engaged there!" Actually, I'm sure we weren't the first or the last.

Dinner was set for Saturday night, and here it was Wednesday, and not only didn't I have a ring, I didn't have the slightest idea what kind of ring I was looking for, or where to get it. Just weeks before, we'd been to dinner with our friend Rachel, her current boyfriend, and a friend of theirs, Carl, who's a jeweler. Now I asked Rachel to hook us up again so I could ask his advice. She gave me his number, and he offered a few suggestions, sending me to a gold wholesaler in the diamond district. Forty-seventh Street between Fifth Avenue and Sixth Avenue in Manhattan is the largest concentration of gold and diamond merchants in the world, and many, if not most, of those merchants are either Orthodox or ultraobservant Hasidic Jews.

By the time I went to the store he recommended, it was Friday. The saleswoman wasn't the intimidating type, yet I still broke into a sweat over my surroundings. I asked to see a simple gold ring with a comfort-fit band, per Carl's instructions. As I tried it on for a test (though I had no idea if Andrew and I wore the same size ring), it occurred to me that it might be odd for a man to be trying on a gold band. *Is this what straight people do, or is it obvious that I'm buying this for another man?* I wondered. *Do women buy them for their husbands, or what?* Even though it was perfectly possible that straight men buy their own rings, it suddenly seemed that the store's Orthodox personnel had peeked inside my bedroom, and frowned.

Once I had the ring, I went to see Carl, who has a business nearby. He said he'd buff and polish the ring as a favor, and I took him up on the offer. We talked about my plans to propose to Andrew. Even though this was a much more personal conversation than the one I had in the store, I wasn't uneasy. The difference was, I think, that he was an acquaintance rather than a total stranger. Also, I knew he wasn't an Orthodox Jew.

At the time, I couldn't possibly know this would be the first in a long series of interactions that shared a key element. For the next two years, many of our decisions would be directly influenced by the degree of religious conservatism that we faced at any given moment. For a largely secular Jew like me, this was a new and not entirely welcome feeling.

Carl wished me a sincere good luck, and I called Rachel when I got back to work, to thank her for helping me accomplish my mission so quickly. She sounded excited for us, and sent me off into the weekend with a wide-eyed, tingly anticipation.

Saturday, Andrew's twenty-ninth birthday, I went out to buy him flowers. I wondered if he had a hint of what I had up my sleeve. Since I have the polar opposite of a poker face, it seemed possible he might read my hand. But as we got dressed for dinner that night, I was confident he had no idea.

We took a cab across town to Sign of the Dove, and when we entered from the snow and chilly wind, the room was warm and inviting. I hoped we'd get a corner table for a little more privacy, but we wound up front and center in the corner dining room. We weren't the only gay couple in the room, but we were more of a minority than usual in this city.

Dinner sped along like any other, albeit with great food, but by the time the waiter asked if we wanted dessert, my butterflies were working overtime. I planned to take my chances with the ever-popular hiding-the-ring-in-the-dessert number, despite my fears that if anyone could wolf down a ring with his dessert, it would be Andrew. It's not that he has a sweet tooth . . . It's more like a chemical dependence to confectioner's sugar and chocolate.

But I hadn't addressed how I'd approach the waiter about the arrangements for the ring. Would I slip him the ring and ask him to slide it under the dessert, or would I chicken out and attempt to distract Andrew while I did the dirty work myself?

The choices for dessert weren't what I would have hoped for. In fact, the only one that appealed to Andrew was a pear tart, which happens to be one of the few desserts I'm not fond of. But after all, I thought, if we're about to enter into a lifetime filled with give and take, isn't it appropriate that it start with a compromise?

After the dessert was ordered, I excused myself from the table, caught the waiter, and gave him the ring. I'd decided he was probably gay, and if not, judging by the rest of the staff, he undoubtedly had some gay comrades. He smiled sweetly and said it would be taken care of.

My palms were moist with sweat by the time the tart arrived. At first I didn't see any of the gold poking out from under the front "V" of the tart, as I'd requested of the waiter. Visions of sitcom farce loomed before me as Andrew cut a piece from the tip and stuck his fork in. Would the ring wind up under another patron's dessert, the scene ending with my forced announcement to the room that the ring was really intended for my, ummm . . . boyfriend? Then, just as he carried the pear with its crumbling crust to his mouth, I could see the ring clearly on his plate. The buffing job showed off nicely in the light, and I was sure Andrew would stop his chewing and spy the glittering object jutting out beneath his pear tart. But without interruption, he dove right back in. Just as he was cutting off the next piece, I was forced to ask, "What's that under your dessert?" Andrew stopped, lifted his fork, and his expression went utterly blank. After a brief moment, his lips curled up at the edges into a slight smile, and his big hazel eyes grew very wide. He looked up from the ring and stared at me, his smile growing a little, but still showing me a face filled with surprise.

Finally I asked, "Well, what do you think?"

He said the obvious. "I'm surprised."

To which I replied with the even more obvious "Will you marry me?"

ANDREW We used to talk about it. "Maybe we'll get married one day . . ." And then we'd half joke, "Who would ask who?" In fact, I always thought I'd be the one to ask. In that particular area, I figured I'd be more gutsy. It was a brave thing to do, and I didn't expect Doug to go out on a limb with that first step.

Until then, I hadn't even fantasized about the specifics of what our wedding might be like. When Doug and I daydreamed about it, it was more of a vague concept, never an attainable goal.

But when Doug proposed, it changed everything. When I first

held the gold band and examined it, I wasn't playing dumb. I really hadn't gotten it yet.

Then Doug said the words. "Will you marry me?"

My immediate reaction was shock.

Of course, I said yes, but I was nervous, even scared. Just how scared, I didn't realize until later. Those feelings were hidden deep.

DOUG   There we were, sitting in the middle of this restaurant. I took Andrew's hand, and we looked a little longer into each other's eyes. But in an instant I realized that we weren't going to have a kiss in this place, at this time. It wasn't a bitter disappointment, just a fleeting, unfortunate reminder of how far we were from the world I wished for.

Over coffee (definitely not Folger's, by the way) I asked if he'd suspected what I was up to.

Andrew answered emphatically, "No. No way."

We started brainstorming when we'd want to marry, and where. Since our respective friends are spread over the continent, from West Coast to East, United States to Canada, we agreed we should have it on a holiday weekend. Andrew preferred getting married after his psychology internship ended, and that would put the date at Labor Day of '96. A year and nine months was a little further off than I imagined, but I wasn't in a hurry. I had one warning for Andrew: September is always the beginning of the new television season, making it one of my busiest months for work. That date would limit us to a very short honeymoon, a week at most.

ANDREW   One minute we're having a regular dinner out together, then all of a sudden a casual daydream is turning into a reality. Rather than succumb to the urge to panic, I began to obsess on every detail of the wedding and reception. I thought about my sisters, and what it had been like when they'd announced their engagements: from that instant, they'd been surrounded by a hoopla that hadn't ended until well after their weddings. And what weddings. Lavish, hundreds of guests, great food, photographers, the works. Every detail was attended to with great care. The material minutiae weren't important, though; it was what they signified that counted. All the trappings meant that what they were doing *mattered*, that it was important enough to warrant all this *stuff*.

I assumed that my nuptials would be attended to with the same excitement and enthusiasm. Only later did I realize how wrong I was.

DOUG   By now I'd had enough of the nuts and bolts. I wanted to know what was going on behind Andrew's glazed gaze.

I asked again, "So you were really surprised?"

"Totally," he said.

Our relationship had always been both loving and intense, and it had taken a number of zigs and zags over the previous three and a half years. It all started, as they say, when . . .

ANDREW   . . . Martin, a gay classmate, told me about a dating club called Brunch Buddies. It was the summer of 1991. I had just finished my first grueling year of graduate school in New York, and I had nothing to look forward to but heat, humidity, and a summer job in the neurology department at the Albert Einstein College of Medicine doing memory research. I was just coming out of a brief one-month, long-distance relationship with a nice Jewish doctor from Montreal (my mother would have been proud) that had ended painfully. Martin and I were riding the bus to school when I told him how depressed and dejected I felt about having been dumped. When he mentioned Brunch Buddies, he had only a vague idea of what kind of dating service it was. We both came to the conclusion that it was probably a group of guys getting together for Sunday brunch, and if you met somebody you liked, you'd exchange numbers.

DOUG   I'd lived in New York for over a year and had dated a few men. My latest boyfriend had been introduced to me by a colleague at work. After being on the wrong end of a particularly unpleasant dumping, my workplace became an inescapable connection to this man and our best-forgotten relationship. I swore that the next man I dated would have no relation to my current circle of coworkers or friends.

I read about Brunch Buddies in the *Village Voice*, and I called to set up an appointment.

ANDREW   They sent me some ridiculous questionnaire to complete before my initial visit, asking me to indicate my favorite movies, books, hobbies, magazines, etc. Obviously their methods were far from scientific, but I figured I had nothing to lose. So off I went with my completed survey, determined to make this a fruitful (pardon the expression) venture.

After a few uneventful dates with different "club members," I set up a date with a thirty-year-old television writer and producer. He was promotion manager for *The Joan Rivers Show*, and I'd watched it more than a few times. I figured if things went well, hey, maybe I'd get to meet Joan.

I hadn't seen his picture, so the only person who'd seen us both was the Brunch Buddies rent-a-yenta. We had only a vague idea of what each other looked like. I was "very tall, curly dark hair, hazel eyes" . . .

DOUG   . . . I was "not quite that tall, curly dark hair, green eyes." These sketchy descriptions meant that I spent a good three or four minutes stationed in front of Patzo's, surveying the crowd. It wasn't my favorite restaurant, far from it. But I had already met three other blind dates over the last four months at The Boulevard on Eighty-eighth and Broadway, and I wouldn't have been surprised if the waiters there were starting to wonder if I was a hooker—or looking for one—what with all the furtive, exploratory looks I gave while taking tables alone, saying I was waiting for someone else yet never looking quite sure who that person was supposed to be. It had come time to change venues. So here I was at Patzo's.

ANDREW   Finally I locked eyes with this guy who'd been hiding in plain sight, sheepishly scoping out the crowd for several minutes. He was wearing short shorts to dinner—tennis whites that wrapped around his thighs—and a body-hugging T-shirt, all a bit too snug for dinner wear. Though I wasn't fond of the airtight packaging, before we finished dinner I had decided the gift inside was sweet.

Over the next two weeks, we went out a few times, but our relationship remained chaste. Our fourth date was a group affair— my first trip to Jones Beach, an hour from the city on the Long Island Railroad.

DOUG   The plans were in place prior to meeting Andrew. A few friends suggested lugging their portable volleyball net to the beach. While the stuff was on the unwieldy side, it promised to be a welcome diversion from another day of gay beach rotisserie tanning and cruising while sucking in our guts, with the possible bonus that a volleyball game might prove to be a man magnet. Of course, by the time of our outing, I already had a man in tow, but since Andrew and I had never so much as held hands, I considered myself a free agent in the volleyball draft.

Soon after we finished our first game, and lay on our towels, Andrew questioned a few of my friends about their coming-out stories. As he listened with rapt attention, I realized that his interest wasn't mere flirtation. He was taking in the information as I must have done with other acquaintances a half dozen years earlier. *He's just come out*, it dawned on me—*or perhaps it's been a year already, maybe more even* . . . but I could see him looking for something in each coming-out story. *He's trying to put his story into a broader context* . . . Until now I had perceived him as self-possessed beyond his years, and it hadn't occurred to me that he might still be fighting for self-acceptance. I had dated too many people who were in the throes of inner turmoil over their sexual identity—and I'd been there too long myself. *Is this still a struggle for Andrew? Or is he at peace with his sexuality, and merely compiling anecdotes to add perspective to his own experience?* The evidence was inconclusive, and I was far too cautious to inquire outright.

Instead I asked, "You want to go for a walk?"

"Sure. How about going in?"

I didn't really want to swim, but I did want to look game. When we waded up to knee level, it was immediately apparent that this was the first time Andrew and I had been alone together. Of course, there were plenty of people at the beach, but this moment of shared solitude created a connection between us. It was only an illusion, but for that instant we seemed sheltered, safe, and alone. Then somebody made a move.

And it's been a running joke ever since. A friend will ask: When did you first get "involved?"

Doug: Well, Andrew asked me to go for a swim, and once he had me out there—

Andrew: Are you talking about the afternoon when you threw yourself at me at the beach?

Doug: Me throw myself at you? You attacked me!

Andrew: No, you attacked me! I was just standing there in the water . . .

Doug: You're a full head taller—if you were standing, I'd have to climb up your leg just to give you a hickey! I attacked you? Oh my God . . .

Suffice it to say, it was a nice kiss.

ANDREW If I said the first kiss was magical, I'd sound cornball, but how else to describe it? On our way back from Jones Beach, I was drained but excited. That kiss suggested to me that there was more fun in store for the evening. The wheels of lust began to spin in my head as I strategized the best way to get Doug back to my apartment. The task was easier than I had anticipated. All I had to do was tell Doug that I knew where to get the best sesame noodles in New York. In fact, the tasting menu included much more than sesame noodles, and we picked up where we had left off at Jones Beach. After gorging on Chinese food, and exchanging our views on the sesame noodles, we moved to the "bedroom," which in my small, cramped studio apartment meant walking two feet toward the double bed. We lay side by side and began kissing. I felt a hesitation on Doug's part. His response to my kiss was more tentative than it had been at Jones Beach, and I could not understand what was causing his sudden discomfort. I eventually asked him what he was feeling. He replied that he wanted to take it slowly.

Whoa! That was a new one.

Historically, once I got to the point where I was lying with a prospective sexual partner on my bed, there was really no question as to what would happen next. I was somewhat put off by his request. At the same time, I thought, *Putting on the brakes? What a concept.*

DOUG I've had a few hormonally charged lapses, but by and large, I've been very "fifties," as in the couples in a Technicolor fifties romance. Kind of like Troy Donahue and Sandra Dee, with Tab Hunter subbing for Sandra. Well, you get the idea.

Anyway, I could see Andrew wasn't used to hearing the word *no*, but I told him I didn't want to move so quickly, and after one last kiss good-night at the door, I headed home.

ANDREW In the weeks that followed, we spent every available moment together, and the days—and nights—were filled with a sense of discovery. And we shared a mutual fascination with each other's professional worlds. Getting a real behind-the-scenes look at what was involved in the promotion of a major talk show like *The Joan Rivers Show* was intriguing for a starstruck guy fresh from Montreal. I would frequently visit Doug during his nightly edits, when he educated me on the process. He handled himself like a pro. I was impressed.

Although my world—that of the struggling graduate student— was certainly less glamorous than Doug's, he displayed a keen interest in psychological issues and would inquire in a genuine way about my day and the patients I'd seen. I was struck by his analytical skills and insight, and was wooed by his sensitivity and kindness.

And after a few weeks of dating, I finally got lucky.

DOUG   I felt connected to Andrew, and was ready for greater intimacy. And the evening was certainly intimate. Our night felt passionate but sweet. When we snuggled in my toy-sized single bed (two bodies couldn't fit on it *without* snuggling), Andrew said the most adorable thing (and somehow he managed to say it so it didn't sound nearly as cloying as it looks on this page): "This is how it's supposed to feel, but never has. Until now."

ANDREW   It was a lovely night. But I have to confess, I don't remember saying that.

DOUG   *Men.*

Anyway, it eventually became clear to me that we were bonding deeply in the way that attaches two people for good. Once I could no longer imagine living without Andrew, it made emotional sense to talk about getting married. We'd had the conversation at least a half dozen times. The first time was purely theoretical, as we'd only been dating a few months. Andrew said he wouldn't want to get married until he'd been with someone a very long time, five years, maybe longer. Years later, and just six months before I surprised Andrew with a ring, we were on the roof of our old apartment building on Riverside Drive. We sat on the broad ledge overlooking Joan of Arc Park and the graceful curve of "Little Paris," the prewar blocks that stretch north from the Soldier's and Sailor's Monument.

In this romantic setting, we were talking about all the press that gay marriage was receiving.* Andrew tossed out casually, "My mother asked again if we ever thought about getting married."

True, we'd been talking about weddings, but this was such a non sequitur.

"What did she say?" I asked, although I'd heard him perfectly

---

*Garry Trudeau's "Doonesbury" cartoon had just gotten pulled from some papers for a same-sex-union story line. As it went, Mark, a newly out character, says to the dismay of a conservative listener: "[same-sex unions in medieval Europe] were just like heterosexual ceremonies except that straight weddings, being about property, were usually held outdoors. Gay rites, being about love, were held INSIDE the church."

well. It was enough of a surprise that Roslyn had asked this question, but it appeared she had asked it *before*, and I'd never even heard about it. I always admired her progressive attitude, but I never dreamed Roslyn would be the first to pop the question.

When Andrew repeated Roslyn's question, I asked simply, if idiotically, "Well, what did you say? Were you surprised?"

"I guess. Not really. I don't know," he waffled.

"Would you ever want to?"

"Yeah. You?"

"Sure . . . How would we do it? Maybe have a reception in our apartment?"

"There's only room for twenty or thirty people."

"It must cost a ton to have it in a restaurant or a hotel."

"It depends on how you do it, and how many people you invite. My parents would probably pay for part of it, at least."

"Really?" The thought left me feeling both awkward and relieved. In June of '94 my financial picture was looking healthy, but not secure enough to seriously consider covering all the expenses for a real, full-tilt wedding. On the other hand, I hadn't been on the receiving end of any financial support since high school, fifteen years earlier, and I knew I'd never be comfortable talking to Sheldon or Roslyn about money. Outside of business, I'd never learned how to talk about financial matters at all.

"What makes you think they'd want to pay for some of it?"

"They'd probably offer to pay for all of it. If we did it reasonably, I don't think the money would be an issue. They paid for both my sisters' weddings, and believe me, nothing we'd have would come anywhere near to costing what theirs did."

"How many people did they have?"

"God, I don't know. I think Bonnie's was over four hundred and fifty. Debbie's was smaller, but still huge, around two hundred fifty."

"I'd have to pay for half at least."

"You don't know my father."

"I can't believe your mother asked about it. She's something."

And it seemed Andrew was probably right. Not just about the

money, but about the *subtext*—that his parents were so supportive, so remarkably even-handed, that such an event was not only *possible*, they might take it to their hearts as they would any other wedding. As optimistic as that sounds now, that conclusion didn't seem in the least naive at the time.

Once that conversation was over, it didn't feel like a matter of *if* we'd tie the knot, but when, and how.

Six months later we were sitting at Sign of the Dove, and Andrew was wearing an engagement ring on his finger. After dinner we held hands in the cab, but since we'd been engaged, we still hadn't exchanged a single kiss. On the way home we passed Barnes & Noble at Eighty-first and Broadway, and on the spur of the moment decided to start our research on the spot. We bought several books on wedding planning and hopped another cab home.

When we finally stepped into our elevator, I pressed my lips against his. It was an intense relief, and we got lost for a moment, just the two of us finally, all the way up to the ninth floor.

When we got into bed it was colder than usual, and I felt like we cuddled together a little closer than before.

The next morning, before we'd even gone into the kitchen for breakfast, Andrew said he'd go and phone his parents. We rarely made calls from the bedroom, so I knew that meant he'd make it from his phone in the kitchen. I didn't plan on telling my parents until later. Much later, it turned out.

When Andrew left the bedroom, I stayed behind, affecting indifference. While he was gone, I paced a lot around the bedroom, which, due to its Manhattan-sized proportions, meant I covered the same ground twenty times in two minutes. Then I edged into the living room, where I could better hear the burble of conversation through the rickety glass doors. Then it happened. I heard the click of the phone hitting Formica. The conversation was over.

I walked through the doors.

ANDREW   Since my mother had already broached the subject, I wasn't particularly concerned about calling my parents. She had also told me that she'd already discussed the idea with Mark, a gay co-worker of hers. Mark and my father get along famously, and he'd offered to get on my father's back if he didn't OK the idea. So when I called my parents the next day, not only was I unconcerned by their possible reaction, but as surprising as it may sound to some people, I thought they'd be happy.

It's not that I expected each of them to respond in exactly the same way.

My father will just deal with it, I thought. *My mother will* make *him deal with it. And that's how it'll be.*

That's how it's always been. On the rare occasion that my mother supported me and my father didn't, she would work on him until she won him over.

Between the two of them, they'd never let me feel rejected, so I had reason to expect they would take this news in, and everything would work itself out. I thought my father would be a bit uncomfortable at first, but that he would adapt quickly.

Just like I *thought* he had adjusted to the news that I was gay. I came out to my parents almost seven years before, and we all seemed to make it through that trial unscathed. At the very least, I figured they'd put a happy face on it for me, since it's pretty obvious that when you announce your wedding, you expect people to express joy for you.

When I called my parents, Doug stayed in the bedroom, and I headed for the kitchen. My mother answered. *Or at least, that's how I remember it.*

Like many other weekend mornings, my father was out playing tennis. This felt like good news, since my mother is the one you go to when there's a topic to discuss that's more on the emotional side than the financial. I thought she'd be pouring with enthusiasm. If anything, I was afraid she'd get off the phone, find my father, and coach him on how he ought to feel about this news before I'd get a chance to talk to him myself. And if she couldn't change his feelings about it, I figured she'd at least try to program how he'd respond to me, to be sure he'd sound supportive.

I told her right away. "Doug proposed. We're engaged."

It's not that she went into cardiac arrest. But given what I expected, it was a letdown. It's just that there was no pretense of happiness for *us*. There is a clear difference between *"I'm* thrilled" and *"You* must be very excited." I didn't hear either. I didn't hear support of any kind. And there was a hint of hesitation, even discomfort. It was a short, quiet phone call.

DOUG   Andrew looked discouraged, even depressed, but not dismayed. Though he'd hoped for more, he said his father's response was typically muted, and thoughtfully restrained.

That's right, *Sheldon's* response. That's who *I* remember Andrew said he'd spoken to. Roslyn wasn't home, so Andrew told Sheldon.

SHELDON   I also recall that I was the first to hear the news. It was a Sunday morning, around mid-March 1995. Roslyn was out, and I picked up the phone. Andrew gave me the news right off the bat.

"We exchanged rings."

I had to think about it. Back in our day, when Roslyn and I first dated, you gave a girl a pin. It didn't mean anything more than you wanted to go steady. So it was no surprise if they wanted to give each other rings—they'd been living together for over a year.

"That's nice," I said. "But what does that mean?"

"We're engaged," he says.

Then I asked what seemed a logical question. "Engaged to be what?"

For a moment he didn't answer, so I went further. "Where's it going to lead?"

He said their intent was to go through either a marriage or a commitment ceremony, depending on what you call it, and it would be in a year and a half. So my initial reaction—I didn't say this to him—was, *Well, a year and a half away, there'll be a lot of water under the bridge by then. Maybe it'll be watered down, if it doesn't disappear altogether. I don't have to give it too serious a consideration.*

It's not that I thought they were kidding, it was just so far in advance.

Maybe I looked at it from that angle because of my training, the experience I had as a counselor at camp when I was in my teens. If a kid came down and said, "I want to go home"—he didn't like camp—you'd try this approach: give it a shot for a few days, come back to me, and we'll see what happens. And somehow, in the interval, an experience occurred that made him more comfortable. Maybe the kid made friends, or the fear he had was forgotten. Usually the problem straightened itself out, and I wouldn't have to deal with any further complication.

I was hoping this would turn out the same way. I almost felt that if I let time elapse, it would just disappear by itself. Here it was March, and they were talking about Labor Day of the following year for their ceremony. So I just thought it would melt away and be forgotten.

I did make the leap of imagination, and tried to picture what they meant by "getting married." The only way I could see it was in the surroundings they had established for themselves. It seemed logical to me that the circle of friends they had was in New York, and it would take place there.

Maybe if I had to suffer—if you want to call it that—through a particular day, it would be with a handful of relatives or friends, ten or so. I couldn't see just everyday friends of mine picking themselves up from Montreal to go to New York for something called a commitment ceremony.

I knew this term, *commitment ceremony.* But I wasn't really aware of other rituals that would mirror a heterosexual marriage, with a traditional sort of ceremony (with the obvious amendments to the verbiage) and the same kind of sit-down dinner, dancing, and the rest of it. I saw a more private type of ceremony. When I say private, I don't mean just immediate family, but, say, including friends, as many as fifty or sixty people.

If you want to take it to the extreme, I imagined a commitment ceremony might amount to a couple on top of a mountain under the moonlight, exchanging vows in their own way. But without utilizing the clergy in any form.

I'm not saying that's what I thought Andrew and Doug wanted. And that's not the kind of ritual I would ever want for them, either. But you could definitely say I pictured the average commitment ceremony as more than a little far out.

I conjured up these images, basically, because of inexperience. Where was I supposed to witness something like this? At that point I was sure that there hadn't been any ceremony of same-sex commitment in the Jewish community in Montreal. I knew of one commitment ceremony that had taken place elsewhere, of a Montrealer's daughter, but I didn't know of one other ceremony that had taken place in our community. Not one.

ROSLYN   Like my husband, and Doug as well, I remember Andrew told Sheldon first. But there the similarity ends. As I recall, Sheldon got the news at his office. *Why?* I asked myself. *Why did Andrew call Sheldon at his office to deliver news like this?* I didn't even *find out* about the proposal, and the wedding, until Sheldon told me after he got back home from work on Monday night.

It's not that I minded hearing it secondhand so much. It was more because I've always been the one everyone in the family would turn to for a supportive shoulder to lean on. And surely this was news you'd want to deliver to a friendly ear.

A proposal . . . The concept of something similar certainly wasn't a shock. But it was surprising that Andrew described it using that specific word. This terminology was so heterosexual that it did kind of strike me, like . . . *Oh wow, they're doing what* we *did.*

At first I said to myself, *Well, you know, what's the difference?*

It sounded romantic, and it sounded wonderful. To me it was a natural outcome of their love for each other, and they wanted to formalize it in some way.

But then I chewed on those words again . . . *Proposal. Fiancé.*

When I repeated them again to myself, they reminded me of what marriage had meant for me since earliest childhood. When we grew up, you were conditioned, you got messages. Everyone models relationships. And at that time the rules were, you were brought up by parents who were obviously heterosexual. Your uncles, aunts, got married, had children. Marriage was seen as the union of a man and a woman who had children, had a family, and all the traditional things that went with that. Father being a breadwinner, mother staying home, taking care of the family. Sure, it all sounds cliché, but it became a cliché by being *true*.

After all these years, I've learned the hard way that the rules of the game change all the time. But sometimes it happens so slowly we hardly notice. Marriage meant one thing to my mother, another to me. And of course, it means something altogether different for most young women today. In the context of this never-ending change, the news of the engagement didn't seem so dramatic.

But when I stopped thinking theoretically, and got down to hard reality, I got scared. Because I knew that it wasn't going to be easy. And a little further down the road, when I got an inkling of what really lay ahead for us, I felt that we were embarking on a kind of journey to some serious place. I didn't know how this was going to change us, but I knew we'd have to change.

ANDREW Doug was hovering around me in the kitchen. He wondered about their reaction.

"My mother didn't have much to say."

That was a half-truth. I didn't have much to say either. Buried feelings were rising to the surface. *Am I ready for a lifetime commitment to one person? What will that be like?*

Those fears were magnified by cultural myths. I'd hear the old cliché about gay people not being able to maintain an exclusive commitment. Logically I know stereotypes like that exist because society discourages our relationships. But myths are powerful. Like it or not, they burrow inside your head. And for the same reasons, the concept of marriage doesn't have a place of priority in most gay minds.

But it was more than that. It's the same thing many people—men, particularly—go through when it comes time to take a stand about commitment. Daytime television is filled with talk shows in which women lament the inability of men to commit. And I know plenty of straight women with the same hesitancy.

So I was feeling something I'm sure most people, straight or gay, can relate to. But on top of it was layered cultural prejudices and internalized homophobia. And on top of *that*, I started to picture a sort of epic coming-out ahead of me. If we were going to get married, it would be a public announcement of my homosexuality that I wasn't sure I was ready to make.

If Doug was ready to ask me to tie the knot, he must have made peace with these issues, or maybe he didn't even have these qualms in the first place. For now, I kept my fears to myself.

CHAPTER 2

Coming Out

ROSLYN, SHELDON, AND ANDREW

1960–1990

ROSLYN   When I first suspected, Andrew was sixteen. His behavior had changed. He became very troubled, and stalked around the house, crabbing constantly. It seemed he never cracked a smile. At least not around me. Something specific was weighing on him.

The second he barreled through the door on his way home from school, he'd start putting me down. One day I had redecorated the entryway. "I don't like the color of this chair." When I failed to rise to the bait, he asked, "What are you making for supper?" "Macaroni and cheese, your favorite." "Oh, I hate that." You name it, he hated it.

Since we were already redecorating, I said he could do his bedroom over. First he asked for dark green wallpaper, and then he insisted on painting the ceiling red. I blanched at the thought. "It's my room, and I'll do it the way I want. And I want it red," he announced gleefully, with a sadistic laugh. In a few weeks, up went the wallpaper, and then the dreaded paint. It looked like a brothel at Christmastime. It made me ill every time I walked in. (The first thing I did when Andrew moved out after college was repaint the ceiling. And let me tell you, it wasn't cheap: it took six coats to cover the red with beige.)

Nearly every day when Andrew came home he'd glower at me, make some derogatory critique, and head downstairs to Sheldon's office to study. I knew his behavior wasn't an attack on me, but a reaction to some problem he couldn't discuss. And I wanted *him* to know that *I* knew. So I tried to reach him through his stomach. I'd climb downstairs with a tray of his favorite chocolate chip cookies, and—yes, it's true—a glass of milk. I kept my words to a minimum. He grunted and looked up indifferently. That was it. I knew this was meant as thanks, but I wasn't going to get the satisfaction of hearing the words. We both knew there was something eating at him, but he didn't want to acknowledge it to me. And when I tried to acknowledge *that*, and comfort him, he pulled away.

I know, every mother describes their teenager like this. But to paraphrase Tolstoy, happy teenagers are all alike, but every unhappy teen is unhappy in his or her own special way. It took a long time to identify what it was that distinguished Andrew's acting out from other kids' garden-variety teen angst.

SHELDON It was obvious to me that something was bothering him, but I had no idea what the source was. In hindsight, Andrew's behavior could be directly linked to him struggling with his sexuality, and maybe I should have seen whatever signals he was giving us to that effect.

You see, several years earlier, our oldest child, Mitchell, told us he was gay. But the circumstances for him and Andrew were quite dissimilar. Mitchell had long been different from most other kids, with a whole other set of interests from the average teenager. Intellectually he was at a completely different place from the rest of his friends. He read at a much higher level. Simply, he was much smarter. He was atypical in so many other ways that when he told us, somehow it didn't come as a very big surprise.

ROSLYN   Not long after Mitchell came out to us, I had my first serious foray into gay studies at school. While working toward my bachelor's degree in applied social science at Concordia University, I was enrolled in a yearlong course on human sexuality. We spent a couple of classes talking specifically about homosexuality, and looked at some films depicting gay relationships. It wasn't pornography certainly, yet it was eye-opening, with same-sex couples touching, holding hands, holding each other . . . in the nude. It helped desensitize me, removing some of the shock value from gay sex.

At last I found the courage to ask myself the question . . . *Is Andrew gay too?* If it was true, it explained a lot. Like how he didn't seem to hang out with "the boys." And when Andrew was sixteen I found out that Lorne, one of his few close male friends, was gay.

Lorne had come over one afternoon. He's always been a live wire, bouncing around like a pinball, talking your ear off. On that day he slipped right up to Andrew's room, visibly disturbed. He told Andrew, although he wasn't sure what was wrong with him, he was afraid he might be gay. He wanted Andrew's advice: should he tell his parents? After Lorne had left, Andrew came into my bedroom for what amounted to a consultation.

"This isn't about me," he qualified immediately. "And don't tell anybody. I think Lorne is gay. What should I say to him? How can I help him?" Typically, Andrew was anxious to help a friend. The irony was, he didn't know how to help himself.

I struggled to come up with some words of wisdom. Then I got stuck on something Andrew said. *This isn't about me.* It had the ring of denial, like "I'm not a crook." He repeated variations on that theme at least three or four times in our conversation. "I'm not talking about me . . . I'm asking for my friend . . ."

Preoccupied with what Andrew was saying, or more accurately, what he wasn't saying, I couldn't think what guidance to give. Except for one suggestion. And maybe, subconsciously, I intended it for Andrew as much as Lorne. "I think it would be best if Lorne could tell his parents. No matter how difficult it might be, it's the only way they can hope to communicate honestly."

Once Andrew had left the room, all I could think was, Andrew's best friend is gay . . . his other close friend, Peter, is different (*different* turned out to mean *gay*, when I learned Peter had also come out, about five years later), and the closer I looked, it seemed Andrew was shaping up to be pretty different too.

As I sat down on the edge of the bed, I thought about the girls in Andrew's life. Now I began to see those relationships in a new way. Suddenly it seemed he was *trying* to be heterosexual. It looked like work. And it looked like it wasn't working. He would go out with girls, like Diane or Maxine, his closest girlfriends. He was even Diane's escort at her sweet sixteen. I can still see them all dressed up like a bride and groom—literally! Diane, in her faux bridal gown, arm in arm with Andrew in his tux. It looked like dress-up in more ways than one. Everything about it was *artificial*. There wasn't a single spark of sexuality between them. Or between Andrew and Maxine. Here he was, this tall, handsome kid, with dark curly hair. I got to thinking about the other girls who were interested in him, and there were many, yet he wasn't interested back. Then it occurred to me . . . He's got this special relationship with two different girls. Why not just *one*?

The clues were adding up.

Immediately I hopped onto a seesaw, bouncing between *Aha! That's what it is!* and *Oh, forget about it, for heaven's sake. It's too painful even to* consider.

One day, not long after, Andrew and I went out to lunch together at a little cafeteria downtown. Sitting opposite each other, I sensed that he needed to talk. But he couldn't articulate what was really going on.

"I'm having trouble with relationships," he said. "I don't feel like being with anybody. I'm not happy. Really, I'm miserable."

I tried to coax some specifics out of him, without success.

When it was clear we weren't getting anywhere, I said, "Look, I can't be your therapist. I'm your mother. I'm concerned. I'm worried. I think you should get some help. Let me get you the name of somebody you can see. What do you think?"

It wasn't the first time I'd made this suggestion. This time he didn't say no, he simply didn't answer. Translation: *I'll think about it.*

A couple of weeks later Andrew announced to me that he would give therapy a try. I was ready with the name of a psychologist who had been highly recommended by a friend of mine. Through the several months he saw this man, Andrew never told me how badly it was going. He just quit. It was five years before I found out the truth behind his terminating the therapy, and the disturbing story of his next experience with a mental health professional, this time a prominent, respected psychiatrist.

Soon after Andrew quit therapy, I shared some of my suspicions about Andrew with Sheldon for the first time. Sheldon didn't comment. He just listened.

SHELDON   I honestly can't remember ever discussing the possibility that Andrew might be gay. Years before, Roslyn and I had talked about Mitchell, but I never recall considering the possibility Andrew might also be gay until much later.

I do remember Andrew entering therapy, and the conflicting thoughts I had about that. On one hand, I was not the greatest fan of social science, primarily because I've always found it hard to call it a "science," it's so inexact. I believe any intelligent, sympathetic, patient person willing to serve as a sounding board probably could serve the same purpose as a therapist in many cases. On the other hand, I knew Andrew was interested in psychology, and Roslyn was in fact a social worker, so if that was what Andrew wanted, I thought it better not to upset both of them. When he stopped therapy, I wasn't concerned. I thought maybe he'd worked through his problems.

ROSLYN   For the next three years, I teetered between the reality I feared and the fantasy I prayed for. It was a precarious balancing act.

All the while I was looking for a hopeful sign.

When Andrew told us he was going to Greece with Diane, I thought I'd found reason for optimism. They were nineteen.

Great! This looks promising! I told myself. Once they started planning their trip, I convinced myself that maybe there *was* something between them after all. Although I wasn't knitting baby booties, I continued looking for good news wherever I could find it.

When they'd been gone for a week, Andrew called home.

"Are you having a good time?" I quizzed.

He sounded good, and I could tell he was having fun.

"Did anybody rob you? Is your money belt on at all times? Did you put your sunblock on? How is your stomach tolerating Greek cuisine? You're sure nobody mugged you?" I ran down the Jewish mother's checklist.

Andrew confirmed the typical traveler's dietary complaints. Then he moaned about Diane being fussy. He said they didn't always agree on rooms.

While we're on the subject of rooms, I thought, *how many* beds *are there in your room?*

In fact, the closest I got to asking if they were sleeping together was when I asked Andrew suggestively, "Are the beds big enough for you, with your long legs?" I can be nosy, but I have my limits.

While they were still gone, I ran into Diane's mother, Rhoda, on the street in front of our house. At the time we were neighbors. Our little corner of Hampstead is pretty, and comforting, in a *Father Knows Best* kind of way. It's a suburb, though not in the current connotation of the word, just some speck in a massive urban sprawl. It's only a stone's throw away from the city proper, and its character isn't much different from many residential areas within Montreal's city limits, except that it's almost 100 percent Jewish.

As we stood on opposite sides of our little Hampstead street, the setting was so homey I might as well have been going over to ask Rhoda if I could borrow a cup of sugar. Rhoda was one of Andrew's biggest fans. (Forgive a mother for bragging, but he really did have what amounted to a fan club.) Over the last few years, as Andrew and Diane had grown closer, Rhoda would often extol Andrew's virtues, nearly always concluding with "He's so special!"

That particular summer, we always checked in with each other as soon as we got a phone call from Greece. "Have you heard from the kids? Where are they now?" Rhoda inquired.

"Mykonos. They seem to be having such a good time together!" Rhoda smiled warmly.

"I'm so happy for both of them," I blurted. Filled with hope, I'd overflowed.

She looked at me oddly.

Then I let my enthusiasm take me right over the edge. "Wouldn't it be funny if they got married, and we ended up *macha-tunim*?" (That's a chummy Yiddish expression for in-laws.) I probably beamed.

Rhoda couldn't even look at me.

Then she made an excuse for leaving, gave me a look that said, *You poor thing, you don't even know,* and took off in a hurry.

I felt my face flush, and my hands were clammy in an instant.

It was at that moment I realized that she knew something I had suspected for a long time. Andrew was gay. She had been told, and I was, after all, only his mother. Why should I have been told?

I was so very angry. Standing alone, there, on my corner. A moment ago I'd been fully dressed; now I was suddenly stark naked, exposed for all my neighbors to see. I escaped into the house, and climbing the stairs to the privacy of my bedroom, I was overwhelmed with such sadness, it was close to grieving. As I lay down on the bed, I wept rivers.

Within minutes, my sorrow turned to rage. I directed it first at

Rhoda, which was ridiculous. I felt betrayed, because she knew something I didn't. Something I *should* have known. I wondered how many others knew. For years after that, every time I saw her, I was very apprehensive. I was experiencing a textbook case of displaced anger, though for all my training and experience, it proved so much easier to diagnose a patient than myself.

How could my neighbor know this most personal news when I didn't? Of course, the signs had always been there. But discovering for myself that Andrew was gay was like studying for a difficult course. I'd gather information, and try to digest it. Only it wouldn't sink in at first. I'd have to relearn the same lessons over and over again before I could make sense of it all.

About three years and two therapists later, Andrew and I were riding together to dinner, just the two of us. He'd just turned twenty-three. It was winter and we were driving across Mount Royal in the family's beat-up second car, an old Honda. We were on our way to meet Sheldon and our other kids at Moishe's, the see-and-be-seen restaurant for Montreal's Jewish community.

Andrew and I were running five minutes late, as usual.

"I'm happy. Things have really changed, and I feel much better," he told me.

"I see that. I'm happy too. I'm happy for you." I glanced over at him quickly, then back at the slightly icy road.

"I've really changed," he said again.

For the next minute or so, he dropped that phrase a half dozen times, like a mantra, a code.

"You're trying to tell me something," I observed.

There was silence in the car. We weren't more than a few minutes from the restaurant. If there was a revelation to be made, it had better happen soon. It was time to take a big risk. Really, I can't believe I asked it so bluntly.

"Are you trying to tell me that you're gay?"

He acted really taken aback, although I think it was a performance. I could swear he set me up.

After he let out a little chuckle, he said "Yes. I am. How did you know?"

"Well, I've watched you grow and develop, seen you being tortured by something, and I figured there had to be something major going on to affect you the way it did. Also, there was a kind of pattern to this. I've been preparing myself all along for it. I'm so glad you told me."

Andrew looked relieved.

"I'm so glad you accepted this about yourself. You know I love you. This is not going to be a problem for me. If I had my druthers, of course, I'd wish you were heterosexual. That's a normal expectation, isn't it?"

He nodded.

"But don't worry. We'll deal with it. It's more important that you're happy about yourself and your life."

We pulled up at the restaurant. In the car, it was just the two of us, sharing this earth-shattering information. Now we had to get out and face the Moishe's crowd. Before this bombshell, I was prepared to be *on*; now I felt defenseless. I'd just heard this tremendous revelation that left me totally at conflict with myself. Lord knows that in this instance I would have welcomed being wrong. Still, this was a confirmation that my long-held hunch was right.

As we got out of the car, I said to Andrew, "Ready or not, we're going to dinner."

"Please, don't tell anybody now."

"Don't be silly. But you'll have to tell Daddy later," I said.

"No. You tell him."

"I'll help, but I think you have to tell him yourself."

ANDREW The truth of the matter was, I was stoned.

Why else would I blurt out to my mother, "I'm gay," then laugh out loud once I realized what I'd done?

We were driving to dinner, and she had prodded me in her intrusive way, "How's your therapy going?"

"Fine." *Enough about therapy,* I said to myself.

We were heading down, on the other side of Mount Royal, overlooking the city. I wasn't particularly enjoying the view this evening, but it was easier than looking at my mother while she headed into the unwelcome vicinity of my therapy, and next, my sexuality: "Have you been talking about relationships?"

Stop with the grilling, already, I yearned to shout. *You want to know what I've been talking about in therapy?* All right . . .

"I'm gay."

My words hung there between us, splattered into the air, too late to reclaim. When my breathing slowed, I was numb, in a state of shock. I couldn't fathom that I'd actually said the words. Certainly none of this was planned.

But oddly enough, my mother seemed less stunned than I was. Her reaction was tempered. No histrionic outbursts. No "My God!" Or even "Dear, I love you so much!" Instead, at first, she just stiffened a bit, and exhaled, "Oh . . ."

Of course, when she rebounded from the surprise, she said, "I love you no matter what." And "I'm glad you told me."

I was relieved . . . but still freaked out beyond belief that I'd done it.

For a moment, I wished I'd never started smoking the stuff. But marijuana was helping me drown out the anxiety I'd been feeling. The whole process of smoking had become, for a time, the easy escape from reality. I'd been at war with myself for years, part of me struggling to get out, another part fighting to hide. It was like there were two of me. The boy who desperately wanted to fit in, and this other person I didn't want to know. I tried to turn my back on this stranger, maybe because he scared me. All this inner turmoil left me simultaneously weary and agitated, eternally on edge.

The conversation in the car couldn't have happened, pot or not, just a year or so before. No amount of loosening up could have made me divulge something I hadn't accepted internally. Now here I was, twenty-two, just out of school, and suddenly facing the rest of my life. I'd worked so hard to obtain my B.A., finally the good student my parents always expected me to be. I'd invested myself totally in the experience, studying feverishly, pouring myself into it. But now that it was over, what was I left with? Without school, I was left with just *me* . . . and the frightening question, who *was* that?

I'd begun exposing the answers to myself, but I wasn't prepared to make this revelation to my mother. By this time, she was grilling me.

"Are you going to tell Daddy?"

I tried to ignore her, staring out the window.

"Well, when are you going to tell him?"

"I'll tell him, OK?"

"Soon?"

"Mmmm-hmmm."

"You really should tell him as soon as possible."

I was getting mad, because I wasn't ready to be pushed. The fact that we were having this conversation was a fluke in the first place; now here was my mother, dictating my next move.

"Just don't tell Daddy. I want to tell him myself."

ROSLYN   On the ride back from the restaurant I was silent and thoughts were racing through my head . . . *I won't have any grandchildren from Andrew . . . He'll never walk down the aisle . . . Now I'll only get to make two weddings . . .*

When we got home, I was the one to give Sheldon the news. I told myself I did it to pave the way for Andrew. Truthfully, I felt the need to unburden myself. Who else was I going to talk to?

I saw a wave of pain wash over Sheldon as I broke it to him. After the initial shock, I could sense his tension ebbing. Although I could see for myself how he felt, I pushed him to talk about it.

SHELDON   It was the day of the Super Bowl, coming home from a restaurant, when Roslyn told me outright, Andrew is gay. It was a real shock, although I suppose it shouldn't have been. Years before, when Mitchell told us he was gay, I almost took it in stride. But finding out I had *two* sons who were gay really depressed me.

Even though I was fully cognizant of the prevailing scientific view that there are genetic causes to homosexuality, I still felt a sense of guilt. Here I was the father of two gay sons, and Mitchell was adopted.

Each of them came from different genetic backgrounds, so either the odds were just stacked against me, or I had to ask myself, could I have contributed somehow to this? How could I ignore the possibility that environmental matters entered into the equation?

I won't give myself a gold medal as a father, though truthfully, I really thought I was above average. I certainly wasn't a disciplinarian, aggressive, or domineering. On the contrary, I would usually give in to my kids' every request, perhaps to a fault. My friends make fun of me, in fact, for the time I've spent with young kids over the years. I seem to have more patience with children than I do with adults. Now that Roslyn and I are blessed with grandchildren, I spend the whole day with them when we visit Toronto. Other friends of mine say they love to visit their grandchildren, but after a half an hour, they've had enough. Not me. So I'm certainly not the "absentee father" some claim contributes to a gay male's sexual preference. Is it possible that I was a good father, and still raised two gay sons?

In addition to my own guilt feelings, I worried about their future. It's tough enough to succeed in our sophisticated and complicated world. Why did both of our sons have to carry this extra burden? Being gay could only make their lives harder.

ANDREW   I know she told him anyway, even though she promised she wouldn't. My plan was to tell him when I was ready. But truthfully, I wasn't ready as soon as I thought I might be. The way my parents remember it, I turned around and told my father in a few days. But as I recall, it took a couple of months. It's funny how some recollections get compressed, or smudged until they're almost obliterated. I don't know if this is just one of those details that fades with time, or if they blocked the memory.

In any case, I certainly wouldn't blame my parents for not wanting to recall the scene that played out when I summoned the courage to tell my father myself. Or, I should say, when I made my first, failed, attempt.

ROSLYN   Like Sheldon, I was concerned about what barriers might be put up before both Andrew and Mitchell, just because of their sexual orientation. I could relate to that fear on a very personal level, because twenty-five years earlier I'd had my own experience of failing to live up to society's expectations. We adopted Mitchell because I hadn't been able to get pregnant.

A little over two years after Sheldon and I were married, we planned to start a family. It never dawned on me that I might not be able to have a baby when I wanted one. After many months of trying, it became clear, it wasn't working. My *body* wasn't working. There comes a moment when you say . . . *What's happening to me? What's wrong with me?* I would compare the panic I felt at that time to what somebody feels when they first think they might be gay.

Then there was the anxiety I felt over telling people about my infertility. I think that's a lot like what drives gay people into the closet. I feared I'd be humiliated if people knew the truth that I couldn't conceive. So I kept it secret, and created a "closet" of my own. And, of course, keeping the secret made everything worse.

Because of our secret, I'd have to take insensitive comments; for example, one day, sitting at the hairdresser, as I was held hostage in curlers, a woman said to me, "What are you waiting for? You're too into yourself!"

The most innocent question could drive my shame even deeper. We'd be gathered around the table for Sabbath dinner. "So, *nu?* When are we going to become grandparents?" Sheldon's mother, Goldie, would ask. We'd be at a bris. "So, when by you?" an old aunt would ask, expecting a firm answer that we knew we couldn't give. Another relative would approach me. "So, next by you?" I just smiled and shrugged.

Meanwhile, my friends were almost sadistically prolific, multiplying like mad. After two years of seeing them, and their friends, and their friends' friends, all celebrating baby-centric occasions, from brisses to birthday parties, I wanted to punch them. I longed to scream, "What do you think? *Don't you know I want to have a child?*"

And of course, as I got more frustrated, I got more tense. While my anger and resentment mounted, my chances of conceiving certainly weren't getting any greater.

After the doctor's diagnosis and his encouragement to adopt, we finally told our parents the truth. "We don't know why. There doesn't seem to be any medical reason, but we're having trouble having a baby. We're putting our name down for adoption."

It was such a relief. And once we knew we had this other avenue, we could put it out of our minds and relax. Once we'd publicly announced our plans to adopt, the outside pressure practically disappeared, as if cut off by a secret edict. It's true that adoption bore its own stigma in those days, but it was nothing compared to the sin of childlessness.

It didn't take long before we'd adopted Mitchell. What happened next was an enormous surprise at the time. Almost exactly eight and a half months after we adopted Mitchell, our first daughter, Debbie, was born. After years of hoping and praying to conceive my first child, suddenly I became fertile, and with a vengeance. After Mitchell's adoption, my next three children, first Debbie, then Bonnie, and last, Andrew, were born in less than five years.

SHELDON   I had never faulted Roslyn for our situation. Neither did I feel any shame. I knew she was anxious about having a baby. So was I. I remember her being tested by doctors. I was tested too. I know Roslyn doesn't remember it like this, but I recall one doctor telling us she was not infertile, and could conceive, but because of some chemical or acid in her system, her potential was not the greatest. He added that if we were thinking of adoption, we should go ahead. We were, and we did.

When we found out about Roslyn being pregnant, I was doubly thrilled. First for having Mitchell, and secondly for the baby on the way. I felt so lucky to have two healthy babies of our own. And let me add this thought, sincerely felt: From the day we took him home,

I never thought of Mitchell any differently than my other children. I never gave any thought to the fact that he was adopted. He's mine and that's it. I love all of our four children fully and equally.

ROSLYN You may have heard an infertility story like ours before. A woman struggles to conceive, then fails, turns to adoption, and suddenly she's pregnant. Maybe it happens because all the external pressure women feel to conceive makes it even harder for some women to do just that. I think the relief I felt after admitting my infertility and deciding to adopt may have actually helped free me to bear children.

My experience with the shame of infertility helped me identify with the societal pressures Andrew was surely feeling. And this gave me an advantage that Sheldon didn't have. When I told Sheldon that Andrew was gay, he had handled it, though it obviously wasn't easy for him. Now it was time for Andrew to tell Sheldon himself.

ANDREW Even after I'd told my mother the truth about my sexuality, for months that revelation was still effectively a secret. I finally felt forced by my mother, and compelled by my impending departure for New York, to speak with my father. With just a few weeks remaining before I would leave for graduate school, my mother was hounding me more than ever, "Have you told Daddy yet?"

I had just returned from a week's vacation in Provincetown with my friend Lorne. It was an appropriate setting for the first trip I'd taken since coming out to myself. For the first time, I saw men and women openly showing affection to members of their own sex, arm in arm, holding hands or kissing, unashamedly, on the beach, in restaurants, on the street.

With one foot in Provincetown the other halfway out the door to New York, I was as ready as I'd ever be to sit down with my father. I announced to my mother, "I'm going to do it tonight." We had plans to go out for dinner, and before we left, I said to my father, "I need to speak to you about something when we get home.

I'd appreciate it if we could talk alone." He must have known what it was about. And even though I knew in my heart my mother had already told him, I didn't really believe that was going to make it any easier for either one of us.

We spent dinner, I think, all ignoring the silent partner seated at the table with us—my almost unveiled secret. After we pulled into the garage, we all walked up from the basement, and my mother asked me to put the dog out. I called out, "Cashew!" but I didn't hear any paws scuttling across the floor, so I headed up one more flight to the top floor with my parents. As we got to the landing, we all saw it.

Green barf covered the last few steps leading up to the top of the staircase. By the time I asked, "What happened?" the extent of the problem was apparent. There was more of the sickly green stuff all over the carpet. The next time I called out "Cashew!" it was more a desperate cry of concern. My parents found our handful of a poodle dozing in the den. When Cashew woke, she batted her eyelashes, innocent as a babe, hopped right up, and bounced into the kitchen, begging to go out. Meanwhile, I noticed a mess that emanated from my bedroom, and walked in to find a small pile of bottles, baby powder, and dental floss strewn across the carpet. At the center was my open toiletry kit. Lying next to the bag was the bottle Cashew had chewed open. It was Immodium that had been prescribed before I left for Provincetown, a preventative measure against traveler's stomach. Cashew had downed the bottle's contents, then thrown them up all over the house.

When I came down to tell what I'd discovered, my father flew into a rage the likes of which I'd never seen before.

"How could you be so irresponsible? How could you be so stupid? Leaving your bag on the floor? What were you thinking?" He was just getting warmed up. After what seemed an interminable time, he hit his stride and really started hollering. He went on and on and on.

Of course, I felt terrible already. I was shaking, pleading, "I'm sorry, the bag was closed, I didn't think she could get into it! It wasn't my fault!"

My father was having none of it, and just kept needling me with variations of the same accusations. "It's so thoughtless! We can't depend on you for anything!"

"Don't you think I feel awful? Don't you think I feel bad that I did this?"

Defending myself was a waste of time. He just came back at me again, shouting, utterly out of control.

By now my mother was trying to calm him, I think because she realized he was overreacting. "Sheldon, it's not his fault!" Still, he was spewing a stream of accusations, and wouldn't let up.

Finally I shouted back in tears, with language I'd never used before at home, "You're a fucking asshole!" and ran up to my room.

A few days later, I tried again to say the words to my father. We sat down together in the den, just the two of us. I looked at him, and said it simply. "I think you know why I want to talk to you. I'm gay."

Despite the ugly scene of the other night, I knew somehow that he would now react calmly and offer support, and if he felt some reservations or even anguish, he would keep it private. And that's just what he did.

SHELDON   When Andrew said he wanted to speak to me, it was the same week that he told Roslyn, but it wasn't the same day, or even the day after. It seemed he had anticipated that Roslyn had spoken to me. He told me simply, "I'm gay."

"I can't say that I'm thrilled, but I accept you for what you are. And I love you just as much." I didn't say just how much guilt and pain I'd been feeling since I'd heard the news.

Andrew replied, "I'm not so happy myself. Do you think I would choose this if I had a choice? I know it'll make things more difficult for me in my life."

No matter what my disappointments were, it never crossed my mind that Andrew's sexuality could change. I think I'm sophisticated enough to realize that fact, even without claiming to understand exactly what caused him to be gay in the first place.

ROSLYN   Later we talked about who we'd share this news with. I said I didn't want to keep it to myself, and that became a bone of contention between Sheldon and I. If we were all together, eating at home, and I said someone should know Andrew was gay, Sheldon would change the subject, leave the table. If the two of us were alone and I brought it up, Sheldon would say, "Why do you have to talk about that now?" He had a really hard time talking about Andrew. It was just too painful.

ANDREW   It was clear that my father had one overwhelming preoccupation, a concern that caught me by surprise.

"What's your understanding of why people are gay?" he asked.

I said the usual things about the nature versus nurture debate. He wanted more. Absolution, perhaps.

Then my father offered what were surely intended as words of comfort, and to some degree, they were. "I just want you to be happy. I'm not saying I'm glad to hear this. I would rather you were straight."

Again, though, he returned to the apparent bottom line. Was it his fault? "Do you think it had anything to do with anything I did, or didn't do, for you?"

"No." Since he'd offered me solace, it seemed it was my turn. Although I exonerated him quickly, my heart wasn't in it. On one hand, I didn't like the feeling of having to acquit him, while I failed to see the crime. At the same time, if he wanted to talk nonjudgmentally about responsibility, my feelings were conflicted.

I had long regarded him as distant. The "distant father, smothering mother" theory that's been used for decades to ascribe guilt to parents hadn't yet been discredited. I didn't necessarily believe that was why I was gay, but I wasn't prepared to reject that possibility yet, either.

When I was much younger, six, seven, eight years old, my father was loving, very attentive to me. He was the kind of father who would sing me to sleep. It was a fairly idyllic childhood, until I felt certain expectations were made of me—prospects I simply couldn't fulfill. For one, I wasn't interested in sports. Although my father would deny that was ever an issue for him, I couldn't help but be aware of how important sports were in his life. His office is filled with pictures of his many basketball teams. He was even captain of McGill's varsity squad, and later a member of the YMHA Canadian championship team. And as long as I could remember, tennis and golf seemed to occupy his every free afternoon.

Maybe it was only my projection; perhaps I wanted to believe he was disappointed in me because I wasn't the jock he had been. Or conceivably he was frustrated, and still isn't in touch with it. Regardless, by the time I was twelve, he was very angry with me. Basically, I felt he didn't like me. I wasn't doing well in school, both in terms of academics and behavior problems. I knew too well his hard-earned, unblemished reputation. Family history recorded that he was Mr. Perfect as far back as elementary school, always the proper child, student, teammate, notary, husband, and father. What must it have been like for him to get calls from my teachers, saying, among other things, that I had a big mouth? I was embarrassed, and it was clear: I'd let him down.

My mother also seemed to want to change me. She was anxious for me to be outside, and active. If I was watching television when I heard the garage door opening, I shut it off and ran upstairs to pretend I was doing something busy. She egged on my involvement in sports more than my father. Though I don't know if my mother consulted with him, she was almost always the one to push me into it.

She'd ask me regularly, "Why don't you play tennis with Daddy this weekend?" He'd ask too, but he seemed to sense my lack of motivation. And since I saw myself as a constant source of aggravation and disappointment, I figured he was probably happy to play tennis with somebody, anybody, other than me.

At school I was pretty much a loner, depressed, disgusted with myself, struggling with feelings of inferiority and inadequacy. Until later in high school. Then something clicked. People started to appreciate my sense of humor. I felt better, looked better, and suddenly, it seemed, I had more friends than I knew what to do with. I started to connect particularly with female friends, like Diane and Maxine, and a few male friends who (not coincidentally) revealed in the next few years that they were gay.

Lorne was the first one to come out to me. And as incomprehensible as it sounds, when he told me, I didn't identify with what he was saying at all. That's how separated I was from what was going on inside. I tried to be encouraging, and sympathetic, but when he went to a support group, rather than offering to go with him myself, I asked Maxine to go with him. (After Maxine attended the group, her parents told her not to go again. They felt she was "impressionable" and feared that she'd become a lesbian. Where exactly did this concept of contagious sexuality come from?)

Over the next few years, I lived vicariously, though subconsciously, through Lorne. I would get a thrill out of hearing about what he was doing. Things that I couldn't do. I knew why it sounded exciting, but I was so isolated from my own desires that I couldn't imagine that I wanted to do any of these things myself.

Things continued to get worse at home. I was constantly butting heads with my siblings, and my parents both seemed perpetually angry with me. My mother had suggested several times that I try to go for therapy, and by the time I entered McGill University, I finally agreed.

The therapist I went to see was a psychology professor at Concordia University, with his own private practice. I think he was recommended by my mother's friend Ida. A couple of my friends from high school had seen him before, and I'd been warned about the way he'd chain-smoke through sessions and blow the smoke out his nose, like a dragon. The "presenting problem," or in layman's terms, the reason I gave for seeing him, was that I wanted a girlfriend. With this therapist I was able to verbalize the unknowable, the unspeakable, at last. I shared experiences I'd had in camp, fooling around with other guys. I knew it was the sort of thing a lot of adolescent guys do, and it didn't mean they all grew up to be gay. Next, I confessed to fantasizing about men. He suggested that I could try to change this. The way he put it was, "If that's what you'd like to do, I can help you with that." I'm not sure if he came from the school that believed being gay was something to *fix*, but he was absolutely willing to help me "change." At that point in time, homosexuality had already been removed from the third edition of the *Diagnostic and Statistical Manual of Mental Disorders* (the official reference book for mental health professionals) and was deemed a normal variation of sexual behavior. But it was also several years before news spread about the damage that was being done to gays and lesbians in so-called reparative therapy.

He asked me to fantasize about women when I masturbated, with the hope that I would eventually find it arousing. He told me to practice doing that. It never worked.

I expressed a lot of shame and guilt to him. Still, I never said I was gay. It was still a concept I couldn't grasp, because it was a notion I didn't like. I didn't like my own instinctual drive. It wasn't *normal*. And yet my best friend was gay. How could I care so much about him, never judge him negatively at all, and still be so deeply in denial?

After a few months of therapy, feeling frustrated, defeated, and depressed, I quit. I had started smoking marijuana. It helped anesthetize the pain, and for a while I could forget the battle that was being waged inside of me.

It took me a long time to rebound from the disappointment of this therapeutic experience. It's not that he was so bad. To a great extent, this therapist was just doing what I'd asked of him. I only wish he'd known how futile it is to change the source of erotic desire, and had helped guide me to self-acceptance instead of certain self-defeat.

Not long after, I discovered the book *Being Homosexual: Gay Men and Their Development*, by Richard Isay. Reading it was a breakthrough in my life. I devoured it in a matter of hours, and when I was done,

I said, *This is me*. The book provided many case studies of different people, many of whom I could identify with. Dr. Isay confirmed some generalities I'd believed by instinct, and shot down others I'd been less sure of. One key cliché he debunked was the idea of the "distant father." He reframed it, and showed that sons aren't gay because their fathers are distant, but rather that fathers distance themselves from sons when they sense they might be gay. The book touched on every aspect of homosexuality and dealt with it from the position that it's normal—not a pathology to be treated and cured.

Now that I felt differently about homosexuality, and myself, I sought a new therapist. At the time I worked at the Jewish General Hospital as a research assistant. I went to the hospital's outpatient psychiatry clinic for an evaluation. "Brief therapy" was recommended. That's the kind of therapy you might recommend to someone who is struggling with a stressful life event that might be treated successfully in a brief period.

I was assigned to begin treatment with the head of the Brief Therapy program. That sounded good, until my first appointment. His office was right across the street from where I was working, doing neuropsychological testing and Alzheimer's research. When I walked in, I waited for a bit in his secretary's office. There were separate doors for patients to enter and exit, so we could all avoid seeing each other. It's not an unheard-of practice, but I've never seen another therapist, before or since, who actually used this method of maintaining client confidentiality. It offers privacy, but perhaps there's more to it. Maybe it's appropriate for a doctor who sees human nature as a cause for shame. Once I entered his private office, I found myself surrounded by pictures of his wife and children.

I told him why I'd come.

"This is an illness," he stated flatly. "I won't be able to support you in getting comfortable with it. If you want to deal with issues related to relationships, such as with your parents, that's fine." But the one thing I wanted to talk about was verboten.

"This is my bias. I think it's abnormal. It's a sickness," he reiterated.

I began regurgitating all I'd read in Richard Isay's book. I didn't come up for air for five minutes, at least.

The doctor wasn't impressed. He wasn't any more impressed during the rest of our eleven remaining brief therapy sessions either.

You might ask, why did I bother? What made me remain and argue until I was blue, for three months? Why didn't I just say, *Fuck you and good-bye?* A curious thing happened. After twelve appointments, all spent debating this virtual brick wall, I realized that in attempting to teach him, I was the one actually being instructed. Thanks to those intense hours of standing up for my convictions, I found I finally believed, not only in what I was saying, but in myself.

Though I had finally come out to myself, it would be months until I would say the words outside of therapy. First I told Lorne. We were in the car. (Inside the car again . . . I must like a captive audience.) I understood why he was so stunned. He had gone through so much on his own, and I could have been there with him. But how could I, when I didn't accept that I was gay? When I looked at Lorne, and considered the five years that he'd been dealing openly with his sexuality, I couldn't imagine what I'd been thinking all that time, how I could have existed on the cusp of awareness, but remained in such deep denial.

SHELDON I don't believe I was in denial over Andrew's sexuality once he'd told me directly. Yet I still harbored a lot of guilt feelings. After I had a few days to think about it, and I looked back on our parenting, I didn't feel either Roslyn or I was "responsible" for Andrew being gay, but this had come as such a surprise, it was going to take time for me to adjust.

This was also harder for me than Roslyn because she and I came into this situation with very different professional backgrounds. The different positions that Roslyn has worked in over the years have always related to people and their behavioral patterns. First she was a teacher, so she was always dealing with children and their disparate personalities, and then she continued on in the social sciences, eventually getting her master's degree in social work. All along, she's been examining people's psyches, their emotions, their motivations, their interpersonal relationships. It's a world made up largely of gray area, and she spends her day navigating the space between what's on the surface and what's lying underneath.

In my world I deal with something far more concrete, and while my job involves some interpretation, it's of a very different kind. I'm a notary, which is something altogether different in Canada, where we live, from the guy in the United States who signs your personal documents at the bank for a few dollars. In Quebec the term *notary* translates to the equivalent of a real estate lawyer in the States. When I transfer a property, while it's not exactly a matter of science, it still has to be precise. It's not as if you're dealing with issues that are open to widely differing interpretations, at least, not if you do your job right. You're dealing with legal documents. Of course, you're working with people, sizing up their needs, their agendas, but there isn't the same level of subjective judgment and analysis that Roslyn's job requires. In addition, the "product" that Roslyn comes out with will change every day, shifting with every client. At the end of every day I'll come up with pretty much the same thing that I came up with the day before.

With her background, Roslyn was busy scrutinizing, analyzing what was happening with Andrew, trying to figure out how we should cope with it.

I just looked at it as a reality. That's the way it is; now let's get on with our lives. Move ahead.

And if you'd asked me then, I'd have told you we'd taken all the sexuality-based trauma that could be dished out to one family.

I would have been wrong.

CHAPTER 3

Coming to Terms

DOUG

1960–1991

DOUG   My own memories of coming out are, alternately, excruciating and mystifying . . . agonizing in the piecemeal pace of my growing self-awareness and mystifying in the lengths to which I'd go to willfully ignore the truth. No doubt there were many pivotal moments that shaped my experience of coming out that I don't remember at all, and perhaps the experiences that I do remember aren't recalled with pinpoint accuracy. But as with Andrew's coming-out story, maybe it's the way I've filtered the key moments, rather than any definitive fact, that has shaped who I am.

For me, the clues started arriving early. In fact, my first attraction to men dates back nearly as far as my memory itself. At

four years old I remember watching westerns and perking up whenever the shirtless Indians were on-screen, then curling up on the
couch with professional wrestling. (Yes, wrestling was on TV thirty
years ago, and even this four-year-old could have told you it was
every bit as phony back then.) Several years later, I remember greeting a nine-year-old friend who had come by our house on his way
back from a football game. The smell of sweat, grass, and something
else indefinable all wafted through my screen door on that sticky
summer afternoon, stirring an irrepressible craving in my gut. Like
most gay kids, though, I couldn't fathom quite what I was supposed
to *do* about any of it.

No doubt I was "different" in a dozen ways. Admittedly, I was
a cliché gay child. Listening to cast recordings of too many Broadway shows, shying away from most sports, afraid of the ball. I wrote
poetry, played piano . . . You get the picture.

There are countless kids who grow up gay without any of these
giveaways, boys who make the football team and conform to all of
society's expectations. And childhood may be a whole lot easier for
them—on the surface, anyway. I'll never forget a story told by an
old roommate. He had been a languid, light-footed teen, growing up
in Memphis, when a girl came up to him at recess in front of a
big group of kids, and announced, real loud, "Honey, it sure *shows*
on you!"

Well, you could say my entire adolescent experience was like a
visceral version of that encounter. Someone was always letting me
know, with a kick, a taunt, a jeer, it *showed* on me. And, like chicks
establishing order, I was getting pecked mercilessly, relentlessly,
nearly to death. Hardly a day went by during my three years of
junior high that I didn't pray for the courage to kill myself. What
is it they say about unanswered prayers?

As a result, when I hear today's debate about discussing homosexuality in school, the fear that it will teach students that gays and
lesbians are regular people, it rouses mighty, righteous indignation
left from some ancient scars that will never heal. When you grow
up facing fear and loathing on a daily basis, broad societal issues

have a way of becoming inextricably linked with individual trauma. This is how, for me, the political has become forever personal.

One day I carried home another wrecked piece of clothing. This one, a jacket, had been written on by a particularly opportunistic bully, a boy who sat behind me in history. He threatened me day in, day out, until I let him cheat on tests. To repay my spinelessness, he regularly drooled onto small strips of notebook paper and surreptitiously placed them on my head until I felt the nauseating drip of his spit on my scalp. This time he'd done something relatively minor, but it *showed* . . . A mere slash of a pen on my jacket. Unfortunately, it happened to be my only jacket.

On a cloudy winter weekend afternoon, as I walked with my parents, I asked my mother if I could have a new one. My father was a few feet ahead, and my mother asked, "What's wrong with this jacket?" I decided it was necessary to show her *what*, although I'd never tell *how*. I slowed slightly, and turned my back to her as we continued down the street. Once my mother saw the mark that ran down my back, she turned forward again and her head dropped, her eyes turned down, glued now to the sidewalk, and her voice fell close to a whisper.

"Don't tell Dad. He thinks the kids pick on you." Well, what could I say to that? *He's right? They do?*

And that's how the cycle of shame begins. I'm humiliated, and I don't want my parents to know what happened. My mother knows anyway, and she's afraid my father will find out, and he'll be ashamed of me too. And she's right, he will be. So no one talks.

This pattern of noncommunication was hardly unique to my ever-more-obvious sexual orientation. When I was born my mother experienced severe depression. I believe that today it would be classified as postpartum depression, though at the time it carried a tremendous stigma, much more than it might bear today. Whatever my family's life was like before, my birth turned everything upside down. Not only was my mother now ill, my father and mother were both, for their time, extremely old to be welcoming a baby into their family. The year was 1960, and my father was forty-six, my mother forty-three. My sister and brother were already sixteen and thirteen years old, respectively.

My parents sent me away to live with relatives. Clearly, no parent gives up a child, even temporarily, without a serious reason. My father and mother sent me off with the best intentions, hoping to give me a more stable beginning than could be offered at home. This difficult decision was made under even more difficult circumstances. I believe they did the most any parent can: they did the best they could with what they had. They sent me to Toledo, Ohio, to live with an aunt and uncle. My parents had almost no family on the West Coast, so my aunt and uncle were the closest relatives even though they lived two thousand miles away. My parents had left New York during the Depression, in the late thirties, leaving behind enormous families, and settled in Los Angeles during the early forties. Our family never recovered from this geographic separation, and perhaps the added strain of my mother's condition made it even harder, after I was born, for us to retain contact with relations spread out across the eastern seaboard. In fact, until I was out of college, I'd met only a handful of my enormous family, and only on one or two occasions at most.

When I returned home from Ohio, at age seven, our family appeared happy. This was my true home, yet somehow, I felt as much an outsider as I had when I was sent to live in Toledo. Now that I was back, both my parents doted on me, and I felt loved, but still, never quite at home. Not that they didn't try. My father all but made himself my private tutor, constantly quizzing me with vocabulary flash cards, setting up math and spelling games on magnetized boards all over the house, testing me on arcane trivia. And my mother tended to me with embarrassing care.

Before long, though, my mother struggled with depression again, and the family fell under a shroud of secrecy and shame that's never fully lifted. It's ironic that this shroud fell over my nuclear family long before my sexuality was suspect. This pervasive clandestine aura was best summed up by my sister's ex-husband, Bob, when he observed that our family operates "on a need-to-know basis." If information isn't absolutely vital (and even, sometimes, if it is), keep it to yourself. And, of course, once something has been rendered unspeakable, it's also been imbued with terrible power. In this back-handed way, secrets came to rule our house. *And everything in our house, it seemed, was secret.*

The summer I turned twelve, my parents and I were on a self-styled camping trip, which consisted of driving to a recreation area in our station wagon, which my father had outfitted with thick foam padding in the back. It was an ingenious method of stretching the budget for a quick weekend getaway, but even the thinnest family would have a tough time squeezing into the back of that car. I don't recall which order we three sardines wedged in, but there was hardly room for a deep breath. We'd done this once before, the previous summer, and since then I'd grown an inch or two in every direction.

It was near sunset; we'd come back from a drive in the forest and parked the station wagon in its spot. The ruggedness of the outing was grating on me, and I complained. I have no idea what I said, but my delivery must have had some drama, a hair too much flair, or maybe even a flounce. My father, walking around the car, carrying some extra pieces of padding into the back, flinched visibly. I kept on with my kvetching until he cut me off, acidly. There were an infinite number of far harsher words that were traded in our family, but his rueful remark, spoken with no great anger, just a weary air of hopelessness and somber resignation, may have cut the deepest:

"I'd hate to say what you sound like."

I knew he wasn't referring to how I sounded. My father was talking about—or really, just barely avoiding the awful declaration of—*what I was.* There was a subtext even a twelve-year-old could decipher, at least subconsciously: *I know what you are, and it's so disgusting, I can't even bring myself to say it.*

When it came time to cram ourselves together into the back of the wagon, I was especially bitter. It's one thing to have to sleep with the enemy, another altogether to be forced to spoon with him till dawn on an inch of foam padding.

You might think I would have been accustomed to derision by now. I'd been taunted so intensely at school, I could hardly think above the din of ridicule. I guess I was stubborn. Because for every kid who called me queer or faggot, I was that much more determined to ultimately prove them wrong. The big problem was, though they were brutal and heartless, they were right. With the transition from junior high to high school, the brutalization dwindled until all that remained for me was a vestigial fear.

The summer of the passage between schools was marked by a relationship that became a passage in my self-awareness. A tall, handsome, slightly wild and hyperactive boy, Mark, had taken a liking to me. Although I could tell that he was only sexually attracted to girls, that didn't stop me from developing an all-consuming crush on him. He came as an irresistible package, with parents much younger than mine, who had created an atmosphere at home for which I'd yearned ever since my family had erected barriers against all communication. We spent the entire summer together, and as my feelings for him grew, it helped explain the attraction I'd felt toward men since early childhood. I was jolted into the realization of what those desires actually signified, and that this was the kind of relationship I really craved.

Perhaps it sounds odd that after years of public humiliation at the hands of countless bullies, I still needed a shock to my system to clarify my own nature. Those taunts, however, seemed to be aimed at someone I didn't know. Since the thugs were, in fact, addressing only a part of me—my "queerness"—and ignoring the whole, it was possible for me to deny the accuracy of their base observation. Labeling someone "queer" implies that's all the person is. But I knew, in my heart, I wasn't one of "them." Until I connected with Mark, I somehow convinced myself that, since the bullies were wrong about me in whole, they were also mistaken about that one specific area, my sexuality, as well. I'd managed to isolate my desires into a separate compartment. If I ignored them, I thought, they wouldn't exist.

I walked a fine line in my relationship with Mark, aware of my consuming desire, yet fearing he didn't want me the same way. When

I finally stumbled over that line, it yawned into a gaping rift that we could never cross again. We were listening, funnily enough, to Queen, in his bedroom. Santa Ana winds had kicked up on a November afternoon, heating the air with the hint of electricity. Mark was lying on top of his bed, wearing only his shorts.

"You won't believe what Steven did on Saturday night." Steven was his next-door neighbor, and best friend from earliest childhood.

"I was sleeping over on Saturday night, and I was on this folding cot across the room. The lights were all out. I thought he'd gone to sleep, and then I felt something land on my lap. When I reached to feel it, I couldn't believe . . ."

"What?" I tried not to sound too eager.

"His underwear! I looked over, and I could see him in the little bit of light from the porch lamp that leaked through the slats in his blinds. He was lying there totally naked, and I could completely see his dick. Then he asks me to take mine off, and toss them to him!"

"Yeah?" My own fantasy life seemed to be spilling into somebody else's hands, and I was anxious, excited, and jealous over what he might say next.

"Yeah, what?"

"What did you do?" I hissed, impatiently.

"What do you think! I said, 'What the hell are you doing?' He says, 'Do it, come on.' So I get up, throw my clothes on real fast, and come home. Is that bizarre or what?"

The story left me so conflicted—awkward, confused, and exhilarated—that I didn't respond. Then Mark sprang out of bed, went across the room, turned on the television, and sat down on the floor, his back against the side of his bed frame. As usual, I sat down next to him, and settled in to watch TV. But this time I edged in a little closer than usual. Perhaps I looked at the story, subconsciously, as some kind of repressed foreplay, and as we watched *Happy Days*, I reached behind Mark and tentatively brushed my hand across the back of his arm. No response. Moments later, I tried it again, a hint more obviously.

"Excuse me, but you're making me sick." As he said it, he glared ahead at the television.

Well, at least he was to the point.

I backed off, but it was too late. After I'd had dinner with his family, I heard the hum of my father's station wagon as he pulled into their driveway.

Peering through the shutters in Mark's room, I saw my father step onto the pavement. I turned away. I was wounded, flushed with disgrace, unable to conceive that Mark might have betrayed me. My face burned, I went light-headed, my fingers tingled. Consumed by a desperate need to disappear, I suddenly felt enormous, a gigantic object of contempt and scorn. My father stowed my bicycle in the back, and we drove home silently, never to speak about why he'd been called on to pluck me out of Mark's house and cart me off, like a criminal.

After high school I was enrolled in U.S.C.'s revamped acting conservatory. Despite the achievement of being admitted to the competitive program, news of my decision was greeted by my family with a resounding cry of foul. This had become, it seemed, my greatest transgression, a slap in the face of the family's reverence for higher education. Never mind that I considered the mastery of the acting craft a worthwhile goal. I wasn't so naive as to expect my parents to weep with joy. But neither did I see my choice as tantamount to family treason.

A rotten carrot was dangled in front of me: If I chose to study law or accounting, my grandmother would foot the bill. If acting was to be my choice, I was on my own. The bitterness I hear in my own description is only a trace residual; it doesn't weigh on me, or my feelings for my family, any longer. But for at least ten years after college, I felt keenly their abandonment, imagining them as the rabid fans of an opposing team, salivating at the prospect of my failure.

In the end, I received enough scholarships and school loans (this was pre-Reagan education slashing) that I was able to wait tables and scrape by for the four years. But the lousy hand I felt I had been dealt has left a peculiar mark. Reading the morning paper will always be an exercise in frustration, because any miscarriage of justice rankles me to the core of my being. Every story of a little guy who gets the short end of the stick makes me seethe.

The wrongs and betrayals I perceived caused me to feel something akin to an orphan. And my parents had moved to Florida soon after I graduated high school. For much of the next ten years I rarely saw them. While I was in college, my sister gave birth to her daughter, Michelle. I spent a good deal of time at their house, occasionally baby-sitting. However, the friends I made at U.S.C. became, to an extent, my family, and an emotional safety net. If I crashed, they were there.

In our junior year, a few new faces joined our small program. One belonged to a bright-eyed, charismatic, curly-haired, swaggering good old boy from Alabama. For a sturdy six-footer, Charlie had a childlike charm, tinged with a taste of black-Irish wickedness. We were instantly inseparable.

Since I'd moved to college, the background noise of my desires had increased steadily until it became nearly impossible to hear above it. Yet I continued to try to ignore reality. I still attached myself to heterosexual guys, hoping that their companionship would suffice. After five weeks with Charlie, this promised to be more of the same—the latest in a long string of straight-boy crushes.

We spent weeks together, staying up late, eating at all-night downtown dives, hanging out between classes, engaging in catty gossiping, and laughing over my pathetic attempts to cheat at gin rummy. I'd already slept over at his studio apartment a half dozen times. He was the first friend I'd made who lived alone, without a roommate to navigate around. In two full years of college, I couldn't claim a single sexual experience, a dubious distinction that hardly any of my classmates could match.

As far as I could tell, Charlie was straight as an arrow. I imagined our attraction was because we were two people who shared much in common. I had already had several other intimate bonding experiences with other young men and women in our class, and none of them involved sex, so why should this one?

We'd been up till one playing gin and drinking. I made a move to grab my backpack, but Charlie gave me orders.

"Put that down. You're stayin'." I smiled, dropped the bag like it was poison, and walked over to the pull-out couch I usually used.

"Forget about it, I don't feel like makin' it." As he walked through from the kitchen to the bathroom, he turned down the corner of the bed, which I took as a signal to hop in. It looked big enough to comfortably hold the two of us. It still looked like any other night.

Once we were in bed, and the lights were out, I turned over, away from Charlie, toward the barred windows. I could hear him snoring lightly. Soon after, I dropped off. I haven't any idea how much later it was, but I woke to find his thigh bearing down on mine. In a flash, both his powerful legs had pinned me. Now his entire body was smack on top of mine, and he was mumbling incoherently into my ear as he pressed against me. For an instant, I thought I must have been imagining all of this in some feverish dream. But by the time it was all over, perhaps a quarter of an hour later, there was no question that in most respects this was as real as—no, more real than—anything I'd ever experienced. The verdict was in. This was what I'd been looking for.

There was one extremely disturbing thing, however . . . Throughout our encounter, Charlie maintained a sporadic, rambling stream of consciousness, which he whispered and grunted in my ear. Not only did it never approach real communication, it even seemed to imply that he was *talking in his sleep*.

When I tried to talk back, there was never a true response, only more semicoherent gibberish. Sexy gibberish, but nonsense nonetheless.

When we were done, he rolled over and went right back to sleep.

Or was he ever awake at all?

That was the bizarre, self-deceiving question I came to ask myself. It was an impression Charlie was eager to foster. When we woke the next morning, I asked him, haltingly, over coffee, if he'd had any interesting dreams that night.

He looked perplexed. "Why? Did I bother you or somethin'?"

My head spun. Perhaps it wasn't real for him. Maybe he *was* dreaming.

If I said this went on for two years, you'd say I was a fool to continue to question his awareness of our encounters. All I can add in my defense is that three months into this deluded dance, I made a desperate gambit to force us both to discuss, and thereby face, reality.

Charlie was set to return home to Alabama for Christmas break. Money was tight, so he was booked on a train home to Montgomery, scheduled for five o'clock Wednesday afternoon. Tuesday I decided I had to stop the farce. It was just twenty-four hours before he was to leave, and I sat him down in his kitchen, across the table, and fought to find the words. I knew I worked best with a script, yet I entered this conversation without so much as a moment of mental rehearsal.

Now that Charlie looked back at me expectantly and asked, "Yeah, what?" I realized how absurd I would sound.

What could I say? "Oh, by the way, Charlie, did you know we've been having sex for the last three months?" If he knew it was true, he obviously wanted desperately to suppress discussion of it. If this were to come as a shock to him, it would, as far as I could imagine, end our relationship.

Yes. That was, sad as it may be, my ultimate priority. For me, clinging to this mute, muzzled affair was of paramount importance. More important even than the truth.

Suddenly I decided the only way out was to make *him* say it. Somehow, I convinced myself that if the revelation came from his own lips, if I could corner him into confessing it, he couldn't blame me, and perhaps our relationship could continue.

"There's something we have to talk about."

"Yeah?"

"It's really difficult, because I'm afraid."

"What's to be afraid of?"

"What do you think's been going on between us?"

"Well, we have our fights and stuff, like anybody. But I like bein' with you. You know that. We have a good time."

"No. Really," I said. "Why do I stay over all the time?"

"I don't know, why do you?"

"That's not what I mean."

"Then what do you mean?" Again he turned my question back on me.

We played this volley-return, volley-return game until, after several minutes, he got up to start packing, and asked me to help him. This kept us off the topic for a few minutes, until I asked him if we could go for a drive. We talked about anything else, it seemed. We stopped for dinner at an all-night diner, then got back on the road and drove late into the night, just marking time on the freeways of L.A.

For the next eight hours, I made several vain attempts to steer our conversation back to the point. We must have traveled all the circles of each highway cloverleaf in a dozen zip codes before it seemed, finally, that Charlie was going to crack.

I started talking about a guy in the acting class one year ahead of us. He was notoriously gay and had flirted with each of us, Charlie in particular. Until now, we had always made a joke of his attentions, but I tried to suggest that perhaps Charlie enjoyed it.

"Do *you?*" Again he shrewdly turned my question against me.

"Yeah, I guess. How about you?"

"What? What's the problem?" he suddenly hammered at me. "Are you trying to tell me you're gay? 'Cause that's fine. You know I've got gay friends. It's no big deal. OK? Is that it?"

I turned away. Sunrise was slashing through the cracks between the towers of downtown as we crossed the Harbor Freeway, but it appeared we were destined to spend the rest of our relationship, however long it might last, in the dark.

I had been in some very deep denial myself. Now I was face-to-face with a new, stupefying level. After all this buildup, after twelve hours of wrenching effort, this was as close as we were going to come to honesty. He wasn't going to talk openly, but he managed to send a message loud and clear:

The concept that I might be gay is so scary, even if I can have sex with you, that I can't discuss it or acknowledge it. And don't even THINK about suggesting that I'M gay. Communication will not be tolerated.

Accept me in silence, or not at all.

An experience like that could send you hurtling out of the closet, or shut you down even more profoundly. I retreated further into my shell.

Finally, two years later, when I was twenty-four, my soon-to-be best friend (and, a dozen years later, my best man) George finally dragged me out.

From that time until I met Andrew, seven years later, I was openly gay to my friends and most of my coworkers. My relationship with my parents remained rather distant, both figuratively and literally. When I was twenty-six I moved to Boston, and a few years later to New York. By the time I put down roots on the East Coast, my parents had moved from Miami, where they had retired, back to Los Angeles. Once again we were settled on separate coasts. During these years we saw each other only on Thanksgiving, when I made an annual pilgrimage home. Given our minimal correspondence, and the still tight-lipped atmosphere, pronouncement of my homosexuality would have seemed like passing gas in synagogue — surprising, inappropriate, and pointless. I knew, given their liberal political and social views, that they would never display disapproval. The news would merely be met with thunderous silence. Perhaps a shrug, and weak smiles. After all, they had both known for years that I was gay, and nothing — *nothing* — was discussed openly in our family anyway.

I could never have imagined the strange turn events would take when my engagement to Andrew pushed me to write my parents with the news, and finally, officially, come out to them.

CHAPTER 4

Coming Home—and Making a Home

ANDREW, DOUG, ROSLYN, AND SHELDON

July–August 1991

ANDREW We'd only been dating for a month when I asked Doug if he'd like to drive up to Montreal together for Labor Day weekend. I was looking forward to showing him around and giving him a better idea of where I came from, my background. And I wanted him to meet my family.

DOUG Stepping into Andrew's world was unlike anything I could have imagined. This small sphere of Montreal's Jewish community was fascinating and unnerving. Montreal is no backwater town. It's an enormous, lovely, and cosmopolitan world-class city. And yet when we strolled around the neighborhood mall, it seemed *everyone* knew Andrew by name. Cars pulled over in the parking lot, rolling down windows. Shoppers stopped us throughout the mall. "How's school?" "Andrew, how's your father?" "Give your parents my best!" "How long you in for, Andrew?"

I always thought of Van Nuys, the L.A. suburb where I grew up, as insular, but I could still walk the streets with a feeling of relative anonymity. Montreal, or at least certain Jewish neighborhoods, seemed a parochial village. Though this provincial familiarity was certainly quaint, I couldn't have possibly guessed at the time how, four years away, it would make our eventual plans to wed infinitely more difficult.

It suddenly felt too soon to be making this intrusion into Andrew's territory. I didn't feel we had connected nearly enough for me to be brought into the heart of this tightly knit community. Fortunately, Andrew's parents were away for the weekend when we arrived, and they weren't returning until Sunday afternoon. At least their temporary absence gave me a little breathing room.

ANDREW   I introduced Doug to many of the family friends and acquaintances who approached me that weekend, but when I did, I just said, this is my friend. What else was I to say? Apart from the fact that I wouldn't have been comfortable offering anything more personal to these people, I sensed we were in a period of transition, from dating to something deeper.

DOUG   As usual, I spent my first twenty-four hours in Montreal with Andrew overanalyzing every aspect of the experience. We went together with his friend Lorne to a bar in the gay section downtown. We perched at a table, where Andrew held my hand—under the table. Was he shy about public display of affection? Or did he want to remain looking unattached, in case something better came along? Did he include me enough in conversations with his old friends throughout the weekend, or was I being dragged around like an unavoidable inconvenience?

Sunday afternoon Andrew took me to the country club where

his parents hold a family membership. We sat out at the pool, and I opened up to Andrew, allowing a new vulnerability, telling him my qualms and fears about his feelings for me. I felt the need to explain my furrowed brow and strained conversation, though I worried he would find my display of insecurity annoying and off-putting. Instead he thanked me for my openness and revealed an even more concerned, caring, and sympathetic side than I had witnessed before, a side that drew me even closer.

We were only a few hours from his parents' scheduled arrival, and now I had a slight boost to help me face our evening together.

ANDREW   Doug was the only boyfriend I ever introduced to my parents. I wasn't nervous about it, though. It was a good feeling to know that they were about to meet someone with whom I felt so close. And I knew they would like him, and approve of him.

ROSLYN   Sheldon and I had left town for the first part of Labor Day weekend, and we came home Sunday afternoon to find Andrew in the kitchen with his new friend.

Until this moment, Andrew had never felt the need to introduce us to anyone he was dating, male or female for that matter, and when he said he was driving from New York with this new person, I definitely became curious. I restrained the impulse to ask Andrew any questions. This time I kept my motherly prying to a minimum, preferring to allow things to unfold as naturally as possible.

Initially I was really happy to hear that Andrew had met someone whom he really liked. As a parent, I was also proud that Andrew felt he could trust us enough to introduce us to Doug. After all, many parents never get to meet the significant person in their gay child's life.

In spite of these warm, fuzzy thoughts, however, the old fantasy resurfaced unintentionally: *Why couldn't it be a girl?* Meeting the "boyfriend" would force us to face the reality that Andrew was in fact gay. Since even the smallest denial of this reality would not be helpful to anyone, I told myself repeatedly, *Think of how you would*

*behave if Andrew were about to introduce you to his female love. Now behave
the same way.* This thought process helped me focus on what was
really important, and that was being the best parent to Andrew that
I knew how to be.

For all my preparation I was realistic enough to admit that this
would be a tense moment for all of us.

Our preliminary encounter in the kitchen went well, but it was
so brief, I couldn't draw any conclusions. But one thing seemed
apparent: *With the last name Wythe, he's not Jewish . . . Oh well, what
can you do?*

SHELDON   Somehow I knew—while Roslyn didn't—that Andrew had met Doug through a service. So I feared the worst. "Service" sounded suspiciously like "escort service." It seemed to me
that anybody who seeks companionship in that fashion is looking
for one thing only. Therefore the image in my mind was of something
purely sexual. Of course, even if that were true, I suppose it's better
than meeting somebody at a bar. Given these impressions, I was
pleasantly surprised when I met Doug. He seemed normal, sophisticated, bright.

DOUG   While Andrew and I got showered and dressed to go to
dinner, my nerves began to fray. I'd never met the parents of anybody I'd dated.

"Do you think they liked me?"

"Oh, come on, of course."

"You could tell?"

"Yeah."

"I don't know. Your father was kind of quiet."

"That's normal."

"Normal for anybody . . . or normal for him?"

"Oh, for God's sake, relax!"

ANDREW   We drove together to one of Montreal's best Chinese
restaurants. It was quiet in the car. When we sat down to dinner,

everyone was extremely courteous. After we negotiated the order, my father loosened up and started drilling Doug about television . . . Joan Rivers . . . the state of talk shows in general. Doug asked all about the city, the different neighborhoods, the politics, revealing his tendency to seek a perspective on his position in a new place, trying to find out where he is in relation to everything else.

Dinner was going well. So far, so good.

ROSLYN   Back in the car on the way home, Andrew was in the backseat with Doug; Sheldon was driving. There'd been a long silence, and a question came to my mind . . .

ANDREW   She said it in such a way, like she was trying to be very cosmopolitan, very "with it" . . .

ROSLYN   All I asked was, "Where did you two meet?"

DOUG   There was a tiny pause as Andrew and I shot each other a look in the backseat.

ANDREW   Doug's face said, *We're not telling her it was a dating service.* For some reason he'd been tight-lipped about the origin of our relationship since we'd met, whereas I got a kick out of people's reaction to this news.

ROSLYN   After a brief pause without either of them offering me an answer, or even a hint, I decided to follow up with what was, as far as I was concerned, a logical question . . .

"Was it in a gay bar?"

DOUG   Sheldon, until this moment, had been silent, and appeared to be concentrating on driving, but in a spontaneous reaction, as if shielding a baby's ears from some gruesome, fearful words, he made a grab for the car stereo, which had been humming softly in the background, and cranked the volume up . . . *waaaaay* up.

ANDREW Perhaps my mother had unintentionally conjured up images for my father that he'd rather not associate with his own son . . . sweaty men boogying to disco music, making out on the dance floor . . . But whatever quickened that connection, those choice words made one seriously snappy neural trip from my father's ear to his fingertips.

DOUG Between the unintentional tawdriness of the question and Sheldon's split-second knee-jerk reflex, Andrew and I couldn't help ourselves, and the burst of laughter that exploded from us—in unison—cut right through the music blaring from the stereo.

ROSLYN What's wrong with wondering if they got together in a bar? People meet in bars. It's a perfectly reasonable possibility, isn't it?

Well, apparently Sheldon didn't much like the question either, because, with one determined turn of the volume control, he *literally* tuned us all out. (By the way, I never did get Andrew and Doug to answer my simple question until years later—when we were planning the wedding.)

When we got home and headed upstairs, Andrew and Doug said good night and slipped into the guest bedroom, on the opposite side of the staircase from ours. As Sheldon and I opened the door into our room, I asked him, "How do you feel about them sleeping together across the hall? Do you have a problem with it?"

Without missing a beat he simply replied, "No."

And I said, "Good, neither do I."

I was surprised that he was so accepting of the arrangement. And though I like to believe that the response was sincere, I question his motive since, as anyone who knows Sheldon will tell you, he does not welcome confrontation at ten-thirty in the evening.

DOUG As I got ready for bed, I pondered over whether I'd given a good account of myself. Andrew said I was fine, but I wasn't convinced. One thing was certain—Sheldon and Roslyn had been splendid, charming hosts.

ANDREW Some people might have had great trepidation in this situation. Doug and I were about to cuddle up together only twenty feet away from my parents' room. I knew this to be a liberal house, however. Since my mother had been a sex educator, books about sexuality in all its forms were all over the place. I just didn't look at this like it was a big deal.

When I climbed into bed with Doug, I felt so close to him. It was a new level of intimacy, an intensity I'd never experienced. I laid my head down on his stomach, and looked up toward him.

Suddenly I had to say it, regardless of the minor risk of seeing him back away . . .

"I . . ."

But once the words started out of my mouth, they got caught somewhere between my brain and my tongue. It was too late, but still, I worried . . . *How does he feel about me?* Each of my short relationships flickered before my eyes in an instant. Every one of the times when I felt more strongly about the other person than he felt toward me.

". . . think I . . ."

By now he knows what I'm about to say. Is he thinking the same thing? I tried to read his expression in the moonlight.

". . . think I'm falling in love with you."

Regardless of my last-moment fears, I was glad I'd said it.

He hugged me very close.

DOUG It came as such a surprise. I hadn't ever played out the scene in my imagination, and somehow the words Andrew had reason to expect from me in return didn't come. Maybe our embrace said enough, at least for that night. Even though I didn't respond in kind, it was, for me at least, an indelible moment. A moment put on hold by an unmistakable call from the hallway.

ROSLYN   As we went through the nightly ritual of ushering Cashew out of the bedroom, I took advantage of having Andrew back home and called out across the hall to his closed door, "Andrew, could you put the dog outside?" Then I shut our door and sat down on the bed next to where Sheldon had already gotten under the covers.

"What do you think of him?"

He said, "He's very nice."

"Do you think he's Jewish?"

"No. At least I don't think so."

"I don't either. But I'm glad Andrew found somebody he cares about, and who cares for him."

I waited for a response.

None.

"What do *you* think?" I pushed. "Are you happy for Andrew?"

"Mmm-hmmmm. I suppose." And, after a pause, "But you know that just because they're seeing each other now doesn't mean they'll be together long."

"For the moment it's good. And you never know."

"Why do you have to make such a big thing out of it? Nobody's saying they're going to be together forever. Enough, already." He sealed the conversation. Closed.

That's my hubby, the proverbial realist, avoiding any projection into the future for fear that he could one day be proven wrong, preferring to deal with the here and now. By contrast, I am the dreamer. And I found myself fantasizing a future for Andrew and Doug, praying that they were as right for each other as it seemed, and that they'd stay together, happily ever after, no broken hearts.

A few months later, Andrew and Doug flew in for the Passover holiday. We held the traditional dinner, or seder, at home. For those who've never been to a seder, it consists of a great deal of eating, and even more talking. The readings tell the historical significance of the holiday, and in our house many of us read it in Hebrew. With the last name Wythe, we assumed Doug would be reading in English, so while trying not to single him out, I asked everyone to read in whatever language they were most comfortable in.

We went around the table, Sheldon, then Andrew, both reading in Hebrew, and when it came Doug's turn, lo and behold, *"Adonai elochanu melech ha-olam . . ."*

He's Jewish! I exclaimed silently. And I smiled as I thought, *So we won't have to do a conversion!*

DOUG   A few months later, I went in for sinus surgery. Nothing serious, but I came out of it with my nose packed with gauze, which started to unravel. I have a phobia about suffocation, and when the bloody gauze dripped down from my sinuses into my throat, I had a panic attack of mammoth proportion. Even for me. Andrew was at his apartment when I called him.

"I'm dying! The packing is coming loose—I can't breathe!"

"Have you called the doctor?"

"It's eight o'clock—I'm sure he's left the office . . . What am I going to do?"

"Call his office. There'll be an emergency number on the machine."

"God, thank you." I called, then beeped the emergency number. Five minutes later, no return call, and more gauze had dripped down, dangling against my tongue. I freaked. I ran around my tiny apartment like a caged rat smelling smoke. The enormous window that overlooked the street seemed the only way out. As a rule, I've never been the suicidal type. But this seemed a worthy exception. I ripped open the window frame and looked down three stories, seeing the pavement below as the only break to put an end to the frantic pounding of my heart and the screaming of blood pumping in my ears. I called Andrew again, with a breathless, hushed threat that sounded like it was coming out of someone else. *"I have to jump.* I can't take it anymore. I can't reach the doctor. *I have to jump."*

I don't remember much of the rest of the night, except for Andrew coming over, taking me to the emergency room, and later helping me pick up a strong sedative to conk me out. But I do remember a couple of things I learned that night. For one, real love isn't about caring for someone at his best. It's about seeing him at his ugliest and sticking it out. Andrew had done that, and more. I couldn't imagine looking at a person as deranged as I'd been, and staying calm, focused, and caring. Yet Andrew had. That night he proved himself a better person than me. In a way, I'd given Andrew an unintended test. One that I would have failed. And once he had passed, I was hooked.

Over the next two years, the relationship Andrew and I built together deepened and grew. One gap that remained between us, however, continued to separate our views of both the world and our relationship: the difference in our ages. Five years younger than me, Andrew was still in school and dependent on his parents, at an age when I'd been completely on my own for almost a decade.

I've always been subconsciously obsessed with time, running my life against an imaginary clock, a race with some idealized version of myself that I couldn't win. Now that I was in the longest relation-ship of my life, and soon to enter my mid-thirties, I felt it was time to move in with Andrew. To a significant degree I was motivated by personal goals outside our actual relationship. Perhaps I should have waited longer before pressing the point, but I was convinced that if the two of us had a future, I needed to see if we were meant to spend our lives together, and living under the same roof seemed the next logical step.

ANDREW Moving in together was entirely Doug's idea. Maybe I would have been ready six months or even a year later. But he wanted to do it too early, and I felt pressured. I was just becoming accustomed to having someone sleep in the same bed with me, and here he was asking me to move in with him? In some ways I saw advantages to living together; after all, moving to a larger apartment, a one-bedroom, was appealing. Not only that, but I loved Doug. However, I found myself focusing on reasons why it wasn't a good idea. The biggest problem I had with Doug was the way he handled conflict. I can recall countless times when he would explode into a rage and storm out of my apartment. Conflicts would often go unresolved, leaving us both silently dissatisfied. I have to admit that there were many times that I unnecessarily provoked him, criticizing him for his choice of clothes or hairstyle, for example. In fact, this critical position was the norm amongst me and my siblings, and I hadn't given it much thought until Doug came into my life.

After doing some research on the rental market, Doug and I learned that the rent we would pay together for a small one-bedroom wouldn't be any less than the sum of what we paid separately. In fact, it would probably be somewhere in the vicinity of fifty dollars more a month. We each had a very cheap, tiny studio apartment, but we knew we'd kill each other if we had to occupy that small an area together. With a one-bedroom, we would gain more living space, but my father chastised, "You're supposed to save money if you move in together, not spend more!"

I didn't believe that fifty dollars a month warranted repeated carping, but my need to seek his approval further fed my ambivalence. And while it's true that at least one of my siblings received similar financial support while seeking an advanced degree, that didn't cancel out the significant factor that he was still supporting *me*. So I was tied, ultimately, to his final decision.

SHELDON I didn't see anything wrong with the two of them moving in together. In fact, I would encourage anybody who is moving into a new environment to find a roommate. What I did question was why Andrew wouldn't see any savings in rent if he were to share an apartment. It wasn't that I discouraged him from moving in with Doug, I only discouraged him from moving into a fancy place.

DOUG I could understand Sheldon's financial concern, theoretically. However, it sounded to me like he was disturbed about something other than forty or fifty dollars a month. One phrase of Sheldon's that Andrew repeated to me struck a chord. "I can understand you wanting companionship. But why do you have to live together?"

Was that a question you would ask a heterosexual couple?

SHELDON   I saw this as two people moving in together, like roommates. For some reason, I never put it on a different level than that of two friends. Perhaps I blocked it out of my mind, even after they'd been seeing each other for two years. Maybe I didn't want to think of their relationship in any other way.

ANDREW   As usual, my father capitulated, but not without tremendous effort on my part. Another agreement needed to be made — this one between me and Doug. He had to agree to enter couples therapy with me. He resisted mightily, but soon he realized that this was the only way I would agree to move in with him.

And as it turned out, I had reason to be concerned about the conflict living together might create. Our first three months under the same roof were nearly our undoing. Like cats vying to mark our territory, each decision about living space instigated a turf battle that called for bared teeth and sharpened claws, leaving both of us scarred from the combat and wary of the other.

ROSLYN   I heard the rumblings of trouble as soon as they moved in together. Sheldon and I were visiting New York, and Doug was away at work. The three of us, Sheldon, Andrew, and I, went out to a cute little breakfast place near the apartment they now shared.

"I don't know if it's going to work out with Doug," confided Andrew, with a resigned, fatalistic air.

"Just because you're having troubles, you're going to run away from them?" I chastised. Andrew looked away, staring back at one of the little teddy bears that eavesdrop from the tops of the semicircular booths, hanging just above eye level. "Don't you think there's another way before you give up? Daddy and I have had our share of problems, but we didn't run away from them, we dealt with them.

In the beginning we had a lot to iron out. We had to learn to compromise and work things through."

Though I tried to sound cool as I counseled Andrew, I was scared. I liked Doug, and loved Andrew, and didn't want to see them hurt. And I feared Andrew would slide into a deep depression if he couldn't work this one out. At least he needed to give it a serious try. So I kept at him.

"The issues between the two of you, finding your place in the relationship and defining your space, they'll exist in every relationship you'll ever have. You have to learn to negotiate—both of you—and not at the expense of the other, so you can both have a share in the relationship, so that you'll both feel understood."

ANDREW   We turned a corner with our first serious purchase. For months we had two mammoth mismatched couches crowding our living room, the leftovers of our prior, individual lives. I finally talked Doug into selling his sofa, with the understanding that we'd go out and purchase a new couch and love seat. Once we found the new furniture, I'd get rid of my own sleeper sofa.

After what seemed like aeons of furious, fruitless couch-hunting, we heard Bloomingdale's was having a sale. I prayed that maybe, finally, our long home-furnishing nightmare would be over.

We made a beeline to the sale area, and immediately gravitated toward a simple set in what they called "seafoam green." *This is surprisingly quick,* I thought. Doug went to find a salesperson to set up the purchase. He took too long, because during those few minutes I had time to doubt our decision. I slowly wandered the merchandise floor and surveyed the many options. By the time Doug returned, salesman in tow, I had settled on another set. Actually, it was the same style, in a chocolate brown.

"OK, we're done," Doug announced.

"Have you run it through on the credit card?"

"Yeah. Is there a problem?"

"Well, it's just that I don't really like that color. What do you think about this one?" I stood proudly by my find.

"It's way too dark. Besides, we both said we liked the green."

"I didn't really like it that much."

"You liked it enough to agree to buy it two minutes ago."

"I don't like that shade, and it'll show dirt."

DOUG The salesman must hear this kind of argument all the time. He stepped back and glanced down at nothing in particular. It was a nice effort, but he hadn't become invisible, and I was suitably embarrassed over having a brawl in front of a stranger.

"What's wrong with the brown?" asked Andrew.

We picked apart and debated the pros and cons of seafoam green and chocolate brown as if the fate of Western civilization hung in the balance.

As I saw it, Andrew made a decision, then once I left him alone, he began to interpret it as a compromise. Compromise was still tough for both of us, and when it came to decoration decisions, it was especially challenging to him. I couldn't move a chair or purchase a candle without his questioning my judgment and then overruling me.

After an interminable argument, during which we paced half the length of Bloomingdale's, losing the salesman somewhere between bedding and china, I stopped suddenly and stared him down. "I'm not leaving this store without those sofas. Every furniture salesperson in Manhattan knows us by name. This is it. I'm not looking anyplace else. If we can't agree on this now, we'll be stuck with those two crappy old couches till we're ready for retirement! You were happy with this set, *in seafoam green*, then you got cold feet. If we can't compromise now—how can we ever do it?"

No reaction. I'd have to get tough.

"You leave *with a couch*, or you leave *without me*."

Nothing. So turning on the drama wasn't going to do it. I had one last idea that I hoped would demonstrate how ludicrous this struggle was. "So why don't we flip a coin?"

To my dismay, his eyes lit up.

"Forget it," I snapped. "If we're ever going to make *us* work, we've got to be able to make *this* work. We're making a decision, and sticking with it, and leaving this store with a new set of living room furniture."

We stood, locked eye to eye, stock-still.

He blinked.

And two months later, we took shipment of the furniture that graces our living room to this day. Two lovely Bloomingdale's couches.

ANDREW   And yes, they were seafoam green. So don't let Doug tell you I can't compromise.

After that, it became apparent that everything would work itself out. And eventually it did. With counseling and mutual understanding, we both made it through a frightening time. And we had a new, stronger connection. It was as if, having weathered the tempest of our first months, we were survivors of the same catastrophe, sharing the bond of veterans.

DOUG   Our small circle of two was much stronger, but there was a subtext that I began to sense lurking almost imperceptibly around the edges of our familial dynamic. On the surface, Sheldon and Roslyn were uncommonly open and accepting of Andrew, and me, and our relationship. Speaking for myself, I never felt Sheldon and Roslyn treated me like a lesser person, or somehow different because of my sexuality. And yet I began to recognize an undercurrent that suggested that Andrew and I, as a couple, were indeed seen as different.

At least they saw us as some kind of couple. Until our engagement, the independence I'd long had from my own parents—and the communication we'd never had—allowed key truths to remain veiled, and pushed Sheldon and Roslyn to the center of our increasingly pressurized extended family, placing a great unspoken burden on them.

As it would for so many things, the wedding eventually exposed many of the unexplored issues that had quietly chipped away at the foundations of our familial relationships. It would force new awareness on many fronts, from the distance built up between me and my parents, to the conflict spurred by my moving in with Andrew.

ROSLYN The conflict Doug sensed in our family had been brewing for a long time, although I did my best to smooth over any potential problems, trying to keep everyone happy and comfortable. One night, however, so much that had been below the surface bubbled up.

Sheldon's sixtieth birthday party had been in the planning stages for months. I had gone all out in an effort to make it unique, to personalize it for Sheldon, reserving one of our favorite restaurants, putting together a menu with all the food he liked, creating a multitiered sports-themed birthday cake (one layer was a basketball court, another a tennis court), laboring for weeks on a video I planned to show that night. By the evening of the event I was on overload, from the basic logistics to the menu, seating, video, music, and the comfort of our guests.

From the minute we began getting dressed, Sheldon became another person, harsh, overbearing, overreacting to anything and everything. By the time we arrived at dinner and sat down at the head table with our children and their respective partners, I had an idea of what had set Sheldon off.

Here we were with Bonnie, her husband, David, Debbie, her husband, Abraham, our son Mitchell, and Andrew—with Doug. This was the first time we'd all been together in a public spotlight, outside of family gatherings that were strictly in the family.

DOUG Getting out of the house that night was an ordeal.

"What are you doing?" Andrew fumed. "Your hair is fine!" He tried to take my "fro" comb out of my hand.

"Leave me alone!" I combed my hair out farther.

"You're getting poofy!" Andrew warned. I kept right on poofing. "Come on, my father's pacing downstairs. He wants to get out of here."

"I need a minute."

"You need a haircut! Stop playing with it, you look fine. Would you hurry up!"

I obsessed over every article of clothing, like I was deciding on the clothes I'd get buried in. An apt comparison, it turned out. The evening turned into a three-ring circus, of sorts. Once at the head table, we were the center ring.

I'd met many of the extended Merling family at holiday dinners, but this was my introduction to the community at large. And though I'd fretted about each of those events, this was a heart-pounding, hangnail-pulling, shirt-dampening night.

ANDREW   The evening started out downstairs at the restaurant, where cocktails were served. People approached us warily. Whether it was because they didn't know Doug or because he was male, I couldn't tell. An uncle who is usually very gregarious seemed to avoid any contact with Doug. I wasn't constantly on the lookout for slights, but I couldn't help but notice some people avoiding contact with him. None of this struck me personally; rather I was concerned that Doug, sensitive as he is, would feel stung by the few cool responses.

ROSLYN   I must have had some discomfort of my own about this, since I was concerned with how other people were reacting to the presence of Andrew and Doug together at our table. Throughout the evening I was hypervigilant, looking to see who was avoiding Doug. I was playing the role of gatekeeper, a position I'd held in my parents' home. The present circumstances only exacerbated this tendency. I was observing to see who was being warm, who ignored him. It was an exhausting evening of surveillance. I grew more sensitive, and watchful, as the night wore on.

DOUG   I was on hyper overdrive as I groped for names of the family I'd met. After a minute of talking with one table of cousins our own age, I turned around to find Andrew was gone. My Siamese twin was ripped from me, and I had a gaping hole where my confidence should have been. Suddenly I couldn't think of a word to say to anyone. I excused myself and headed for the bathroom, hoping to find Andrew there.

It was the only thing I got right all night. We were alone at the urinals. "Don't leave me alone out there tonight, please?" I pled nakedly. As he shook his head and chuckled, all I could think of was that line from *Broadcast News* that goes something like, "Wouldn't it be nice if insecurity and neediness made us more attractive?" Well, if it did, I was downright gorgeous that night.

So you might expect that I would have been more sensitive to Roslyn's predicament as one-woman envoy between the heteros and the homos. Unfortunately, I was too self-obsessed to see what she was up against.

Once all of us were seated at the head table, it was quite a while before any of the Merling family's friends stepped over to say hello. When one woman finally did approach the table, it came time for Roslyn to make a round of introductions. You could sense that everyone was curious as to how she would navigate the uncharted etiquette challenge before her.

Roslyn stepped squarely into the breach, without batting a well-mascaraed eyelash. "You know Bonnie and her husband, David, our son Mitchell, Debbie and her husband, Abraham, Andrew . . . and his *partner*, Doug." We all smiled politely; amused glances were exchanged. (What did we *expect* Roslyn to say? In our discomfort with the situation, we all reacted like schoolchildren.) At last, amid the titters, Mitchell cracked a wicked, insinuating smile, and chimed, "Andrew, I didn't know you two were in business together!" The table erupted in laughter, leaving Roslyn twisting in the breeze.

ROSLYN   All my hard work was going down the drain. The audio for the band and the videotape weren't working, my family was imploding in squabbles that don't warrant repeating, and Sheldon was on a rant.

"It's too hot. The service is too slow. What's wrong with the tape? Are the wires connected? What's the problem? When are we going to get the music back?" He wouldn't quit.

I was going down, and hard. And no one seemed to care. No one even attempted to help work out the glitches or to offer advice on how to deal with what was fast becoming a tragicomic opera.

By the end of the night, I was ready for a rubber room.

SHELDON   Roslyn has long insisted that my bad mood that night was in response to Andrew and Doug being at center stage with all my friends present. And I've always told her it simply isn't so.

Perhaps I wouldn't have chosen Roslyn's words if I'd been the one to introduce Doug. I'd have said, "This is Andrew's friend, Doug," and let it go at that. This was the full extent of my discomfiture.

The truth is, I was angry at myself that evening, because I felt stupid and embarrassed. We'd arrived at the party, and as I gazed around the room at my assembled friends and family, it dawned on me that I had inexplicably forgotten to invite a friend with whom I have lunch each and every day. He's also a tenant in the same office building as myself. The next Monday I spoke to him about my oversight, and he accepted my abject apology. But on Saturday night I was miserable, and it had nothing to do with Andrew and Doug.

ROSLYN   Sorry, Shel.

At the risk of sounding analytical, I have to wonder why he took all of the anger he said he felt toward himself, and directed it at me? How did it help to continue dwelling on the negative to the point of excluding any of the evening's many joys?

Anyway, the fact that I was on the receiving end of a barrage of complaints leads me to believe that this irrational behavior was coming from something deeper than a forgotten invitation. I still attibute it to the "partner"-ship at our table.

And while I've confessed that I felt my own unease about Andrew and Doug, I don't believe I'm projecting my fears onto Sheldon. This was an altogether new and unpleasant side of my husband—or at least a side that, after all these years of marriage, I'd never witnessed myself.

When Andrew announced his engagement to Doug, it was that night that appeared first in my mind. Not the usual visions of a ritual imbued with joy and honor, or the elation that I shared with my daughters on the word of their intended betrothal, but a bitter struggle fought between the lines, the true sources of anger never addressed, and therefore without hope of reconciliation.

Having already been involved in all aspects of both my daughters' weddings, I knew that under the best of circumstances an affair of this complexity is a trying business. And this promised to be anything but the best of circumstances.

Reflecting on the night of Sheldon's birthday party, I honestly wondered if our family was capable of surviving this wedding.

PART TWO

Collision Course

People might not get all they work for in this world,
but they certainly must work for all they get.

—FREDERICK DOUGLASS

September 1995

One year until the big day.
And Montreal was talking.

. . . This sort of thing isn't done in our community.

. . . Why does it have to be so big?

. . . Why does it have to be here?

. . . After all, this thing isn't really necessary—is it?

. . . This is radical.

. . . Why can't they do it in New York?

. . . It's so selfish of them.

. . . Why are you doing this to Daddy?

. . . You're simply ruining our Labor Day weekend.

. . . Where's Doug from—can't they do it there?

. . . A lot of people don't like this thing.

. . . Why do you have to put us through this nonsense?

CHAPTER 5

The Bad Guy

SHELDON AND ROSLYN

July 1995–September 1995

SHELDON   When Andrew made the announcement to us, no one was sure what he and Doug had in mind, in terms of a ceremony or a celebration. Then, over the summer, their vision of the event took shape. To our surprise, they decided to hold it in Montreal rather than New York. What's more, they wanted all the usual trappings of a traditional wedding—and on a large scale. News of these plans spread through our community. And people began to express their opinions. Some were more hurtful than others.

I certainly identified with their feelings. Yet it didn't help to hear one close friend say, "Why does it have to be in your face?" Or to have another friend, a very sincere person whom I think very highly of, tell me, "Look, I would support my child one hundred percent, up to a point. I would tell him, a commitment ceremony at the house, fine. Anything else, count me out." If I was hearing this from good friends, I could only imagine what mere acquaintances were saying out of earshot.

Some blamed Roslyn. "What is she doing to you?" was a thread woven through many responses.

Others, I sensed, were wagging a finger at Andrew. Their muted, subtly disapproving reactions suggested they held Andrew culpable for the crime they imagined being perpetrated against me. *"Who the hell does he think he is? He knows who his parents are! He knows this isn't comfortable for his father. Can't he realize there's a reason why he's not comfortable?"*

ROSLYN   A ceremony in *Montreal?*

That news was the fuel that switched Sheldon's simmering discomfort on high.

Andrew called me a few weeks after he had announced their engagement to report that they'd decided to marry in Montreal.

"We're trying to figure out the best weekend to come up and look for a hall. Do you have any ideas?"

Taken aback, I didn't make any suggestions.

"Well, you'll come with us when we go?"

"Mmmm-hmmm." My ambivalence may have shown.

And Sheldon's initial discomfort was very understandable. I empathized with his objections to the wedding as the boys were now envisioning it. What I had trouble coming to terms with was his worry about how the community would judge us. For me, there was a fine line—but a crucial one—between worrying about our own comfort level and worrying about the approval of friends and acquaintances.

A few weeks after the boys' decision to hold the ceremony in Montreal, I approached Sheldon several times to discuss the new arrangement. On my third or fourth attempt, Sheldon finally opened up a bit. "You know people aren't comfortable with this. It's never been done, and you know I'm not the one to be the first. The community isn't ready."

"It's not just the community, it's *you*. Either they will respond positively or negatively, but that's not the issue. This is your son, and this is what he wants. Give me some concrete reasons why he shouldn't be able to have an affair of this style."

Until this point I'd been somewhat restrained in my support of these new plans. I was denying my own feelings, both those of pleasure and of dismay. Back in January, when Andrew first announced the engagement, I was stunned by how traditional it all seemed. Doug giving him a ring, then finding a hall; it was so identical to what heterosexuals do that it shocked me. I didn't imagine they would want to incorporate formalities, rituals, that were so linked to men and women. It just shows how rigidly placed these values are in our psyches. My first thought was *Oh my God!* rather than *How nice!*

As Sheldon reiterated his reservations, "This community doesn't want this here, I keep telling you . . ." I was finally forming a stance of my own. I answered back: "If all you can say is the community this, the community that, to me it says you're ashamed of your son. You want to hide him, you want to do it some place that isn't Montreal. It's hiding from society, and from yourself. It's playing a game. We'll go to New York, we'll have sisters, brothers, and a dozen friends, we don't have to face people. If you really love your son, you won't hide. Since when do you allow your friends to tell you how to react to your own child?"

Over the past several years, I had done much of the work of coming to terms with the fact that both of our sons were gay. I had felt keenly all of the classic stages that parents suffer, from sadness to anger to shame; much of this even before our sons disclosed their sexual orientation to us.

As Sheldon repeated his fear, for the fourth or fifth time, "It's never been done! What will people say about this?" I had an epiphany that stirred me to an astonishing self-realization.

I looked at Sheldon, and his negative reaction to the news of the wedding. And to my shock, I saw myself in him.

Oh my God, is that me?

I lay in bed, next to Sheldon, staring up at the ceiling, but I might as well have been looking in a mirror.

I've been holding back. When Andrew talks to me about this, I clam up. I'm not overjoyed. Why have I been behaving this way?

I've never seen myself in this light.

That's not me, I said.

When it all came to me so clearly, I wanted to shout it out, to turn to Sheldon and say I'd figured out why I'd been so cool to Andrew since the engagement. But I held back. I couldn't share this with him. He was so relentlessly negative about the whole subject, and anything I might say now would sound like a pointy-fingered accusation. I just turned over and tried to go to sleep while he read. It was the beginning of a rift in our communication that would quickly deepen.

Once I'd seen myself more clearly, my attitude took a sharp U-turn. I started getting very involved in the planning of the wedding. Whatever advice Andrew asked, I was there with my party-planner hat firmly in place. Rolling up my sleeves and warming up my dialing finger, I set the action into high gear, helping the boys find a band, a deejay, a photographer, all the usual wedding acoutrements.

Along with my newfound desire to make this event a success on a personal level, I started to look at its potentially positive impact on our community. While the wider Jewish community has traditionally supported many liberal causes, gay rights is a unique matter. For many Jews, supporting civil rights for blacks may be an easy decision, since it has reverberations in the world at large but does little to change our daily lives, in our own homes. But when a child discloses he or she is gay, a societal problem that we'd rather keep at arm's length comes rushing toward us with outstretched arms. And rather than mustering compassion for an *issue*, we become consumed by a dilemma that's struck us, literally, where we live. Or if it's the child of a neighbor, or friend, it's a problem that many of us treat like it will disappear if we only ignore it. This reflex to hide homosexuality, indeed to hide homosexuals themselves, had gone on far too long, and taken far too many emotional casualties in our community. And I'd already been working for some time to change that.

It was a hot sunny day in the spring of 1986 when I walked through the gates of McGill University. I was fifty-one years old and about to embark on a path that would eventually lead me to a master's degree in social work. I was on a high. I had been accepted into the Special Bachelor of Social Work program, which was specifically designed for mature people with experience in the helping professions. Starting a new career at this stage in my life was exhilarating and also scary. How would I balance the demands of family with full-time schooling? Sheldon and the kids were most supportive of my new adventure.

I noticed a nice-looking young man surrounded by his own entourage, and he had everybody in stitches. I'm a sucker for blue eyes and a great sense of humor, so I joined the group. A few weeks after we met, Mark Mazer confided to me that he was gay. My questions concerning his coming out and his family's reaction were rampant, and he always answered everything. Then I caught myself wondering, how did he make love?

I became utterly fixated on that. I think many heterosexuals are. And every time I saw another person I surmised to be gay, that's what I would think of . . . how do they "do it"? And specifically, what was the "it"? Getting to know Mark helped rid me of some of the ridiculous fantasies I'd had. I soon learned that their lovemaking isn't much different from ours. He helped me see gay people like any other people, with concerns and issues, family problems, the same things the rest of us face, with the extra stress of dealing with other people's reactions to their sexuality. This is how I came to realize that their sexual orientation doesn't change them in any way. That was really an awakening. I gained a new perspective on homosexuality, and we bonded very quickly.

As luck would have it, we did our internship together at the Montreal General Hospital in outpatient psychiatry. We ran a group together, and ate a lot of muffins and drank a lot of coffee and put on a lot of weight. We became the "odd couple," and dining out on Thursday night became a ritual. We often bumped into my couples friends, who always raised an eyebrow when I introduced my "friend" Mark. One night when Sheldon had tennis and couldn't accompany me to a screening of *Shoah*, Mark escorted me. Once again, the eyebrows were raised, and there was whispering. The following morning, by coincidence, the hospital was making a break- fast for outgoing interns at 7:30 A.M. at the Ritz Carlton. You can just imagine the stares we drew when some acquaintances who had seen us the night before at the movie (*Shoah* is five hours long, and let out after midnight) saw the two of us standing outside the hotel together at dawn.

When Mitchell came out to us that fall, he was twenty-five years old. Mark had become an invaluable source of advice and compas- sion. Exposing myself emotionally, I asked Mark the countless ques- tions that burned inside me. We talked for hours and I cried. I remember dropping him off at his apartment after midnight, hardly able to see my way home, blinded by tears. After months of seeking Mark's counsel, I had a much deeper understanding of the hardships of being a gay person in a largely straight society. I also felt that somehow I had healed and that I could go on with my life. But I wanted the answer to one more question. "What do other parents do?"

"About what?"

"Who do parents of gay children talk to about all this? If I hadn't been able to talk to you about all this turmoil, this guilt, this new experience, I don't know what I would have done. I can't understand how other parents cope."

Then Mark had a logical and inspired notion. "Roz, we have to start our own group."

Finally, four years later in 1991, the first impetus toward actu- ally creating the group came from the rabbi at one of the conservative synagogues in Montreal. Rabbi Len Wasser contacted a Jewish organization for lesbian, gay, and bisexual people called Yachdav, which translates from Hebrew as "together." The members wanted to take part in the same rituals as other Jews, but for a variety of reasons, couldn't observe them with their families. And though they wished to practice their faith in synagogue, they didn't feel welcome in their families' congregations. So they held services together in their own homes, and the group became a community. When Rabbi Wasser called Yachdav, he was looking for counseling services for parents of gay and lesbian children. He was given Mark's name.

"Honestly," the rabbi told Mark, "I don't know what to tell them. I try to be understanding, helpful, but my training doesn't give me the expertise to counsel these parents. If you'll hold a group, I'll find you room in the synagogue for meetings."

Confident that our group would have a home with Rabbi Wasser, Mark and I created a ten-week curriculum for a psychoeducational group where parents of gays and lesbians would learn to address their fears.

We watched parents arrive at their first meeting terrified of merely entering the room, for fear of meeting someone they knew. They couldn't fathom that any other parent in this group was bound to be in the same boat. Some came in hopes of finding a way to change their child. Most were grasping at straws, hoping to negotiate the opposing reflexes to reject the stranger they saw in their child, and to draw closer to the person inside they knew and loved.

The parents who made the fastest progress were almost always the ones who came to the class as soon as they found out about their child's sexuality, before patterns of avoidance set in. One parent, who approached us soon after her daughter came out to her, expressed a typical concern about how her friends would judge her, and her daughter. "We're all invited to the wedding of our son's friend. My daughter's invitation is for her and a guest. What if she brings the woman she's seeing? What will people think? Will they dance together? What am I going to do?" Her catalog of apprehensions piled up.

Months later, after a lot of personal growth, this same woman learned of another upcoming wedding. And she told me, "If they don't invite our daughter along with her partner, well, I'm going to have to call and have a talk with them." Each bit of progress in the group was a wondrous thing.

When our first class graduated, they formed a self-started parents' support group, meeting once a month. As Mark and I have continued to run the more formal psychoeducational groups year to year, many of our graduates have moved on to the support group. And a year after the support group was formed, I received a call from one of the parents asking me if my husband and I would like to be a part of that group. She said that they would be honored to have us. I decided that if we were to join them, I would not attend as the "professional" but rather as just another parent who happens to have two gay sons. They agreed. In my mind I was doing it for Sheldon. Soon I discovered how very much I also benefited from the contact with these struggling parents. It became a springboard for discussion between Sheldon and myself about our own boys. We got so much from the group. We tried to give back too. Sheldon in particular.

You see, one especially righteous parent refused to see his daughter if she came home with her partner. While Marvin (not his real name) didn't go to the extreme of sitting shiva for his daughter (the most severe rejection of a Jewish child is mourning his or her "death" when the child has transgressed in some manner so unforgivable that the parent never acknowledges him or her again), he had effectively cut her out of his life.

Sheldon attended the group with me on a few occasions. And I sensed that he saw this particular man as a personal challenge. I know that Sheldon was disturbed that Marvin could close the door on his daughter.

"I told you, I wrote her off," Marvin told Sheldon one evening. But Sheldon continued to work with him, with humor. They became buddies in the group, sitting near each other when Sheldon came.

Slowly Marvin budged. I'm sure it will be a long road for him, but I know Sheldon helped jump-start the trip.

SHELDON   When I originally attended the support group, it was more of a courtesy to Roslyn rather than a desire to seek comfort. Not that I thought I was beyond help and didn't need to improve. I recognized at that point in time that although I was perfectly at ease and accepting of my son's orientation, I was not at ease in discussing the situation with friends and relatives, let alone strangers. I attended various get-togethers of the group and listened attentively, although, as is my usual custom, without really talking too much.

Generally speaking, I observed that the majority of the group numbers were now accepting of their children's orientation, although there were a few strong objections. When it came to partners, though, they seemed overall to be critical. Some were not comfortable that their child's partner was not of the same faith, but most were obviously uncomfortable, if not downright unaccepting, of two adults of the same sex sleeping together and all the other imaginings that go with that arrangement—especially in their own home.

Now that Andrew had announced his intention to hold their ceremony in Montreal, I had something to talk about. For the first several minutes, the gathering was just as usual, people talking about their experiences, their troubles.

One parent confessed, "My son came home with his partner for Rosh Hashanah, and I felt uncomfortable, what with them sleeping in the same room."

Then I spoke up, with what was certain to be a new subject for the group. "I want to throw something at you, and get your reaction. How would you respond if your son or daughter came to you and said that they want to go through a commitment ceremony, but not only a commitment ceremony—they want it to be a wedding? If they wanted it to be a big affair, a hundred and fifty people maybe, and go through the same kind of celebration as a heterosexual marriage—what would you say?"

Almost every parent in the group expressed sympathy.

"I don't know how I would react . . ."

"Oh, that's a tough one . . ."

"I don't know if I could handle that . . ."

"I couldn't do it," another stated flatly.

And another, acknowledging that this wasn't merely a hypothetical question, offered genuine commiseration. "I feel for you."

I must confess that putting my question to the members of the group was primarily motivated by a desire to prove to Roslyn that my initial objection and discomfort were normal and that other parents in a similar situation would feel exactly the same way. And frankly, I was right.

One parent, however, was very positive.

"Great. Why not?" he countered, brightly.

I took his enthusiasm with a bit of skepticism. This particular father is a very nice fellow and a very intelligent person. His own daughter had gone through a commitment ceremony, in New England. And he acknowledged having attended the ceremony with reluctance. He even refused to participate in the proceedings. The way he depicted his daughter's ritual, it seemed a rather iconoclastic affair. It was held somewhere outdoors, without benefit of clergy. His daughter and her partner exchanged vows in a self-directed, self-written ceremony. He described himself as sitting at the back of the crowd, listening. And as it progressed, he found himself comfortable enough to walk up to the front. So as he painted this picture of his daughter's affair, with his sole intent being to offer encouragement, I was receiving a very different kind of impression.

Now, he's already been through the ceremony, I thought. *Of course it's easy enough for him to say, "It's great, why not do it?" If it was so easy, why is it he barely even took part?*

He had proved my point better than any of the others. He had faced the same situation, and had initially failed his daughter. At least I had stated from the outset that I would be there, no matter what. All I was asking for, if not begging for, was a little discussion, give and take, compromise, to show that my discomfort was understandable and perhaps could be reduced if not eliminated.

When the discussion was over, and I looked back at the various responses, I saw that I wasn't going to have too easy a time. These were parents of gays and lesbians who are accepting enough to want to come to this group. And if they weren't receptive to something like this, how was I going to face the music in the Montreal Jewish community, with all my conservative friends?

That's not to say this is a regressive city. Far from it. Montreal has a well-earned reputation as a cosmopolitan, world-class metropolis. It's also a remarkably diverse one. Beyond the French-Latin character and the English-WASP temperament, there are numerous other ethnic communities, such as the Italians and Greeks. And like other tight-knit ethnic communties, Montreal's Jewish population has largely clung to many of its customs.

But it should be stressed that, unlike most U.S. metropolitan cities of today, where Reform Judaism is the majority and people attend "temple," in Montreal there is a very small Reform population. Most Jews adhere to either the Conservative movement (middle of the road, traditionalist, with men and women worshiping together) or the Orthodox movement (strict and observant, with men and women seated separately), and mostly attend "synagogue." The point is that change doesn't come easily or quickly in Montreal's Jewish community. The population is more comfortable with knowing what to expect; even if they are not strictly observant Jews, they feel more at home in a service that adheres to the general rules that have been practiced over centuries.

Putting aside the Orthodox belief that homosexuality is an "abomination," what right does a member of an Orthodox synagogue such as myself—a man generally respected in the community as a quiet, conservative person, even an outright *square*—have to shock the community by hosting, for the first time in its history, a commitment ceremony on a grand scale?

Don't get the wrong impression. Montrealers are open-minded, by and large. Undoubtedly many people in this city believe that homosexuality is not a "choice," and most are probably accepting, though I've always found the overall attitude to be *don't make waves*.

ROSLYN   And though he's too modest to say so, it's fair to say that Sheldon's sensitivity about the response from our crowd is heightened by his prominence in the Jewish community. As a notary, his work in real estate puts him in contact with a large number of the city's most prominent businessmen, and he's always been a very visible man (at six foot four, how could he not be!) in our synagogue, serving as vice president for a time, and is a man known for his contributions to Jewish charities. When you consider the already tight-knit quality of our community, it's fair to say that Sheldon's a public figure, and a figure known for his staid, conservative nature.

SHELDON   That's certainly the image I convey. And it's an accurate one.

It can't be stressed enough: holding the ceremony here, in this city, in this community, turned this entire affair into an exercise in pushing a boulder up a mountain. As I've said, Montreal is a wonderful city, but there's one vital element to the civic life of our city that permeates every facet of life here. Bear with me, for even if it might not be readily apparent, it will be helpful as you read further if you know something about the stress we cope with day in and day out.

We Montrealers are all participants, willing or not, in a debate over language, namely French and English. It's a dispute that has dominated Quebec life for over two decades, and shows no sign of easing up. In fact, the younger generation of Anglophone Montrealers (as English-speakers are frequently referred to; French are hence known as Francophones) has been so drastically reduced in recent years, it amounts to an exodus. I need look no further than my phone bill or frequent-flier report to be reminded of my personal example. All of our four children have left the province of Quebec. And so have most of their Anglophone contemporaries.

While there is no doubt that Montreal owes much of its charm to its dual personality, the mixing of French and English cultures, the conflict that we all face today has deep roots in the province.

After the French were defeated by the English in 1631 on the

Plains of Abraham in Quebec City, they suffered a sort of cultural humiliation. And for centuries the Francophone majority of the province were ruled by a group they considered an occupying force. Certainly there were injustices perpetrated against the French over those three hundred years. Our very license plates bear testament to the long-festering wound of defeat with the enigmatic phrase *Je Me Souviens*, meaning "I will remember." Well, eventually, the anger of that memory propelled the French-speaking majority to seize the reigns of power with a tight and unforgiving grip. And now that they call the shots, they've not only sought to secede from greater Canada, but to redress past wrongs, both real and imagined, in some arcane ways. Francophones are in the process of evening the score, if you will, over the past subjugation of their mother tongue, with the introduction of Draconian sign laws.

The French language must predominate and French letters must be at least twice as big as the English letters—even in Chinatown! An Orwellian "language police" patrols the city, ever vigilant for the English scofflaw who allows an Anglicized word to stand alone, on a storefront window or inside a shop. The forces of separation have also imposed restrictive education laws, forcing immigrants to attend French schools rather than English ones. All of this, plus many other pervasive irritants, have helped convince our youth that they are not wanted and the future for them is elsewhere, especially professionals who, thanks to their specialties, can more easily find employment elsewhere.

Yet, given this pervasive tone of intolerance, Montrealers are surprisingly accepting when language isn't the issue. It should be noted that in the French section of the city (east of St. Lawrence Boulevard, which is also known as Main Street, or "the Main") there is an area called the "Gay Village," with many clubs. Montrealers, like most other people, segregate themselves, feeling more comfortable with their own. French east of the Main, English west of the Main. There are exceptions, such as Westmount, where both the wealthy French and English reside. In any event, the French, with their fiery Latin character and zest for life, are most inclined to accept differences and change, and therefore I believe are most accepting of gay life. Unfortunately, don't look for gay clubs or a Gay Village in the West End. West Enders either go to the gay clubs downtown or must head east.

All of which is to say that although a "commitment ceremony" in the East End Gay Village may be acceptable and not uncommon, I personally had never heard of any in the West End, especially with a religious content, and I am just not the type of person to want to be the first.

ROSLYN I always put my concern for my child above my concern for the community. But by the fall, when I began to tell friends of our plans for the ceremony, it became harder to withstand the public reaction.

One exchange was typical. Sheldon and I were having dinner with two close friends. Let's call them Carol and Ben. While we leafed through our salads, Carol asked me, "How are the plans coming?"

"They're coming very nicely," I responded. I suppose I betrayed a little excitement, even though I was very conscious of Sheldon sitting across the table from me. I knew that a great display of enthusiasm on my part would send him further back into his shell. Rather than retreating, Sheldon took the offensive:

"I don't know, something's not right about it. It doesn't have to . . ." He searched for the right words. "I don't see why it has to be on this scale."

Then, on Sheldon's cue, Carol pounced. "You know, Roslyn, people are talking about this." She surveyed my reaction for signs of the first squirm. "And they're saying what Sheldon's saying. There's nothing wrong with them having a small affair in New York. But why does it have to be here?" Before I could answer, she added, "It's not *done*, you know." The intonation of that last phrase served as notice that she wasn't interested in asking me anything. She was merely castigating me.

Both Ben and Carol continued to dish out a subtle but effective critique over the next two courses.

Ben: This is really radical. In our community, it's never taken place.

Carol: It's not necessary. Why does it have to be?

Sheldon: You encourage Andrew. Why do you always encourage him to do these things?

Mostly I sat quiet, but occasionally I ventured a defense I was fairly certain would fall on deaf ears. "I didn't *encourage* him. I'm *supporting* him. This is a very important thing in his life."

As they ganged up again, I listened with one ear, stared blankly at Sheldon and my friends, and thought: *Since this is important to Andrew, I don't care how other people are going to feel about it. I can't be responsible for their worries, their prejudices. This is our child. And I'm so angry with all of you. And Ben, Carol, how can you tell us what's best for our kid? How dare you take it upon yourselves to tell me where I should have this, and how many people should attend? And would you ever have presumed to give me this kind of advice if my son had, more conveniently for you, fallen in love with a woman instead of a man?*

Of course, I held all this in. After they quieted down, and my own anger subsided enough to allow me to remain composed, I tried to educate the table.

"I'm sure you know," I ventured, "that gay people have always needed to conceal their relationships. And that's why there's historically been so much promiscuity in the gay community. Liaisons, quickies in out-of-the-way spots, were the norm because they had to hide, and so they couldn't have regular relationships, the sort we all take for granted. I'm sure none of you think promiscuity is a good thing, right? Especially in this day and age! And isn't it wonderful that we can be part of changing that, in celebrating their committed relationship? Won't the ceremony be so much more meaningful, so much more joyous, if it's held together with friends, family, and community?"

"Yes." Carol considered for a moment, exchanged glances with

Ben and Sheldon. "But . . ." And they resumed the barrage of negativity I'd been subjected to since the salad first arrived.

Only minutes before, I had sat down at dinner with my husband and two good friends. Now I was under attack by strangers. Dinner had turned into a shooting match, and I was outgunned, three to one. After the dinner plates were taken, and I set my napkin back on my lap, I wanted to cry. My friends and my husband had shunted me off to the other end of the table—the deep end, so to speak. And they'd done it as a unified group. Until tonight, the "community" concerns that Sheldon had long reported had been a series of volleys in a battle fought just out of my range of sight. Now the war was being waged in full view, and the cannons were tilted straight at me.

Then, when I thought the conversation was over at last, Sheldon piped up, pointing out the painfully obvious. "You see, Roslyn, I told you people would have problems with this . . ."

I cut him off. *"People* will get used to it."

SHELDON   Before, when it was just something Roslyn, or Andrew and Doug, would bring up, I didn't focus on their plans, perhaps in the hope it would just go away. As the controversy became a more common topic of conversation, I slowly came to grips with the strong possibility that something was actually going to *happen.*

Once the reality started to sink in, though, I tried to make my position known. It was never my attitude that they should do what they want, and if I'm not comfortable, I'm not going to be there. Or even that I would go, but not host it. My stance was that we needed to talk about compromise.

I asked Roslyn repeatedly, "Why can't we have something smaller?"

But she was so gung ho, she couldn't hear me. "What, are you ashamed? Is that why you want a small ceremony?"

"That's not what I said."

"To heck with what other people think, we have to do what we feel is right, and if we're proud of our children, this is what they want, and they're going to get it. And I don't give a damn what anybody else thinks about it."

Now, that's all very noble, and even true to some extent. But neither Roslyn, nor Andrew and Doug, could recognize how I was struggling with this. I needed sympathy, and got none. Roslyn was so sensitive to my misgivings, it was as if I were attacking her and our child. And her motivations, I believe, were broader in scope than mine, extending well beyond our own family. If I had to simply characterize my own motivations, I would say, "I have a son. He has a situation. I have to keep my relationship with my son as good as possible, and honor his position. I'll face the facts, and do whatever, in the end, is necessary." However, if I were to encapsulate Roslyn's motivations, I felt she'd say, "Yes, that's all true, but we can do *good* at the same time."

While there's nothing wrong with wanting to do good, that was entirely outside the scope of my motivation.

Then, one day in September, Roslyn suggested we try seeing a rabbi. Together, as a family. It would be the first time the four of us, Roslyn and myself, Andrew and Doug, would sit down together and discuss what was happening since Andrew had first called with the news almost nine months before.

ROSLYN   Sheldon and I had traveled a full circle. Initially he experienced all the isolation, and felt like the victim. On one hand, he insisted I couldn't hear the depth of his uneasiness. But I also found him anxious to dodge a conversation.

Alone, at home, I tried various approaches.

"We're sitting here—you seem to try to avoid the discussion. When there's a topic that isn't pleasant, you change the subject."

"Not now."

"When?"

"Later."

"When later?"

"Later."

We got so used to this perfectly circular discourse, we could do it in our sleep.

So I took to initiating conversations when he'd have the hardest time escaping from me—when we were in the car. Preferably on a long trip.

We were driving to Toronto, to see our daughter Bonnie, her husband, David, and the kids. It's five hours, door to door.

"Can we talk about the plans for the ceremony?"

"Not for five hours. One hour, OK. Five, no way."

I pressed him again on what he planned to do if the boys stuck with their intention of a large ceremony, here in town.

After a number of questions along the lines of "Why is it necessary?" he offered a sentiment he'd expressed before. "I'll be there, no matter what you do." Though I was comforted knowing that he would stand by those words, I also knew it couldn't work out that way.

"You can be there, sure. But you can't *just* 'be there,' because everyone will be very uncomfortable. It'll just be a disaster. I don't want to go through all the planning, all the work, and then see Andrew and Doug have that kind of wedding, if all you're going to do is just show up. We both have to be comfortable with it, we both have to realize that it's *right*. Until we know that, we can't do it. It would be a catastrophe."

I could tell Sheldon what he needed to feel, but for the life of me, I couldn't put myself inside his head and help him travel the distance from where he was to where I wanted us to go.

Later, as most of our friends and family lined up behind Sheldon, I felt I was being victimized, like people didn't understand me. Everyone made it sound like it was so easy for me. Some of what people were saying about me came to my face, and other conversations made their way back to me in subtler, sneakier ways.

"Roslyn knows all about it. She's been working in the field for a long time."

"She's a *professional*. But look at her poor husband . . ."

"Look what she's putting him through."

"This isn't the least bit easy for me," I'd say, to anyone who'd listen. "Just because I'm a professional, that doesn't mean I don't have feelings, fears, qualms. I still have to deal with so many issues that I haven't figured out for myself."

No one was listening. Not my friends, not my husband.

The end result: I was isolated.

And I started to get bitter. I'd tried the best I knew how to support Sheldon when he felt alone. Now I felt he was undermining me at every opportunity. When we were out with Carol and Ben, and on innumerable other occasions, he could have stood up for me. When we'd hear the umpteenth variation on the thinly veiled personal misgiving, passed off as civic duty, i.e., "*People* are going to be very uncomfortable with this," Sheldon could have said, "Maybe they will. But we're working on that."

Instead, he continually let me look like the bad guy.

And his response was always just this side of accusatory. "See, Roslyn, I told you. I said they were saying this."

For a time, I turned to Andrew for solace. Since I assumed he'd sympathize with my plight, I'd call long distance for moral support. Then one day, when I phoned to commiserate, Andrew shut me out.

"I don't want to hear any more," was his cold statement of fact. And as harsh as that was, I understood without his explaining any further. He felt it was his doing, that his plans were causing me this pain. And he had begun this endeavor with hopes of creating a unique occasion, a celebration of love filled with joy. How could he stay focused on that goal if he had to grapple with every angst-ridden argument I'd had to hear, sifted through the filter of my own pain and anger?

What would I tell a parent in my position? I asked myself.

For the life of me, I had no idea.

At this time, September 1995, the parents' group had a home in a Conservative synagogue, Share Beth Shalom, which had as its rabbi a young dynamic leader, Rabbi Barry Berman. Our previous synagogue had made it clear that we were unwelcome in their midst once our old patron, Rabbi Wasser, had left their congregation.

Rabbi Barry Berman had come to our psychoeducational group as a guest. He talked about how the Conservative, Reform, and Reconstructionist movements of Judaism were working to come to terms with homosexuality. He made it clear that his synagogue was looking for ways to make gay families more welcome.

I asked him if he would meet with Sheldon, Andrew, Doug, and me when the boys came up for Rosh Hashanah, in three weeks. He looked down, considered the request for an instant, and replied, "I'm glad to be whatever help I can, but obviously you know I'm not a therapist. You're the therapist. I'm happy to sit down with all of you, though."

My expectations for the meeting were cautiously optimistic. Once Sheldon, Andrew, and Doug all agreed to attend, I coasted along with Sheldon, not making waves, awaiting this new forum. I hoped the rabbi would ask us all to hear each other, and since I knew of his pro-gay stance, I imagined he would bestow validity on Andrew and Doug's wishes. Ultimately I hoped he would ask Sheldon and me to be the best parents we could be.

The rabbi extended a genuinely warm welcome for the parents' group, opening his doors to us, offering coffee and empathy.

I must have forgotten, if only for a moment, that this is Montreal.

CHAPTER 6

Location, Location, Location! *(or: Fait Accompli)*

ANDREW, DOUG, SHELDON, AND ROSLYN

September 1995

ANDREW   The key decision about where we'd hold the ceremony was made in July. From the time of our engagement in January we had vacillated between New York and Montreal as the preferred location. During that time I did some investigative work in Manhattan, exploring the options for reception halls.

One day in May I walked across Central Park and, on an impulse, strolled into the elegant Pierre Hotel on Fifth Avenue and Sixtieth Street. Knowing it was far beyond our means, I inquired if I could meet with the banquet manager. In moments I was introduced to a gentleman who showed me the main ballroom and the cocktail area. He offered information regarding the approximate cost per guest. This was early in my research, so I had no basis for comparison, but I knew it would amount—regardless of how many people we eventually invited—to a whole lot of dough.

While the banquet manager was forthcoming with numerous details, I withheld from him one key detail of my own: the sex of my intended. Why complicate matters? I asked myself. After all, since I knew we couldn't afford this, there wasn't any point in getting into particulars, was there?

I'd also called the Four Seasons on East Fifty-seventh. It's a spectacular new hotel, with a knockout design that combines futurist fantasy with classic deco, and even though I was sure it would be pricey, I was so taken with its atmosphere that I held out hope that we could have our reception somewhere on their grounds. When I asked to speak to the banquet manager, I was connected with a pleasant woman who provided me with all the pertinent facts.

This time, perhaps because it was a conversation by phone, without face-to-face contact, or perhaps because she was a woman, and therefore somehow less threatening than the gentleman from the Pierre, I was emboldened to plainly lay out all of our facts.

I didn't hear the sound of any glass—or any other objects for that matter—come crashing down to the floor on her end of the line. Once I had heard all the prices, and we toted them up, she might well have expected that I'd be the one doing the dropping.

With a few more exploratory phone calls to more realistically priced venues under my belt, I became increasingly aware of the financial difficulty that lay ahead of us if we planned a reception in New York. Since Doug and I had already scheduled a Fourth of July trip to visit my parents, I suggested we consider taking a look around my hometown.

In fact, I'd floated the concept of moving our reception to Montreal several times before, but Doug never offered much response.

DOUG   I'd had many mixed feelings about that idea. I agreed with Andrew that prohibitive prices in New York would mean a much smaller, and more spartan, affair. Yet I wasn't convinced that an event as intricate as a wedding could be planned effectively from four hundred miles away.

New York was obviously the simplest answer, geographically. And some of the friends we'd made together in Manhattan would surely find it expensive and inconvenient to make the trip north of the border. Also, I feared that some of my oldest friends from L.A. would be less likely to venture to Montreal for a weekend, while I knew most of them welcomed a good reason to fly to New York, where the wedding could be the centerpiece of a longer vacation in the city.

I was even more ambivalent about Andrew's desire to keep the ceremony in New York while moving the reception to Montreal. When Andrew and I first seriously discussed the shape of the entire wedding, he talked of splitting up the ceremony from the reception, and more significantly, inviting only a small core of family and close friends to the ceremony, and a much larger group to the reception. This severing of the event unsettled me, but I couldn't determine the true source of my dissatisfaction.

"Why not have it all in one place, at one time, with the same people?"

"I don't like being the center of attention."

"How can you have a wedding—even if it's just the reception part—without being the center of attention?"

"It's not the same thing. I can't explain it. I'd rather have the ceremony with just a few friends and family, and then have a big party afterward."

I had always disliked the idea aesthetically, and more significantly, I thought it would send the wrong message to those attending the reception. I feared it would appear that a ceremony between two men was something to be hidden. And now that Andrew wanted to actually search for a reception hall in Montreal, I was able to articulate the key question that had troubled me ever since Andrew first suggested fracturing our event into two distinct halves.

"Is this about self-hatred? Are you calling it shyness when on some level you don't really think you deserve a wedding?"

ANDREW   It really is true that I've never liked being the center of attention. Perhaps it's because, historically, whenever I've been the center of attention, it hasn't been such a wonderful experience. Part of this discomfort stemmed from a general feeling of self-loathing. It was as if being in the spotlight would reveal to others the person I really was, the person I worked so hard to keep hidden.

It's also true that I was concerned that some guests, especially those of an older generation, might not know how to react to the sight of two men publicly engaging in this hallowed ritual. What if they remained silent, but spoke volumes with looks of reproof? Or worse, if they betrayed their disapproval and snickered?

So yes, I was experiencing a twinge of internalized homophobia, fearing that reactions of discomfort or disdain might be deserved, because I might, in fact, look ridiculous doing this.

DOUG   I wanted to know one thing.

Was he *embarrassed* to marry me?

And if he should answer yes, I contemplated the possibility of asking a question with more serious repercussions.

Which part was embarrassing?

The *marry* part?

Or was it marrying *me* in front of a roomful of people whose approval or rejection weighed heavily on him?

As I quickly played out the possible variations, like plotting out a chess match of emotions, Andrew's eyes searched my face. Without deciding how far I'd go to learn the truth, I swallowed hard and asked.

"Are you embarrassed to marry me?"

He put his arms around me, then pulled away and looked me in the eye. "No way."

"You're sure?"

"Absolutely. That's not what it's about at all."

So while I still didn't like the idea of a separate and therefore invisible ceremony, I didn't want to push Andrew into something he didn't want. And by the time I was on the plane to Montreal that

Fourth of July weekend, I had made peace with the separation of ceremony and soiree.

ANDREW   It was my first trip home since our engagement. No decisions had been made yet about what city the ceremony or the reception would be held in, so Doug and I had no definite indication of how my parents were acclimating to our plans.

When I arrived at the airport, my mother picked me up and we went straight to a Chinese restaurant. My father met us a few minutes after we'd sat down. What surprised me was, we didn't speak about anything related to the engagement. I was hurt, and confused. I showed my father the ring, and he changed the topic.

My brother, Mitchell, showed up for dinner late, upset about some problem at work. The focus became my brother and his difficulties. Here I was, coming to see my family for the first time since the engagement. I thought it would be exciting to talk about the wedding plans. Instead, whenever I brought it up, it would get dropped like a bad habit.

There was much more support when I got together with Lorne and some of his friends later that evening. And somebody made a suggestion that sent our wedding journey on a whole new course.

DOUG   Andrew had just met me at the airport, and he was already pitching a place he'd just discovered. An out-of-town reception was one thing, but I wasn't prepared to have Andrew make all the decisions before I'd even arrived. I have a nickname for him, well earned: "the Steamroller." When he sets his sights on something, move aside or get mowed down.

"We still have places to visit tomorrow with my mother, but you have to see this!" he cooed. "Lorne told me we should stop at Eaton's. A friend of his had been there for an AIDS benefit. The top floor is called Le Neuvieme. That means 'the Ninth,' so guess what floor it's on? Anyway, it's almost never used for public functions. I had a little time after my haircut and before my dentist appointment—" I laughed over Andrew's need to migrate four hundred miles to tend to his personal hygiene "—and I'm just telling you, it's everything we've been talking about, but didn't know how or where to find. Nothing I say will do it justice. You have to see it with your own eyes." I was not about to be swayed, but I didn't say a word.

We left our bags in the car and pushed through the store. Andrew had warned me that the first floor didn't make much of a first impression, filled as it was with handbags, scarves, umbrellas, and other department-store goods. But as we stepped out of the elevator on the ninth floor, rounded the first right turn, walked past the ersatz marble fountain in the foyer, and yanked open the unassuming door to the hall, I felt every hair stand on end.

This really was it.

It was rare for Andrew and me to share immediate and total enthusiasm for an experience. Usually one needs to be wooed into approval by the other. As we stood together and surveyed the room, our silence, and the knowing look we shared, said we both knew we'd found one perfect thing. And it was just as well that Andrew hadn't wasted breath trying to describe the feeling of being in that room, with its magnificent deco detail, soaring ceiling, romance pouring from every inch of its marble and alabaster. I'd never seen anything like it. And no wonder, since the manager later described it as the only remaining original art deco restaurant in North America.

But how much would the space cost? I fretted that such a room couldn't possibly be in our price range.

"Don't worry." Andrew used his soothing psych voice. "I'm sure it's not so bad. Just wait until tomorrow. We have an appointment to come back with my mother."

ANDREW The next morning, my mother, Doug, and I set out for downtown as if we weren't really the first family to shop for a gay wedding reception hall in Montreal history. But of course, we all knew it would be an unorthodox series of meetings.

As we tooled toward our first appointment, my mother stated matter-of-factly that she hadn't clarified the nature of the couple in question when she made our appointments. And while I didn't expect any banquet managers to faint directly upon meeting us, I was certainly concerned over whether any would break into an uncontrollable sweat when they realized there were two grooms, and no, there weren't two brides waiting outside in the car.

The Ritz Carlton Hotel would be our maiden voyage together into this uncharted territory. We strode into the lobby and surveyed the various rooms unaccompanied by hotel personnel. When my mother asked to meet the banquet manager, we were introduced to a pleasant-looking man who displayed refreshing candor by expressing mild surprise—yet without judgment. Acknowledging that this was an unusual arrangement, he stepped up to the challenge by treating us all as I imagine he would any other family.

Since money had always been the main motivation behind moving the reception to Montreal, the answer to the question of cost was absolutely key. And the answers were very good. Not only was the per head cost of catering startingly low, by New York standards, but the lodging costs were a fraction of the price as well.

DOUG   The banquet manager took us to the main ballroom, a large, attractive, somewhat upscale version of the generic reception hall good for bar mitzvahs, weddings, or fancy business affairs. As Andrew and the banqet manager discussed catering details, Roslyn and I surveyed the room in detail.

"Where would you like to have the ceremony?" Roslyn asked.

Suddenly it hit me that neither Andrew or I had ever discussed this with his mother.

"Oh. Well, actually, we were thinking of having the ceremony . . . in New York."

Roslyn recoiled as if from a foul smell, the exact same reaction I'd seen on Andrew's face a thousand times. "I don't like that idea at all. The reception won't have any context, it'll be devoid of meaning. There won't be any connection. People won't understand—or at least, people from around here won't understand—what they're here to celebrate. It'll be as if we have something to hide. And wouldn't it be much nicer to do it all together, at the same time, with the same people?"

"Ummm, well. . . ." I didn't want to get in the middle of a disagreement so soon in the process. But I agreed wholeheartedly with Roslyn. "You're right . . . I mean, I think that's a good point. So we should all talk about that together."

After one more hotel appointment, we made our way to Eaton's. As we rode the elevator up to the ninth floor, Roslyn waxed nostalgic.

"You know, I used to come up here as a little girl. It was always such a treat. We'd dress up in our best and behave very grown-up."

We surveyed the room together. "It's still so gorgeous," Roslyn observed. "Nothing's changed here. It's amazing."

While we waited for the manager to meet with us, we sat down for a snack at one of the dozens of tables spread out over the enormous multitiered floor.

"Hmmm." Roslyn pondered her meal. "*Nothing* has changed here. It's pretty much the same thing they served forty years ago. We'll ask if they allow an outside caterer to work in their kitchen."

"*Bonjour,* good afternoon." We all turned, slightly startled, and behind Roslyn stood an affable thirty-something man in a navy blue suit. "I'm Mr. St. Pierre. You are Mrs. Merlin?"

"Yes . . . Mrs. *Merling*, and this is my son Andrew, and his partner Doug."

"OK, would you like to sit down at a bigger table, up there?"

He motioned to the next level up, to the right, where larger rounded tables were positioned at wide intervals.

ANDREW "The room looks like a grand ocean liner, sort of," Doug ventured. "Like the *Titanic*." The tone of my laugh made it clear that wasn't the most optimistic comparison he might have made. (In fact, we learned later that the room was modeled on the Queen Mary.)

"Yes, it is designed to remind you of the great ships," said Mr. St. Pierre.

And it does. The lowest, and central, portion of the restaurant stretches about thirty yards. Ringing the room at both ends are two curved and elevated areas. And at the center of each of these is a fountain which flows from the wall into a dazzling fixture of iridescent metal and glass, providing illuminated streams which bookend the glorious space. Directly in front of each fountain is a large marble platform, which flows down to a wide staircase leading down a half dozen steps onto the main floor. And on either side of the foot of each staircase is an enormous alabaster torchère, standing over eight feet tall and three feet wide, adding a final touch of surreal elegance.

Once we were seated on one of the upper landings, my mother dove right in. "The ceremony we're thinking of holding here would be a wedding, or a commitment ceremony, for my son and his partner. Is that a problem for you?"

"No, not at all. It's unusual, of course. But no problem at all."

And when he told us the price, we tried, collectively, not to betray our elation.

DOUG   Andrew had been right. The rate was impossibly reasonable. The price for that room, even if it existed in New York, would be astronomical. Suddenly the concept of holding our reception here seemed not only blissfully preordained, but eminently sensible.

A number of other details were hashed out, and Roslyn suggested we all meet again after she talked to Sheldon. Mr. St. Pierre went back to work as the three of us took to measuring the room and brainstorming the logistics. Dozens of blue-haired ladies were enjoying a quiet afternoon lunch. And heaven knows what they thought we were up to, wending our way between tables, examining every detail, from sight lines to acoustics.

"The room is huge. I think you could hold both the ceremony and the reception here," Roslyn suggested.

I looked to Andrew for a response. He mulled it over for a moment.

"Yeah. We could do that."

From that moment, there was no doubt that our wedding would be here, in this room, in Montreal.

As I absorbed this reality, I wondered if it was the romance of the room that changed his mind—or was he just getting more comfortable with this entire concept as this process continued?

ANDREW   Above and beyond all my other reasons for wanting to separate the wedding and the reception, there was always one particular concern. I was abundantly aware that this entire event was a significant stretch for my parents. I thought they would be much more comfortable having the ceremony held before a separate, intimate, gathering. Here was my mother, though, getting into the spirit of this with Doug and me. And lo and behold, she suggested that we hold the ceremony and the reception together. If she thought it was a good idea, maybe we should do it that way after all.

And the room was an inspiring vision, the perfect place.

SHELDON   I knew they had found a place they liked in Montreal. It seemed the rest of our community knew it too. And you already know from the previous chapter what the community was saying. Despite the negative reaction, Roslyn was discussing the upcoming event as a fait accompli. I was becoming even more the odd man out, with three of them on one side, me on the other.

So when Roslyn suggested we all meet with a rabbi, I said, *Why not?* In a little less than a year from now, *something* was going to happen, and my aim was to try and reduce the scope of it. I had hope that this might be an opportunity for all of us to be heard.

ANDREW   Even though I've never been as religious as my father, I agreed to the meeting, hoping that this might help him reconcile the tremendous discomfort he was expressing about the wedding. I went into it feeling hopeful that we could make some movement in the right direction, and deflate some of the tension that had been mounting from week to week.

SHELDON   On the day of the meeting I had no great expectations. We filed into his study, and once we were all seated, Rabbi
Berman said he already knew, more or less, what had brought us
together for this talk. Once he'd heard Roslyn, Andrew, and Doug
give a little background into the ceremony and celebration they envisioned, he looked to me and said, "Go ahead and give me your
position."

I told him, "Look, I'm going to be there. If this is the way they
feel about it, if it has a religious context, it's all right. But if I had
my choice, as a compromise, to take my feelings into account as well
as theirs, and still give them essentially what they want, why can't
we, for example, have the ceremony in a rabbi's study, like this?
That occurs very often, in second marriages, for instance, when both
people have children."

Rabbi Berman listened attentively. Roslyn, Andrew, and Doug
all remained silent. So I continued. Perhaps, this time, they were
really hearing. "If you want me to give my idea, why not have the
ceremony with the immediate family and maybe a best man or what
have you, one or two close friends perhaps, then come back to our
house and have a party with say, fifty, sixty, even seventy people?
The house can accommodate that many people. And that's enough.
We don't have to take ads in the newspaper. When they talk about
a video, a photographer, a band, well . . . to my mind it's all indica-
tive of their desire to make this much bigger than I'm comfortable
with."

And I brought up the same question I'd asked of both Andrew
and Doug many times since last January. "Tell me one other person
that you know who has gone through what you're talking about."
And as always, they had no reply.

"I shouldn't be the innovator," I insisted. "Also, I'd like to know
more about the ceremony as they see it, in some detail. Doug has
talked about wanting to have his friend Geri speak during the ceremony—"

"Geri's one of my two closest friends," Doug interjected, "and she gave me the honor of asking me to speak during her wedding. I want to do the same for her."

"I understand that, and perhaps that's not unusual outside of Canada, but here—well, I've never heard of it. And furthermore, I want to make sure this doesn't become some kind of platform. This shouldn't be about politics, and I need to know that this won't be treated as some kind of endorsement for gay marriage per se. This is about our family, and that's it."

After a long while silent, Roslyn shot out, "What have we got to be ashamed of? If we're proud of our children, we do it openly, we don't have to keep it on a small scale. That's like hiding it, keeping it in the closet."

I'd heard this line of defense before.

And she added, "Either we have it the way we want it, or what's the purpose of going through the whole thing?"

Doug tried another tack, no more helpful. "OK, so we recognize that you'll be very troubled that day, but why don't you pretend that one of your children is marrying someone of another faith. Imagine what that would feel like. You'd be uncomfortable, but you'd get over it." I didn't think that comparison recognized the magnitude of what we were experiencing.

Through all of this dissension, Rabbi Berman didn't say a thing. After almost an hour, he finally spoke for two, maybe three minutes. And I thought his answer was a great answer. I don't think they understood the answer, but I saw it as supportive of my position, so it was a great answer.

"I'm just a rabbi, not a psychologist," he qualified immediately. "So I can't give you a psychological answer. The best I can do is try and translate this into religious terms. The Bible says a person should revere his mother and father. Therefore, relating it to the context that we're discussing now, you should talk this over separately, together—however you like—and try to see each other's positions. Hopefully, on one hand, you get what you want, and on the other hand, you're sensitive and sympathetic to the position of each other. See if you can come to some kind of compromise that satisfies everybody."

DOUG   The rabbi closed with this thought. "And when it's all said and done, in accordance with Jewish tradition, the parents will confer and reach a final agreement. Sheldon and Roslyn must concur, and then present the children with a united front."

United Front? What was this, a meeting of NATO?

"And the children should respect their wishes. At least that's how you would handle this situation if you used biblical Scripture as a model. And, as I said, the Torah is my frame of reference here. I'm not a psychologist."

We had all listened respectfully, and when he finished speaking, I was numb. Why had I, a largely irreligious Jew, acceded to this meeting? If I'd ever given a moment's thought to how this would play out, it should have been no surprise. After all, we were meeting in a synagogue, not a gay and lesbian community center, or even a therapist's office. Organized religion has always left me ambivalent at best, and bitter at moments like this. I tried to remember that millions find lifesaving support through ecclesiastical charity, yet my paltry disappointment reminded me that the good Lord can also taketh away—in the name of a book whose rules I interpret as fiction stuffed with mythic metaphor.

As Andrew and I marched from the synagogue to the car, we crunched dried and crumbling leaves beneath our feet. Breaking from our usual pattern, I was far ahead of him, forcing the pace. I wouldn't dare speak until steel and glass could stand between me and the serene Montreal morning. When we reached the car, I glanced back at the bland cement exterior of the synagogue. No sign yet of Sheldon and Roslyn—they must be chatting in the hall with the rabbi.

The street was nearly silent when we stood on opposing sides of the car, and I heard the jab of Andrew's key in the driver's door. I threw myself into the passenger seat as Andrew turned over the engine.

"Great," I hissed, "just great."

"What are you talking about?"

"Did you hear what happened back there?"

"Yes! What's your problem?"

Andrew made the familiar turns, first onto Sherbrooke Street, then Decarie Boulevard, and finally the Laurentian Autoroute, which was to take us out to the country for an afternoon hike. But the discord during the ride would be bumpier than any terrain we'd negotiate by foot that day. I managed to spoil the scenic drive with an ugly scene of my own. Regurgitating the meeting in the rabbi's study, I acted out each moment for Andrew with a masochistic theatricality. Then I wrapped up the recitation with my interpretation of Sheldon's take on the talk.

"And when we walked out of the room together, did you see how your father sailed out of that room? With a bounce in his step and a song in his heart."

"Yeah, and . . . ?"

"The rabbi basically gave him exactly what he wanted. When, where, how, even *if* we have a wedding is, as far as they're concerned, out of our hands."

"I really don't know where you're getting all this from. I wish you would just calm down and let it go. Nothing happened in there."

"How can you say that?" I was getting really revved up now. It was one thing to have the rabbi subvert what I saw as the real issues, but another entirely to have my own husband-to-be deny that his father was about to yank the plug on our plans. "Even though he had some problems with this, it sounded like your father was coming around. Remember the last time we were in Montreal? We were at dinner at Le Latini? It was the first time we'd sat around together and talked about the wedding. And he actually sounded fine to me. OK, we didn't get into great specifics. You and I hadn't even worked out any of those for ourselves. But he sounded fine. *Fine!*"

Then I dredged up a particularly incongruous moment from a

batch of memories, moments now tainted by this rabbinical encounter:

"Do you remember?" I spun the question into an accusation. "Your father suggested—*he actually suggested*—" I sputtered, recalling the scene now with bitter irony. "He even suggested we do a videotaped invitation! Remember, I was working for Oprah at the time? And he said, 'Why don't you ask if she'll read a line or two on camera.' I could swear to you he wasn't kidding, either. Now, forget for a second that she'd never do it, and put aside the fact that you know I'd never get into an intimate conversation with Oprah, let alone ask her to appear on a wedding invitation videotape—but your father seemed really enthusiastic, even tickled by the idea. I figured it showed he had started to put aside his fears and get into the spirit with us. So what's happened?"

Andrew remained stone-silent, so I answered myself. "We decided to have it here in Montreal. That's what it's about, right?"

He kept right on staring ahead at the road.

I began to imagine a journey through the interior of Sheldon's fears, and as I mapped out the terrain of his subconscious, I grew more agitated.

"He's ashamed. This is totally about shame. When the wedding was in New York, it was one thing, but now everybody will know, and see him being part of it. And accepting us as a couple, publicly, is just too much, right?"

"What are you making yourself crazy for? Everything's fine. Nothing's changed. Nothing happened."

"How can you say that? Did you hear the rabbi? And did you see the look on your father's face? It's like he just won the lottery! Are you in denial about this, or what? How can you not see this?" Now I was spewing, in a fine rage. Andrew's rejection of my perceived reality had left me feeling abandoned.

For the better part of a year, Andrew and I had shared this dream, building a vision of it, together. Now, in one fell swoop, Sheldon was ready to topple it. And for me, it felt like a thunderbolt from out of the blue, tossed by some callous, omnipotent force.

And worse yet, I believed that Andrew was willfully ignoring it.

ANDREW   It was like we'd been at different meetings. And the one Doug had attended was in some threatening place I had no interest in visiting.

"How can you say nothing happened?!" he shouted.

"Because nothing happened. You're driving yourself—you're driving *me*—nuts! *Nothing happened.* You're totally overreacting!"

"No, *you're* totally in denial! It's like we weren't even in the same room together. We're not powerless here. After all, we're still talking about *our* wedding. We are absolutely helpless, though, if you can't—or won't—see what's going on here!"

"I can't—no, I *won't* talk to you if you're going to be like this. That's it."

SHELDON   Doug must have been crazy, to think I was seriously suggesting he get Oprah to do a videotaped invitation! And he was mistaken in fixating on the rabbi's suggestion that Roslyn and I come to a joint decision. I liked that he suggested dialogue and compromise. I didn't think that his words were intended as some judgment from the highest court in the land—*"You must obey"*—nor that any decision Roslyn and I reached should be binding.

ROSLYN   I can't say I was disappointed in the results of the meeting. Rabbi Berman took pains to present himself as a man of religion, not a counselor. His was a religious reply, not a therapeutic one. In fact, his response came from the Conversative wing of the religion, and after all, he is a Conservative rabbi. In addition, I shouldn't have been surprised; Judaism practiced north of the Canadian border is typically a notch more Conservative than its American counterpart.

Sheldon and I have always chosen to attend an Orthodox synagogue. When Doug first came to services with us, he expressed surprise that I would willingly attend services where women are obligated to sit in separate side sections, while men sit together at the center. Actually, it's never bothered me a bit. I've never felt I was being demeaned as a woman. I'd chosen to be there, and if I didn't want to be there, I could always leave.

I wasn't brought up in a particularly religious home; rather, it was traditional, and therefore observant. I never went to Jewish school, because some people believed young women could learn what was important at home. My maternal grandmother moved in with us when I was a girl, and she was my most treasured source of Judaic knowledge, instructing me in all the ritual and tradition.

There was at least one lesson I didn't learn about Orthodox teachings until adulthood when I already had four grown children. I heard it said in my synagogue that homosexuality was considered an "abomination." This was disturbing.

"Why am I sitting here when my sons aren't welcome?" I asked myself. I talked to Sheldon about becoming members at the Conservative synagogue, but it was a halfhearted effort, since I knew he'd never leave the tradition he'd known all his life. And part of my heart was with him on this.

I remember attending Orthodox synagogue as a child, and I've taken comfort from the rituals ever since. There's solace in knowing that it is consistent. There's so much insecurity in the world, everything is in flux today, you have to kill yourself to keep up with technology, culture, societal shifts. Still, you know when you go to pray, every Jew in an Orthodox synagogue around the world is doing the same thing.

There's the paradox. It's not comforting to know my sons aren't welcome there. What is comforting is that it doesn't change.

Although I'm very fond of Rabbi Berman, and he's been unusually supportive of my work in the gay community, he had missed the point as far as I was concerned. He had completely ignored the question of whether there was anything wrong with the boys' wish to have a public union in the manner they planned.

He listened well, though. And his advice that Sheldon and I join together to form a united front was both scripturally sound and good parenting. Any two parents will always have differing opinions, but when your decisions regard the children, the repercussions are greater and demand that the two of you sit down and compromise to reach a consistent position. Our household had always been run this way. It's helped us work together, and it's taught the children that they couldn't split us, that Sheldon and I could always formulate a compromise that would satisfy us and them.

Ultimately I felt the rabbi sided with Sheldon, and that was fine with me. Sheldon obviously needed the support.

ANDREW   That evening, when Doug and I got back from the Laurentians, we got together in the den with my parents. We all, for the most part, reiterated the key positions we'd expressed that morning. What impressed me most was my father's outright honesty about his feelings. I sensed that for the first time, he felt he had a forum where he could acknowledge his deep fears and reservations without being berated by my mother for his narrow-mindedness. He was sincere and honest and made a concerted effort to negotiate his inner conflicts, with the clear goal being to reach a point within himself where he could accept and follow through with this wedding.

Therefore, when I looked back to the rabbi's statement about respecting the wishes of your parents, I really didn't see this as a threat to our plans. Whether I was in complete denial of this possibility, I can't say. But my key belief, from day one, had not altered. I always felt my father would go through with whatever Doug and I felt was appropriate, even if it meant some kicking and screaming on the long journey down the aisle.

ROSLYN   After we got home that evening, Sheldon confronted me. "You're always going along with Andrew, encouraging him."

Only hours after a meeting I'd set up to give him a forum, Sheldon was already back to the same old complaints. So though I'd heard accusations like that before, this time I was incensed. "Encouraging him to do *what*? Something *terrible*? No. To do something *you* don't want him to do. He's not asking to do something illegal — he's not asking me to commit homicide, burglary, robbery. He wants to have this celebration of his relationship. *Why shouldn't I support that?"*

Part of me wanted to hear him out, but I was too emotionally involved.

SHELDON   Roslyn suggested that I talk to a psychologist. "You're not getting anywhere talking to me"—as if I was the only one who needed to travel any distance toward compromise. "We're coming from places so far apart. Why don't you speak to Dennis?"

When it was clear that none of them could ever hear my concerns, I contacted Dennis. I had met him before, and was quite impressed. So I sat down in his office with little trepidation. He listened patiently while I expressed my frustrations.

"Never mind that they don't agree with my position. Let them sympathize that I'm having trouble with this, and then we can start talking. Because until they recognize that there's a problem here, that I'm uncomfortable with this, and that most of our friends are troubled that this could happen in their community, then we have nothing to talk about," I told Dennis. "They're not dealing with reality, they're just being flippant. 'Oh, nonsense, you're ashamed, you want to put it in a closet.' That kind of talk doesn't get us anywhere. It just shuts me down."

As a good professional, he listened but didn't take sides. At the end, though, I got the impression he sympathized with my predicament. By this I do not mean that he expressed a negative attitude regarding the intended affair, but rather that he understood my frustration that nobody could understand that it was possible, if not inevitable, that I would have all these concerns and misgivings.

After I'd seen Dennis several times, I felt some relief in having the opportunity to express my position. But it didn't, practically speaking, do much good. At home, nothing was changing.

ROSLYN   Intellectually I knew I was right to be angry with Sheldon for what I perceived as his unwillingness to accept Andrew as a gay man without feeling shame. Shame is such a powerful emotion that we even feel "ashamed" to admit it. By rejecting Andrew's idea of how the wedding should be, he was symbolically rejecting our son. My heart told me I was being unfair since giving up shame is a big step that needs to be worked through over time.

Meanwhile, Andrew and Doug were moving ahead with their plans, and since it was difficult for them to do some of the requisite legwork from New York, I continued helping them with many of the necessary details. Though many of my friends continued to criticize my involvement in the planning, I was thankful for the support of others, like my colleague Mark, cousin Miriam, and friends like Roma and Lona, to mention just a few.

As the New Year approached, Sheldon—thanks to therapy—felt ever freer to chastise me for my involvement in plans that he disapproved of so adamantly. I found myself at a crossroads. In seeking to create his own marriage, Andrew had unwittingly created one of the biggest challenges for mine.

There was no way I could gently extricate myself from this rift. I would have to make a painful choice.

CHAPTER 7

Standing Our Ground

ANDREW AND DOUG

January–March 1996

ANDREW   Here it was, New Year's Day.

"Exactly nine months to go until Labor Day," Doug observed. "So, you think it'll be natural or cesarean?"

"Very funny. It doesn't look like there's going to be any delivery. Not at this rate."

"What do you mean?"

"I got a call from Leslie Hoppenheim. She never got the checks."

"What do you think that's about?"

"I don't know. I'll call my mother later and see what's going on."

Leslie Hoppenheim is the no-nonsense party planner my mother found to coordinate the wedding. She runs a booking agency out of her home in Hampstead, a few blocks from my parents' house. We first met with Leslie on the last day of "The Rabbi Weekend," as Doug had taken to calling it. That was back in late September, and Doug had brought cash to pay the initial deposit.

Having our first business meeting in her home, in the middle of conservative Hampstead, only reinforced the feeling of having this wedding in my parents' backyard. When we sat down to talk, Leslie was upbeat, with an edge.

"So, this is *unusual*, isn't it?"

"Yeah, it is," I replied, not too defensively. "I guess some people are more surprised than others. But we want to focus on making this a great night for everybody. So whether they're on board with the concept when they walk in or not, hopefully they'll have a good time."

"Well, I'd say if your family is comfortable with this, everybody will follow their lead."

True enough. And no small goal.

She ticked off the details she'd already covered with my mother: photographer, band, or maybe a deejay. . . . Then there was the question of a video. Doug thought it was an unnecessary extravagance. He'd always say it was money that didn't need to be spent. I told him we'd cut back in other areas. "And don't worry, this is going to cost so much less than either of my sister's weddings, believe me." And that would undoubtedly be the case.

From the outset, Doug had been very sensitive about the money. He wanted to keep the cost low enough so that if we needed to pay for it ourselves, he could swing it. There were a few problems with that scenario, however. We'd purchased our apartment in July, and the cost of renovations had sent us deep into hock on a half dozen credit cards. Doug wasn't having his most flush financial year, and if my income were a heartbeat, it would flat-line. But he looked at each financial decision as if it were coming out of our bank account. The way I saw it, we needed to keep the cost down, while creating the best wedding we could.

DOUG   The New Year's report from Leslie Hoppenheim gave me pause. Roslyn had known for weeks that the deadline for payment passed on December thirty-first. I was less concerned about the missed deadline than the reason behind it. Roslyn wasn't the type to miss a down payment. She is nothing if not organized. And while she may be late for everything from dinner to theater, museums to the gym, I knew her well enough by now to know that this deadline having come and gone was a sign of something not quite right.

ANDREW   Later that afternoon, I called my mother. After a bare minimum of the usual chitchat, I told her about Leslie's call. "Did you mail her a check?" I asked.

"No."

"You know the deadline was yesterday, right?"

"Yes."

My mother is never monosyllabic. "What's going on?"

"I meant to talk to you about this before now. I've had to make a decision. It's a decision that's very hard for me. I can't be involved in the planning of the wedding anymore. It's causing too much strain between me and Daddy. He doesn't want to do this, and I have to stand by that. I just can't do it anymore. I can't be involved. I'm sorry."

What do you mean you can't be involved? What's going on here? I thought. The only ally in my family was abandoning me. I got a sense from my mother's tentative statement that she was having a difficult time breaking this news to me. I began to empathize with her as I recognized the anguish that she, too, was fraught with over this decision. I withheld my own reaction and quickly ended the conversation. But nothing had prepared me for this.

DOUG   We both looked at each other, shell-shocked. I heard him repeat the conversation, but it wasn't real. It didn't sound like Roslyn. Or not the Roslyn I've known. I tried to battle back rising anger; Andrew's face was a mask of melancholy. I couldn't recall seeing him look so haunted, as if a switch had shut him down. Unaccustomed as he was to being overtly rejected by his parents, this obviously came as an astonishing blow. I stuffed down my own bitterness and tried to think affirmatively, for him.

"Look, whatever happened just now, it doesn't have to finish our plans. We can call Leslie and ask for an extension."

"She can't do that. That's not how it works."

"OK . . . well, how about we ask how much she needs, and we FedEx the money to her ourselves?"

"She needed it yesterday."

"If you tell her what happened, don't you think she'll understand?" Andrew looked cross, and I assumed that he didn't want to get into the public exposure of this private dispute. "OK, we can be more vague . . ." I vamped. "We . . . we can say there was a *misunderstanding*, and *we* need to send the deposit."

"Let's just forget about the whole thing! It's causing too much trouble."

Too much trouble? Isn't it worth the trouble? I asked myself.

ANDREW "If my parents are really backing out of the whole thing, are we prepared to do it all ourselves?" Doug didn't answer. "Can we come up with all the money? And it's not just the money — there are so many details. Can we do all the legwork from New York? You've never had a family wedding, you have no idea how many minuscule details there are. Managing all that from here in New York will be impossible."

That was the trouble it would cause for us. I was even more worried about the trouble it was causing my parents. If my father was so completely against this that my mother couldn't even be involved, I just didn't feel like it was worth putting them through any more pain.

DOUG I was so focused on Andrew that I didn't discern his unspoken concern about his parents' feelings. As far as I was concerned, this goal was well worth *our* trouble, and I wanted to know if Andrew felt it was worth it, too.

"Maybe this is just temporary. Maybe your parents need more time with all this, and putting the deposit down right now was too big a commitment when they're still grappling with everything. What do you say we put down the deposit as a sort of insurance policy? If they come around soon, then we saved all the plans we've made up until now. If they ultimately decide they won't be involved with our wedding, we'll make the decision later about either paying for it ourselves or giving it up. If we make the deposit ourselves, we can make the big decisions later."

"But we could lose all that money."

"I don't think it's going to be lost. I think we're going to get married, one way or another. If not, I'm willing to take the risk. I think our wedding is worth it, do you?"

ANDREW   With his question hanging in the air, I left the room to do some housework, and avoid the issue.

After a few hours of mulling it over, I went looking for Doug. He was lying on top of the bed, fully clothed, at three in the afternoon. All the eager pragmatism he'd mustered earlier had been squeezed out of him. He had that pursed-up look that tells me he's catastrophizing. "What have you been doing?"

"You know."

"Fretting?"

It's like a domino game of calamities he plays in his head at times like this, conjecturing every possible miserable outcome, tracing the ripple effect it'll have on our lives.

"Is it worth all this?" I asked. "You look absolutely miserable."

"And you?"

"I'm feeling miserable, believe me."

"Don't worry, you look miserable too."

We almost laughed.

Doug's eyes narrowed a little. "This is *our* wedding. Not your mother's. Not your father's."

"Are we ready to pay for it—all of it, *everything*—ourselves?" I asked, though deep down inside it really wasn't the money I was most concerned about. Rather, I was torn between my own dream and my parents' fear of public humiliation in front of friends and family.

DOUG   For the first time since I proposed a year ago, I saw despair in Andrew's eyes, and I knew the joy of our plans was being siphoned out of him, leaving him empty and drawn. A flash of anger detached me from Andrew's pain, and put me in mind of my own. I was flooded with resentment for the position we'd been put in.

Ever since the weekend we first met in Montreal, Sheldon and Roslyn had welcomed me into their family with a casual forthrightness that would surprise many observers. My first encounter with the wider Merling clan was on Passover at the Montefiore Club, in an imposing dining room that looked more like a grand library. Thirty or so family members were decked out in formal dress for a meal around a mammoth square made of four long boardroom tables. And though I went to this first Passover seder with a flock of butterflies, Roslyn and Sheldon made me feel unquestionably welcome. Following their lead, the rest of the family did likewise. And in the years since, even if some of the family offered me more warmth than others, I have always been treated with respect.

Since I had been separated by distance and circumstance from much of my own family, I found a surrogate, of sorts, in Roslyn, Sheldon, and the family they welcomed me into so willingly. And over the years, as I grew more deeply in love with Andrew, I also grew to love his parents very much as well.

Now, sitting in bed on New Year's Day, looking into Andrew's wounded eyes, seeing the reflection of my own feelings of betrayal, I was filled with a new resolve.

"If this is something we believe is right, then I think we should see it through. And I think it's right. What do you think?"

ANDREW   "I do too. But this is a lot of money," I reminded Doug, avoiding the real issue.

"I know it is. But we can also cut back. We don't need the video. With that room you don't need flowers. That would knock off twenty-five hundred at least, right there. And do we need a full bar? Why can't we do a cash bar? Jews don't drink."

"At this wedding, they'll need a drink."

"OK, but we can economize," Doug insisted.

"Economize, yes. But it's not worth all the work, and all this extra stress with my family, if we're not going to do it right."

"OK, let's sit down and go over the budget again, and pare it down to the essentials we both can agree on, then we'll see how low we can get it."

I took my file out of our office, and we convened at the dining room table. We debated the essentials, then crunched the numbers.

"How are we going to come up with that?"

Doug did a little calculating. "I can put away half from what I earn in the next nine months, if we watch our spending carefully. And I have a credit line from a credit union account at reasonable interest. And we won't go on a honeymoon."

"We're going to need to get away for a vacation after this is all over, whether you call it a honeymoon or not."

"Maybe. But it'll have to be simple and short. And we'll put it on a credit card."

"Which one? We're thousands in debt from the renovations."

"I have two more cards I haven't used."

"Do you want to be in all this debt?"

"Listen, all these numbers assume that I'm going to stay in this economic rut. If business picks up, I might not even have to borrow on the cards. We can talk about money until we're blue in the face. You know we're not going to be out on the street. Things might be tight for another year, but we'll be OK. The real question is, is this what you want to do?"

"Yes. Obviously your answer is yes, too?"

"Yes, definitely. And I think our decision to get married should be based on whether we think it's right for us, and not what anybody else thinks. Your parents or anybody."

"I agree." I still had my doubts about the money, but I decided to put my doubts on hold and call Leslie. I apologized about the delay, and said we were having a family disagreement, but that it wouldn't affect our commitment to make the deposits.

"If we sent you a check from New York on Tuesday, you'd get it Wednesday. That's a little past the deadline, obviously. Have we lost anybody?"

"Somebody else wants David Sternfeld, and since I didn't have a check, I figured he could do their wedding instead." Shit. Sternfeld was young and innovative. He was the only person I thought would do our photos the way we wanted. And I knew enough about him to sense he'd be comfortable with a gay wedding. "But since it was the holiday weekend, I didn't do anything about it yet. You'll get me the check Wednesday, definitely?"

"Absolutely."

One bullet dodged.

And for now, at least, we had a little time to regroup. Once we mailed the check tomorrow, we'd have deposits down on photographer, band, and most important, the room at Eaton's.

DOUG   With the challenge Andrew and I faced, we grew closer than ever. The bullets that were swirling around us had helped us create a safe bunker together. Before this, Andrew and I had worked through problems more as individuals with two points of view. This new challenge was forcing us to learn new coping skills, developing strategies to work together as a team. We were creating a third, separate entity: our relationship.

This last insight actually came courtesy of my therapist.

She was also impelled to remind me on several occasions, after hearing stories of Sheldon's increasing angst:

"This is *your* wedding. You're not doing this *to* anybody, you're doing it *for* you." I had to remind myself of those simple, wise words many times over the next year.

ANDREW   In October, two months before the New Year's bomb dropped by my mother, and a few weeks after the meeting with the rabbi, we had another fateful, and thankfully much more successful, encounter with a rabbi of a very different stripe.

Rabbi Elizabeth Bolton came to us, like the other rabbi, through my mother and her parents' group. The rabbi's mother, Rebecca, attended the group. While my mother hadn't met Rabbi Bolton yet, she figured there was a strong chance that a lesbian rabbi would perform a gay wedding. Rabbi Bolton was scheduled to speak before the New Jersey Gay and Lesbian Havurah, a group of gay and lesbian Reform Jews. Since she lives near Philadelphia with her partner and their daughter, New Jersey seemed like a good midway point for our first meeting.

A dozen or so members of the group were already assembled in the home of Karen and Robyn, our hosts. An instantly likable couple, they both occupy the great, gray middle ground between lipstick and dipstick, much as Doug and I fall somewhere in the vast average between nellie and butch. True, Karen has more the carriage of a nurturer, and Robyn is a whiz with all things mechanical, but they're the kind of suburban women who shoot down stereotypes just by being themselves.

Before Rabbi Bolton arrived, we were introduced to the crowd. The purpose of the meeting, we gathered, was to discuss feminism and the role of women in the Reconstructionist movement. As it happens, half of those present had been, or were soon to be, wed. When we told the reason for our trek, sooner than you can say Adam and Steve we were treated to wedding pictures and loads of anecdotes. We also learned Rabbi Bolton had officiated at one of their ceremonies. My mother had already told us that she was a rabbi and cantor rolled into one, performing the dual role of orator and vocalist, the latter talent having been finely tuned from her prior training as an opera singer. We were encouraged to hear her praised on both counts.

When the rabbi appeared, she proved to be young, warm, and gregarious. Hearing her speak before the group about the challenges she faced as a woman negotiating her way through the traditionally male-dominated religious hierarchy, it seemed all the more fitting that a woman should preside over our unconventional ceremony.

DOUG   If anyone doubts male primacy within Judaism, I only have to point out that my father has told me of growing up reciting the traditional prayer ". . . and blessed are you, Adonai, our God, who has not made me a woman." As Rabbi Bolton spoke, I picked up a few basics of Reconstructionist Judaism: a return to spoken Hebrew in both public services and celebrations observed at home (in the Reform wing of the religion, Hebrew had been somewhat eschewed in recent years, in favor of English); a new integrated role for women, redressing millennia of treatment as inferiors and temptresses; and an emphasis on welcoming gays and lesbians into the fold.

Here was a rabbi I could put faith in. She spoke as a woman who put spirituality ahead of dogma and saw literal interpretation of all Scripture as a folly. After all, "abomination," the disparagement invoked for homosexual acts, also shows up in the Hebrew Bible (known to non-Jews as the Old Testament) to describe many minor infractions that no rational person would call by the same name. But "abomination" is still waved like a cross before a vampire when it comes to same-sex love.

Rabbi Bolton evoked an intelligent and compassionate side of the religion that I had been looking for. I could imagine her helping us to create a ceremony that incorporated spirituality and tradition, while nudging the religion forward.

ANDREW   It also struck me how appropriate a female rabbi would be, given that Doug and I had decided to ask four female friends to hold our *chuppah*, taking a role customarily played by men. We had chosen women to support the canopy over our heads because, true to the gay male stereotype (and aside from George and Lorne, whom Doug and I had chosen as our best men, respectively), our most enduring bonds have been with women.

Once the rabbi had concluded the discussion, she suggested we meet at a local restaurant to get acquainted. By now Doug and I had established a rapport with Robyn and Karen and exchanged numbers. The similar time frames of our weddings promised we'd find counterpoint in each other's progress.

The roadside restaurant we'd chosen for our first meeting was a truly incongruous setting for a lesbian rabbi and the gay couple she might wed. The buffet of luncheon meats and Jell-O–encrusted fruit had probably never played host to so diverse a gathering. We pulled up chairs at a wood-grain Formica table overlooking the parking lot, and gave each other a good-natured third degree.

We were surprised, for no good reason, when Rabbi Bolton told us she had performed very few same-sex ceremonies.

"By the way," she asked, "what are you calling your ceremony? A 'wedding' or 'commitment ceremony'?"

Doug and I laughed.

"It depends on who you ask," I answered, enigmatically.

"You each call it something different?" she asked incredulously.

"No—not us! My parents. Sometimes my mother calls it a wedding. Lately she calls it a commitment ceremony. Sometimes, at least. My father has always called it a commitment ceremony. For Doug and me, it's a wedding, and that's what we're calling it. That's it."

"So it's officially a 'wedding'?"

"Definitely. In terms of the name, that's their problem."

And Doug added, "We're the ones exchanging vows and rings, and it's a wedding as far as we're concerned."

DOUG   "Do *you* have a preference?" I asked.

"Well, of course, it's up to every couple. But I'm glad you're comfortable with calling it a wedding. 'Commitment ceremony' can be just fine, but it highlights our differences instead of our similarities. You've got a rabbi performing the ceremony, so there's a strong element of tradition right there. Of course, there's one obvious break from tradition here, but depending on how you organize this, it may be the only major departure from what most Jews expect to see at a wedding."

Andrew and I traded looks of relief, knowing we saw this ceremony the same way the rabbi did. That's when I started thinking of
her as *our* rabbi.

"So you see eye to eye on the terminology. What was the first
thing you discovered you had in common?"

"When we first met?" I asked.

She nodded yes.

ANDREW   Only half kidding, I told her, "Doug worked on talk
shows, and I watched them."

Then the tougher question: "What made you fall in love with
each other?"

Doug and I looked a little desperately at each other for rescue.
I never saw this one on The Newlywed Game, I thought.

Rabbi Bolton prodded, "Andrew, you first."

I just said the first thing that came to mind. "His kindness,
warmth, his big heart, and generosity."

DOUG   I answered, "His strength and caring. His empathy and
understanding." I knew there was some key that I couldn't unearth
under the pressure of the moment, and I was caught up in the
frustration of shortchanging Andrew's virtues.

Thankfully, Rabbi Bolton turned to practical matters. "Do you
want to think about whether or not we're a good fit together, and
talk later?" she asked.

While I was already certain she was the right rabbi for us, I
didn't have much idea of Andrew's response. I turned away from
her, toward Andrew, pondering the standards of etiquette her question begged. I raised my eyebrows and indicated my enthusiasm —
with what I hoped was an almost imperceptible nod yes. I saw that
Andrew hadn't furled his right eyebrow in his usual involuntary sign
of disagreement. He read my response, and answered for both of us.

"No, that's OK. If you'll have us, we'd definitely like you to be
part of our wedding."

"All right, then," she answered. "Me too."

We all breathed a fleeting sigh of relief that this formality was behind us. Rabbi Bolton continued, "How much have you thought about the ceremony, and what do you know about the traditional approaches to a Jewish wedding, versus how you envision yours?"

Andrew and I replayed our *no, you first* pantomime of minutes ago, until I confessed, "I haven't been to as many weddings as Andrew, certainly not as many Jewish ones. So other than a few nuts and bolts we've worked out, like working with you, for instance, I'm not very well informed."

She recommended we buy a book she'd prescribed to other less-than-devout Jews, *The Jewish Wedding Book*, by Anita Diamant. "So, you didn't know you'd be getting homework, huh?" I took notes as Rabbi Bolton gave further instruction. "Come up with an outline for the ceremony, using, if you like, some of the examples in the book. And we should meet sometime in the next four or five months. I like to meet at least three times before the ceremony."

Once we had a rabbi, it seemed the freight train was on the track and there was no stopping until we made it all the way down the aisle. And I'd come this far without telling my own parents.

Yep. For all my tough talk about other people's difficulties in facing reality, I'd never asked my parents to face my own reality. But shame of the realities of human nature had tainted my family's interactions for decades. None of us drank to hide the pain; silence was my family's drug of choice. Now, thanks to the wedding plans, I was forced to break our household's mold.

After Andrew and I returned from our annual Thanksgiving trip to visit my parents, I wrote to formalize the facts they already knew, and inform them of news they surely never dreamt possible.

Daddy:

It's not news to you that our family has had more than its share of stresses and strains. Those very stresses have created an atmosphere where communication between all of us has ranged from inadequate to, during some periods, nonexistent.

Looking back over the only period of our family history that I know personally, I remember a lot of difficult times. But you should know that, in retrospect, I know that you and Mommy each did the best you could under tremendously hard circumstances. That's not to say that I think you made the right decisions in all cases regarding my upbringing, but who could say they'd ever made all the right decisions? Not me, certainly. And you both obviously did a whole lot right, because from all apparent evidence, Lynn, Jerry, & I offer a pretty positive testament to your parenting skills.

We're a long way from our toughest times together, but the hardest years left all of us more distant than I'm sure we would have liked. I spent several years with minimal contact with all of you, with the exception of Lynn. I think we've all grown closer, ironically, since I've moved to the East Coast. But no matter how much, or how little, any of us are in contact, there's also a bit of distance that I think all of us maintain from each other when it comes to our personal lives.

This lack of interaction in personal areas is, I think, the key to our family's dynamic. I'm not saying it's a great thing, but given that atmosphere, I've felt it would be odd for me to bring up somewhat private aspects of my life. But there are some things that need to be dealt with openly here, and I'm sure you'll understand why when you read further.

I can't imagine that I'm telling you anything new at this point, since you've met Andrew at four different Thanksgiving dinners. As you know, we've lived together almost three years, and bought our co-op together last July. If it hasn't been crystal-clear until now, let me say that we have been in a committed, loving relationship for almost five years.

When some people discuss their homosexuality with their parents, they fear rejection, ridicule, or worse. To the credit of both of you, I certainly don't have that concern. However, as I wrote earlier, given the low level of personal communication in our family, there's not really been an opportunity for discussing this in any appropriate context.

You've always been well informed, progressive thinkers, who don't allow dogma to dictate your personal views. And I'm sure your reading habits haven't changed so much that you could have missed the tremendous social changes that have been taking place over the last five or ten years—putting gay and lesbian rights in the forefront of the civil rights debate, where blacks found themselves thirty to forty years ago.

So, if my theory of our family dynamics is true, why am I broaching this personal topic right now? Don't worry, it's great news (at least to us!). I don't imagine that I've said anything so surprising thus far, but you might find the next information astonishing.

Andrew and I are getting married. And the irony isn't lost on me that I should be the only one of your children to have a big wedding. But that's the fact. The date is set for next September 1st, in Montreal, where, as you know, Andrew hails from. We are expecting to have somewhere in the vicinity of 100–125 people, perhaps a bit fewer if the prospect of traveling to Montreal is too daunting for some of our New York and L.A. friends.

Andrew's parents, Roslyn and Sheldon, are very much involved in the planning of the event. It would be safe to say that his mother is much more at ease with the entire concept, which admittedly is nothing if not out of the ordinary. They have always been very supportive of our relationship, and this event has not changed that. However, it is certainly serving as a catalyst for discussion of comfort levels. Nowadays, every wedding presents its individual challenges (i.e., second marriages, interracial marriages, interfaith marriages . . . hey, look on the upside—we're both Jewish!) and many couples find they're creating ceremonies tailored to their circumstances. Andrew's parents are working with us on that process.

I've already told Lynn the good news, and she will be flying out with Michelle. Since we're having it Labor Day weekend, it's ideal to build a vacation around attending, and that's what Lynn & Michelle will do. I'll be dropping Jerry & Roslyn a note very shortly to let them know about it as well.

I know how rarely the two of you get out of the house nowa-days, let alone on an airplane, so I don't expect that you can neces-sarily attend, but I wonder if you think you could consider it? Maybe you could let me know after you've had some time to think about it. We're having a female rabbi, and incorporating a good deal of Jewish tradition into the ceremony. (Andrew's father feels particularly strongly about that, and I concur.)

In case you're wondering why we're doing this (a question not uncommon for those in older generations to ask), it's for the same reason anyone gets married—to celebrate their love and commitment before family, friends, community, and God. And I would also add, because you raised me to believe I was as deserving as anybody else.

Of course, I understand that it's got to be, at very least, surpris-ing to learn of all this—but I hope you can eventually join in our excitement. Dad, I address this to you because I thought you might want to decide how to ease Mommy into this, if you even feel that any extra care is necessary.

I knew this letter would open up a new line of communication between me and my parents. And I imagined that it might set a new tone of openness in the family in general. But I could never guess its direct effect.

My father called the week after the letter was mailed. It was early December.

"You must have worked a long time on that letter."

Twenty years, I might have said. "It wasn't much trouble, I knew what I wanted to say," was the half-truth I offered instead.

My father sounded more upbeat and cheerful than I'd heard him in a long time. Basically he said that although they hadn't been on a plane in several years, if their health held up, they planned on being in Montreal for "the celebration." When my mother took the phone, she effused happiness about the new tidings, and though I expected her to be encouraging, I was still moved by the intensity of her joy.

The stunner came a couple of days later when my sister called.

"Your letter had quite an effect on Mom and Dad," Lynn told me, with typical reticence.

"Really?"

"Well . . ."

"Tell me!"

"It's actually pretty incredible."

I sat down.

"When Dad told me about the letter, he said he wasn't sure about how to handle it with Mom. He'd clipped a 'Dear Abby' article written by a gay man who'd come out to his wife, and asked if I would show it to Mom, to get her reaction. He was afraid she might fall apart if he told her, since she 'had no idea you were gay.' Then he confides in me that he's known ever since you were thirteen, fourteen years old, but that he's always kept this to himself, for fear Mom would go to pieces. So I showed Mom the 'Dear Abby' column. She said it was very sensitive, but looked curious about my reason for our talk. So I said it. 'Doug's gay.' Then I showed her your letter, which Dad supplied me. When she finished reading, she said, 'I'm so glad he told Dad. I've known since he was a teenager, but I didn't dare tell Dad, for fear he'd disown Doug.' "

I couldn't speak. What could I possibly say?

Evidently I knew each of my parents in a way they'd never known each other. I was certain that they'd both understood for years, and were at peace with the fact that I was gay. At the same time, I'd built a wall between them for twenty years, without ever realizing it. Now, with one letter, the wall came crashing down. At last they could speak honestly and openly about me after twenty years of silence.

ANDREW The friends Doug and I had made in New York had been totally supportive ever since our engagement. Nancy and Bennett, Orna and Nigel, Rachel, Regina, Jacqui, Lori, and the rest always behaved as if ours were any other marriage. Of course, as road blocks went up in Montreal later on, all of them recognized that it was our homosexuality, and the reaction of others to it, that made things rough. But each of their responses seemed to come from the same common ground: the assumption that our intention to get married was not inherently inappropriate, and that our challenges lay in coping with those who didn't understand that we were just trying to live a life like anybody else.

That's how the New Yorkers reacted. My close friends from Montreal were another story.

Diane's reaction wasn't as extreme as when I told her I was gay. At least this time she didn't ask, "Are you sure it isn't a phase?" Diane's both cultured and well traveled. And she trained in theater and dance, so homosexuality wasn't a taboo subject for her, I'm sure. Still, I knew she was uncomfortable when all she could offer by way of congratulations was, "This is so *different*, it's so *unusual*." Maxine responded pretty much the same way. Even Lorne wasn't exactly whipping a hat off his head and tossing it in the air.

I was disturbed by their lack of empathy, and I asked myself, again and again, *Can't they imagine how it feels for me, announcing my marriage to them, and they can't even try to* sound *happy for me?*

And, further, I wondered, *If I were marrying a woman, they'd be acting so differently. And these are my best friends. It's not like we're family and they're stuck with me because of blood. Can they like me, and not like that I'm gay? That's who I am. If they care for me, that's part of what they care for. So why should their expressions be so muted, when most of our other friends had been thrilled and delighted?*

As I sifted through the possible factors, I culled one that I hadn't considered before: they're all Montreal Jews. Yes, they're from a younger generation, but perhaps having been bred in this conservative, sheltered enclave has limited the scope of what they imagine possible for me, and in Lorne's case, even for himself. Or maybe they were worried about the community reaction among their parents and peers, fearing the negative reaction that did, in fact, occur.

One additional factor came to mind. I myself had been driven to another country by the political upheaval in Montreal. The very concept of change had come to mean something other than progress;

instead, it represented helplessness, an onslaught on the community by adversarial forces.

Perhaps, when my parents' circle learned of our plans, it may have been seen as another unwelcome change being forced upon Jewish Montreal, only this time, the societal shift came from the inside. Doug and I had instigated this. And my parents had become agents of this change, however unwillingly. So the atmosphere in English-speaking, and particularly Jewish, Montreal, of a people holding together fast against the incursion of an unfriendly future, may have made it harder to proceed with the plans that we were pushing forward. And my old friends from Montreal, while they were of a younger generation, were also reared in a community suffused with this feeling of helplessness. And while I don't know if any of their parents were among those my mother told me of (she usually kept her stories anonymous, to keep me from holding a grudge), it's probable that my friends' parents were far less than enthusiastic in their reception of our engagement.

Regardless of any external pressures my friends may have felt, their reactions, or lack thereof, hurt.

DOUG When they learned of our engagement, my oldest friends, Geri, George, Debbie, and Anita, answered with cheers and toasts. And as Andrew mentioned, almost all of the friends he and I had made in New York were delighted. One of the New York family had been less than hearty in his congratulations, however. Louie has been like a brother for over fifteen years. (He'll "banish me from the kingdom" for making him sound older than twenty-five—so let's say we met in kindergarten.) With a warm heart and a scalding sense of humor, he can always make you feel the heat of either his approval or reproach. You know you're in trouble with Louie when ambivalence is the best he can muster. And so it was with the wedding.

I put it off to jealousy, though I knew that was too pat an answer. And because I didn't go out on a limb and ask him outright, I could never confide in him when the wedding plans were thrown into doubt. I felt more than a little lost without his antic, painfully funny intrusions letting me know he was out there for me. Still, I knew he was happy for us. And we reserved him a special place of honor in the ceremony. The Yiddish term *Badchan* translates loosely as "clown." Louie wouldn't have loved that title, so we told him the other, more modern translation, "emcee."

Like Andrew's, a few of my oldest friends remained guarded in their responses. While they offered halting congratulations, their reservations often surfaced through one not-so-subtle phrase, a refrain I heard from so many people I could hum it in my sleep: "Are you going to have *bridesmaids*?" After a few choruses, it was clear that those who'd ask this vaguely derogatory question were squeamish about the whole same-sex wedding notion, and didn't quite understand what we were doing, or why.

As for the friends we could always count on, their kindness was regularly repaid with calls at ridiculous hours and shamelessly selfish requests. Jacqui even commiserated with me over Howard Johnson's tuna salad the night before she ran the New York Marathon. She repeated loudly a concept I'd heard from Geri, George, Debbie, and others: Why not cancel the plans in Montreal and do it in New York? Jacqui added a more far-flung proposition: If we were drawn to Montreal because we'd found a drop-dead location, why not ask our friends, starting with her, if they could help us—through donation of time, money, and connections—put together an equally special wedding in New York? We both knew there was more to it than that, but the thought was lovely. She wanted us to know the extent of the support that existed out there.

George and Geri were the rocks of support I leaned on every time the going got tough. Ever since high school, Geri has been a font of common sense, good taste, and self-depricating wit. She was one of those friends many gay men and lesbians know and love who figure out we're gay before we do. Still, I had a brutal time coming out to her. Actually, I didn't have to. We were at George's party when she walked in on me midkiss with a friend of the host. In a way, it wasn't an accident that it happened under George's roof. He was the first person to make me feel that it was more than just OK to be gay. By just being himself, he provided a positive example I could watch and learn from. And it didn't hurt that we're both typically—even *stereo*typically—gay in the old-movie/show-tunes department. We became fast friends, and I was impressed by his choice to be bravely, irrepressibly out at NBC, where we met in the page program. Since the old days when we seated guests at *The Tonight Show*, he's been, along with Geri, the place I go to be myself. Now, with the wedding plans under siege, it felt as if we three were one in our frustration.

I also called Karen often. We'd met just months before at her home in New Jersey, but I felt closer to her, in some ways, than to anybody. Our wedding plans were following the same trajectory, in terms of both the calendar and the karma. We went into this with precisely the same motivation: to celebrate our relationships. And we had the same strength: we didn't see ourselves, or our loves, as intrinsically different—neither better nor worse—than anybody else's. One key difference emerged between our experiences. Karen's parents, and her father in particular, were playing the leading role in the planning of her wedding to Robyn. And their attitude, she reported, was one of unquestioning support. Within their extended families, they had their share of turmoil and controversy. But when it came to the planning, her parents were behind them 100 percent. That unquestioning support made a huge difference for her. I could see it in her body language, in her uncreased brow. I lived vicariously through her, watching a parallel, lighthearted universe that I could only imagine. When I told her how justifying my love was grinding me down, she knew whereof I spoke. During those months, Karen was a one-woman validation machine.

Two weeks after the New Year, Andrew and I had a weekend trip planned to Miami Beach, where we've been rehearsing for our retirement for a couple of seasons. My parents have an apartment in one of the de facto senior citizen centers for migrating Jews. The one-room studio has sat empty for many years, since my parents moved back to California in the mid-eighties.

In the first real downtime we'd had together since Andrew's New Year's Day phone call with Roslyn, we sat on the beach, and Andrew cataloged a dizzying array of physical ills. While we're both just this side of being hypochondriacs, Andrew had reached a new summit of somatic complaining. Usually one of us plays a game with the other on the arrival of a new malady. "How do I feel today?" Andrew often quizzes me. That's my cue to guess, "You don't feel good." Then he prompts me to minister to the afflicted area. If it's a tight shoulder, he turns and shimmies his back for a rub. If it's a sore throat, he points to his Adam's apple for me to plant a kiss on it.

This was different. He wasn't joking, and it seemed each piece of his body was in revolt against the whole. From between the lines of our discussion about the wedding, and the recent escalation in the problems within his family, I saw a disturbing likelihood. I asked Andrew to go for a walk, so I wouldn't have to look at him while I shared a theory.

"Sweetie, I'm scared for you. You're coming apart, and I can't do anything about it. And my opinion is, it's psychosomatic. Not just some of it. All of it. Your neck, your back, your tingling, your headaches, your stomach, your bowels, your feet, everything. You told me when all of these started. It was in the two weeks since your mother backed out of the wedding. In my opinion, you're feeling abandoned by your parents, and that's never happened before, has it?"

He shook his head no.

"It's like you're in shock. You can't comprehend they would, in effect, say—" I reconsidered whether I needed to say the next part, but I went ahead "—that in one basic way, they don't accept you. You believed all this time they had. The reality is different from what you've perceived since you came out to them five years ago, and you're having a hard time catching up with it. And that's why I think you're getting so sick."

I had wanted to walk, and avoid looking at Andrew as much as possible, because I was overwhelmed with guilt. I felt responsible for his pain, as if my proposal of marriage had transformed his body into this battlefield.

ANDREW I've always hated when Doug plays analyst, even if he's right on the money. My somatic complaints and preoccupations were torturing me. The only feeling I was aware of was the anger toward my father and the shame that I felt was at the heart of his effort to put an end to our wedding plans. The latter was supported by the aspects of the ceremony that most troubled my father: the video and the photographer.

"Why do you need to spend that much money? What do you need a video for, a photographer for?" he asked, time and again. He was always dealing with the monetary stuff, not the feelings around it.

Back in December, a couple of weeks before the deposits were due, I said to him outright, "You're having a lot of reactions to this, and a lot of what's feeding your reaction is that you never dealt with the fact that I was gay. All those feelings are coming up now, because you're forced into dealing with it."

And he tried to explain to me how he was feeling all alone, by himself, abandoned. He was angry that we couldn't understand what he was going through. "You and Mommy think it's so normal, you think there's nothing wrong with it." And he trotted out his favorite line: "I'm the most conservative notary in Montreal—I don't want to be a pioneer."

So what was it that disturbed him particularly about the idea of having a video and the photographer? Doug and I talked about it a lot, and came up with a logical theory: Video and photos would be a permanent record, and make this event more than just a moment in time that could be left behind and forgotten. They would insure the ceremony would continue to be remembered, like any other wedding. And the mere presence of a photographer and video crew might communicate this to guests, and suggest to them that we saw nothing so different at the core of this experience.

The weekend after we returned from Florida, Doug and I had a family meeting, which in this instance meant the two of us.

"This is *our* wedding. Nobody else's," Doug insisted. "If we want to pay for it ourselves, we'll handle it as we see fit."

"We'll work with everybody to try to allay their fears, but this can't be *about* their fears," I said, picking up the thought. "It's about us, and our relationship. And as long as it's about the money, and what my father will and won't pay for, it can't be about the real issues."

And Doug added, "What's important is that your parents come because they want to, not that they pay for it."

"So pick up the phone after I dial."

Doug has always been afraid of causing any trouble with my parents, so I figured he might back out of calling my father together, as we'd planned. And sure enough, he backed out. "I know this is about our wedding, but isn't it also personal, and in a way, about issues between you and your father?"

"Good try, but that's cheap psychology. You just don't want to confront him. And you want me to do it by myself."

"I think it would make more sense for you to do it. But if you really need me to—"

"Never mind. I know what I want to say."

CHAPTER 8

Common Ground

SHELDON, ROSLYN, ANDREW, AND DOUG

March–May 1996

SHELDON   The call came from out of the blue.

Andrew said to me, "Doug and I have decided we're prepared to host this, and pay the financial costs ourselves, because we're looking for your emotional support, rather than your financial support."

So in effect what he was saying was, "We're going to have it whether you like it or not. Don't worry whether you're going to pay or not going to pay. But if you see fit to come, we'll be happier than if you don't see fit to come."

It was hurtful, especially considering that I had acknowledged in the beginning that I was going to be there, and that there was no way that I was going to be a no-show.

Maybe he and Doug thought this challenge made it easier for me; in fact, it just made me angry. Here Andrew was telling me they would pay for it. As if my concerns were ever about the money. Instead of allowing us to discuss an alternate kind of affair, he had cut off the communication lines on the subject.

After I hung up, I asked myself, *Why does he have to put me through this trial? It's not Abraham and Isaac, but it ranks right up there. It's a test.*

I had been seeing Dennis for individual therapy since October. Before the New Year, he told me he'd wanted to see Roslyn and me together, since he felt my immediate problems regarding the wedding were really couple's issues. Soon after the three of us sat down together for the first time, Dennis suggested, "Why don't we run through the way you see the ceremony taking place. Not the words, but who's going to walk down the aisle, who you're going to walk down with, are your children going to participate . . ."

Andrew and Doug had already told us that they planned on a traditional procession, which I was against from the outset. Like their wish to have a video, a photographer, and a band, it seemed this would mimic a heterosexual ceremony. Despite my objections, they were firm about this.

ROSLYN   Together with Dennis and Sheldon, I attempted to visualize it all. And as I paced through it all, step by step, I was rattled. I must have never walked through the actual event and imagined how I'd feel along the way . . . *the guests arriving, watching them surreptitiously from some cloistered spot at the back of the hall . . . the curious faces, the excitement, and the fear . . .* Then the ceremony itself. As I pictured myself standing under the *chuppah*, casting a glance on the sea of apprehensive faces, I tried to envision a traditional ceremony . . . *my son, together with Doug, in front of the rabbi.* Then I skipped to the final moment. *Breaking the glass . . .* If it's a Jewish wedding, they must intend on breaking the glass . . . *Will they both do it? Or just one? Which one?* And then I saw the thing I must have been avoiding from the beginning. For surely, every wedding ends with . . .

A kiss.

Were they going to actually *kiss*? My mind raced.

Would Andrew stand in front of all our friends and family, and kiss another man? No . . . maybe he wouldn't want to. Maybe they'll . . . maybe . . .

Just another irony, that in grappling with a small detail that suddenly loomed larger than life, I'd made a breakthrough that would allow a real dialogue with Sheldon for the first time since the engagement. He could set aside the image I'd been projecting: the professional who isn't fazed by anything. At last he could see *me*.

SHELDON   *Finally,* I thought, *I have broken through.* Once Roslyn realized she had her own concerns, she could finally hear mine. And now we could discuss how to find a compromise with Andrew and Doug. Something that we could live with.

ROSLYN   No longer adversaries, we could talk like partners. Maybe the words I was saying to Sheldon weren't so very different from before. The tune was what changed. When Sheldon said he was worried about some aspect of the ceremony, I could relate, and he knew it. I might not agree with him on a certain point, but now at least we were on the same team.

SHELDON   "Though it's true that Andrew and Doug have a lot of heterosexual friends," I pointed out in a session with Roslyn and Dennis, "they also have gay friends. Are they going to be dancing together? Will it be in a manner that might be uncomfortable for sixty-year-olds who haven't experienced anything like it?"

ROSLYN   It was another detail I hadn't envisioned until now. If we were going to invite all our close friends and family, I'd have to imagine how I'd feel with them watching every step of the way. Now that I was drawing the image of the ceremony in my mind, I was troubled by an old expectation. My old dream came back, my old fantasy that there would be a girl at the other end of the aisle. I'd held on to this wish for so long, it almost seemed real. If I was ever going to be truly at peace with the upcoming ceremony, I'd have to come to terms with this old fantasy.

It was just another reminder that the pain of finding out your child is gay never disappears completely. It dulls down, and you learn to live with it. That doesn't mean you don't value your child, or that you don't value what he or she is doing. But it's a reality. And ignoring it doesn't help matters. We've all been conditioned to expect something else. So it comes as a loss.

Sheldon raised another issue . . .

SHELDON   *OK, I'm stuck with something public,* I conceded to myself. *But that doesn't mean we have to make a* statement.

It was a concern I voiced from way back, and often. I wanted assurance that this whole affair wouldn't become a political platform. There were going to be a number of speeches, undoubtedly, and I didn't want anybody to politicize the situation, and plead that people in this situation are entitled to have something like this.

In fact, there was only one concrete aspect of the ceremony Andrew and Doug had told us about. One of Doug's friends, Geri, was going to speak under the canopy *during the ceremony.* I understand it's common in the United States, yet it's unheard-of in Montreal. Here the only people who speak under the canopy are the clergy and the couple. So what was this friend, whom we'd never met, going to say? I wanted to see that politics would have nothing to do with it.

Now that Roslyn and I were asking many of the same questions, Dennis suggested it was time to bring in Andrew and Doug.

ANDREW   We came in to Montreal for four group sessions. The first time it was a two-hour session with all four of us at once.

Since my father had been seeing Dennis for several months, and my mother for half that time, our first visit was framed as if we were entering their world. I had heard rave reviews from both parents as to Dennis's skill and compassion as a therapist, and anticipated the same in his dealings with Doug and me. I was relatively calm and felt confident that whatever issues arose, Dennis would guide us toward a reasonable, fair resolution. Doug, on the other hand, was definitely on edge that day as we drove to the appointment to meet my parents. In almost a frantic, frenetic way, he began to prepare both himself and me for potentially heated debates over various details, anticipating a contentious atmosphere. Finally I said, "Just relax! You're driving me crazy!"

DOUG   I went into that first session with a chip on my shoulder, still angry about watching Andrew erupt in psychosomatic illnesses. I imagined that Roslyn and Sheldon had cast these on Andrew, like a curse.

On the other hand, I also knew we were taking a positive step forward, by sitting together with a psychologist, who I presumed would be more pragmatic, and less religiously biased in his counseling, than a rabbi. As the four of us sat down with Dennis, we were all smiles, and you could detect the air of hope we all breathed in together.

So Roslyn's confession came as the first surprise of the session.

ROSLYN   I simply told Andrew, and Doug, what I'd admitted to Sheldon and Dennis.

"I've discovered that I'm not as comfortable with certain aspects of this ceremony as I once thought. I'm recognizing that I've got questions, like Sheldon does."

DOUG   Although she'd been calling it a "wedding" since September, I recall Roslyn now amending her wording and calling it a "commitment ceremony."

ROSLYN   I asked Andrew to go through the ceremony as he and Doug saw it.

ANDREW I resented having our wedding ceremony scrutinized in this way for my parents' approval. But in the spirit of the moment, I did the best I could to outline what I envisioned the ceremony to be.

"It will be just like Bonnie's and Debbie's processions, no different. Bonnie and Debbie will walk down the aisle with David and Abraham. It would be cute to have their kids walk with them, but we'll have to wait and see what Bonnie and Debbie decide to do. Then we'll have close friends, Grandma—"

Before I could finish, my father jumped in and asked, "Why does it have to be so big? It sounds like a typical procession. I don't think people will respond well to that. And what will people call them, 'bridesmaids'?"

Bridesmaids again. "We'll find something else to call them. But we really haven't made any final decisions about the order of events . . ."

DOUG "We're working on it with Rabbi Bolton. We know she's going to sing in Hebrew . . ."

ANDREW "And we've asked Diane, Maxine, and Doug's friends Debbie and Anita to hold the *chuppah*. We're going to have friends come up to read the seven blessings."

SHELDON "How is that going to work?"

ANDREW "We haven't figured out the details, exactly. But we're going to choose close friends who won't be under the *chuppah* to come up from the audience and read the blessings. Rabbi Bolton will probably sing them in Hebrew first."

DOUG *This is progress,* I thought. *And whatever Roslyn's concerns are, I haven't heard anything insurmountable yet . . .*

ROSLYN "How will the ceremony end?"

ANDREW   Doug and I looked at each other for a second, both wondering what she meant exactly. I took a stab: "We'll step on the glass."

SHELDON   This much we anticipated. It's the way every Jewish wedding ends. Some say crushing the glass symbolizes the destruction of the Temple in Jerusalem. Comedians will tell you that when the groom breaks the glass, it's to symbolize that's the last time he's going to put his foot down.

ROSLYN   I hoped that breaking the glass was the last tradition they planned on incorporating.

"And then what?" I prodded.

DOUG   I wasn't sure where this was going, so I offered: "We'll walk back down the aisle."

ROSLYN   "Go back a second. After you step on the glass, were you planning on what you would do? At the point where the rabbi usually says you may kiss the bride?"

ANDREW   Doug's eyes locked on mine. I asked my mother, "What do you mean?"

ROSLYN   "Your father and I were wondering if you were planning on kissing. Because we'd rather you didn't. Believe me, I was surprised when I realized it, but the fact is that when I mulled it over, I came to the conclusion that I'm not comfortable with it."

DOUG   *Stunned* doesn't begin to describe my reaction. *What would you like us to do?* I almost asked. *Have a hearty handshake? Or a high-five perhaps?* I looked to Andrew, hoping he'd know how to handle this, but he looked dumbfounded. Someone had to say something, so without thinking first, I spoke slowly and decisively. "We really are anxious to talk about all of your concerns. But there's nothing to say on this one issue. It's our *wedding*. Of course we're going to kiss."

SHELDON *If we're each going to close discussion on a topic we don't like, what's the point of talking?*

ROSLYN "Does it have to be a long kiss? Can it be . . . brief?"

ANDREW Give me a break! This is the mother who taught sex education in high school, the one with all kinds of sex manuals scattered around the house, the one who I was able to approach in my teen years about sensitive sexual topics, and she was caught up with how long the kiss would be? Or maybe she was just wondering if we were going to use tongues! This line of questioning had gone as far as it could go. "We'll just have to see how we feel at that moment. But don't worry, it's not going to be some big sloppy thing."

ROSLYN Even if the boys didn't respond well to my question about the kiss, at least they knew I was conflicted.

SHELDON I aired my concerns about speeches turning toward the political.

"I don't want this to become a platform."

And I mentioned our concerns about behavior that might come as a shock to the older crowd.

Doug offered something far short of an assurance. "You've met most of our friends, you know what kind of people they are. We can't tell them what to say, what not to say. You'll have to trust them."

OK, that's a logical answer, but it's not too comforting.

DOUG I recall answering Sheldon this way: "Do you trust Andrew and me to behave in a way that will be respectful of your concerns at our wedding?" Sheldon nodded yes, and I went on:

"You know most of our friends. Do you believe that you can trust them as well?" When he said, "Yes . . ." and shrugged, it practically screamed, *"But can I have it in writing?"*

What kind of behavior, I wondered, *did Sheldon, Roslyn, or their friends imagine they might witness at our wedding?* I shuddered to imagine. *Surely,* I thought, *Sheldon and Roslyn know us better than to suppose some steamy porno flick would be reenacted at our nuptials?*

As to Sheldon's "political" concern, I took "politics" to mean "approval"; in other words, a "political speech" was, I imagined, one in which a friend might imply—or state outright—that gay marriage was a fine thing. Andrew didn't have an answer to Sheldon on the "political" point, so my response stood as the last word, for the moment.

SHELDON   In the end, we talked a lot, but most of our questions went unanswered, because they themselves hadn't figured out a lot of the details.

ANDREW   Although a lot of specifics needed to be ironed out, I was relieved by the fact that my father was no longer floundering alone, feeling abandoned and misunderstood. My parents were finally allies and not opponents. This was a significant step for me in relieving some of the guilt I had been feeling about the mounting tension in their relationship.

ROSLYN   Even if that first group session didn't resolve much, the fact that Sheldon and I were finally able to work together made it OK to talk about the ceremony in public again. At the big Passover seder held that year at the Montefiore Club, I felt free enough to make an official announcement of what everyone at the table surely knew already. "We're celebrating the commitment of Andrew and Doug, and we're expecting you'll all join us." Sheldon may have wanted to crawl under the table, yet he sat up straight, and together we projected a new kind of unified front: one of support. Despite my misgivings—or maybe because I could finally admit them—I was able to join with Sheldon and speak the truth plainly for the whole family. I felt a fresh determination to find common ground where we could stand together as a family, and I had resolved that this ceremony, in whatever form it took, wasn't going to be a secret—it was going to be a celebration.

Most everyone gathered around the table offered a *"mazel tov"* or a smile. Even if no toasts were made, it was a positive response.

DOUG   I was working in Chicago the week after our first group meeting, so when I parted from Andrew I had time to think things over by myself on the plane. Sheldon's continuing worry about politics nagged at me. I wondered, *If his friends heard someone stand up and say, "The marriage of two people who wish to be publicly bonded is good for society," what would happen? Does Sheldon imagine he'll be viewed as a conspirator in some great gay underground cabal? "And so what if he is?"* I answered, in my fantasy dialogue.

Though Sheldon had never said the words "homosexuality is wrong," it dawned on me that perhaps he harbored that belief, yet held it in reserve, so as not to injure Andrew. And while I didn't see it then, I had, in effect, morphed Sheldon into a walking metaphor in that moment.

He became homophobe-*lite*.

Sheldon is anything but a homophobe. And yet I had—on a subconscious level—begun to see his inner conflict as symbolic of society's struggle to fit the once comfortably invisible homosexual into the world order. *What would it take to make him see us as a couple, two people in love?* From this point on, I had a hard time seeing Sheldon's struggle for what it was: one good man's effort to balance his love for his son with the pressures that engulfed him. Instead, it came to represent something bigger and far too unwieldy for one man to bear.

As I tried to piece together evidence to make sense of the riddle Sheldon had become for me, I recalled a night three years earlier when Roslyn, Sheldon, Andrew, and I had been out to see a play in New York. It was the story of a pregnant woman who learned, with the help of *Brave New World* technology, that her fetus would grow up to be gay. To abort or not to abort, that was the question. After the play, *Twilight of the Golds*, Sheldon asked Andrew and me, over coffee, *if we were given the choice, would we rather be heterosexual?*

I answered him quickly, to erase any impression that I had a shred of doubt. "No, I wouldn't change."

"Even with all the difficulties? It's harder living in this world and being gay, isn't it? Wouldn't it be easier if you were heterosexual?" Sheldon asked sensibly.

"Easier, maybe. Better, no," was the best I could do in the pressure of the moment. But sitting alone on the plane, contemplating the conversation, I added a coda to my response that I hoped might sway Sheldon. *Yes, I might have been spared tremendous pain and cruelty at the hands of fools and bullies. But the precious lessons I've learned have forged a far better person. Now I understand the pain of others. I chafe at injustice, because I know what it is to be judged unfairly. You know the saying "What doesn't kill me makes me stronger"? Well, without my struggle I'd be a far weaker, lesser man.*

Even if I could manage to spit all that out, would he hear me? Could I ever speak such abstract stuff to Sheldon, who is so well grounded in reality? No. But I saw the wedding as the simple truth that would speak to him of the proper place Andrew and I deserved at life's table.

ANDREW It was a month before our next session with Dennis, and in the interim we talked again with Rabbi Bolton. We came up with an idea that would help the entire gathering of friends, family, Jews and non-Jews, gay and straight, follow the ceremony. And we narrowed down a prospective list for the walk down the aisle. Diane, Maxine, Debbie, and Anita would walk down the aisle first, step up to the top of the stairs, and raise the *chuppah*. Louie would walk next down the aisle. He would be followed by my grandmother and my uncle Ivan, then our siblings and their spouses. We wanted their children to follow, but we weren't sure how everybody would react to that idea. Then, if Doug's parents made it as planned, they would be next. My parents would be the last ones down the aisle before Doug and I walked together to our place under the *chuppah*. Other traditions were incorporated and transformed. And a significant one got dropped altogether . . .

DOUG Roslyn's question about same-sex dancing made me consider one tradition Andrew and I had never discussed. The first and only time I'd ever ask him, we were back in New York.

"What about a first dance?"

"No. I wouldn't be comfortable with that," was Andrew's lightning quick answer. "Would you?"

"I guess not." I wasn't fully comfortable with the mental image either, but I ached to live in a perfect world. Hearing Andrew admit the truth rubbed my nose in reality. The issue was dead.

The thorniest matters had been addressed, and we were ready for Sheldon and Roslyn.

ANDREW Dennis suggested that my father and I come an hour early before the next group session. This would be followed by another two-hour session with my mother and Doug, making it a three-hour marathon for me and my father. I had noted his connection with Dennis in the last session. Perhaps that's what helped him open up. In that last meeting, my father seemed in touch with his own feelings, and I'd never seen that before. It was clear that he was making a serious attempt to work this through. Therapy with Dennis was obviously helping him both to express himself and to resolve the problems he was having with the wedding.

I hoped a meeting alone with him and Dennis would help us discuss the problems I was having with his reaction. My father was forever complaining that we weren't listening or taking his feelings into account. But I saw it as a difference of opinion. I was, in fact, trying to make compromises. I felt, however, that *compromise* meant something very specific to my father. The compromise I believed he sought was an entirely different kind of affair than we had planned, a very small ceremony, out of the public eye.

For years I had felt my father was disappointed that I wasn't interested in sports, in being a lawyer. And that I was gay. All these things I thought he saw as shortcomings. Now I wanted to broach a deeper topic: the suspicion that my father's anxiety about the wedding video and photographer were masks for his own anger and disappointment that I was gay.

Going into the room, just the three of us, was strange. I knew we needed to deal with the suspicions I was harboring, and because of the honesty my father had shown in the last group session, I trusted that he'd be honest with me here. But I was still scared. It reminded me of a time six years prior when my father took me for lunch at a neighborhood deli, where the agenda was to open up the lines of communication between us about my being gay. My father meant well and it felt good to know that he was making a serious effort at improving our relationship. Nevertheless, I remember feeling extremely uneasy and guarded during the meal, since we weren't used to communicating in such a vulnerable way, essentially one on one. This same feeling came over me again in the session with Dennis, although this time I had years of individual therapy behind me and was ready, willing, and anxious to hash out all my feelings and possible misperceptions.

SHELDON   The conversation generally revolved around the fact that the only topic of conversation between Andrew and me seemed to be money. I recall saying that although I recognized my obligations as a parent and intended to fulfill them, and in particular to provide Andrew with the best education available, it was somewhat frustrating to have the feeling (true or imagined) that for a person who necessarily was relying on others for financial assistance, he could better manage his limited resources.

There was also the thought that I should spend some social time alone with Andrew, lunch for example, and without Roslyn—because with Roslyn the time would be mostly spent with the two of them talking shop, and me as the third-party outsider.

ANDREW   Similar to the way I felt my father was focusing on trivial wedding details (such as the presence of a videographer) in order to avoid dealing with more deep-seated feelings of embarrassment and disappointment over my sexuality, I began to feel his constant critiquing of the way I handled my finances was another way for him to displace anger about this same issue.

So I jumped right in covering many of the other matters that I felt placed strain on our relationship. His response was genuine and direct.

"It's not true. When you weren't into sports, I wasn't disappointed. When I found out you were gay, I needed time to adjust, but I've accepted it completely, without question."

This was a pivotal moment in my relationship with my father. For me, the weight of guilt that I was carrying around had lifted. I knew Dennis had helped my parents find common ground together. Now it seemed there might be room there for me as well.

DOUG   Only later would Andrew explain to me the significance of his session with Sheldon. When Roslyn and I joined them for the bigger family session, Andrew and I offered a compromise that was intended to put guests at ease—and by extension, my parents, too.

"We're going to write up a program," I told them. "When everyone walks in, they'll find one on their seat. It'll give everything a 'label' so there won't be any confusion. We'll call the walk down the aisle simply 'procession of family and friends.' Hopefully that'll clear up the 'bridesmaid' issue. The program will explain the religious rituals to the non-Jews. And where we deviate from tradition, it'll explain the new aspects of the ceremony to the older crowd."

ROSLYN   *This ought to help*, I thought. I glanced at Sheldon for a response.

SHELDON   "How many people are going to be under the *chuppah*?"

ANDREW   Both of you. Doug's parents, if they make it. If they're not there, his sister Lynn and niece Michelle. The rabbi. Lorne and George. The *chuppah* holders—Diane, Maxine, Debbie, and Anita. And us—me and Doug.

SHELDON   "And all those people will be walking down the aisle? Anybody else?"

ANDREW   I went through the list, name by name, as Doug and I had set it out.

ROSLYN   It sounded fine to me. Until he got to the end. I didn't get the picture when he looked at me and said, "Then you and Daddy." But when he said, "And I'll walk down with Doug," I saw what was going on, and how sad he was about it.

He didn't think either his father or I could stand by his side through this. In public.

Sheldon and I had already discussed it privately. Days before, I'd asked my husband, "Do you see us walking Andrew down the aisle? "And he said without any hesitation, "Definitely."

Now I was devastated. I felt so terrible for Andrew. It was agonizingly clear: he didn't feel either our approval or our support.

"Andrew . . ." My tone pleaded for him to turn toward me. Once he did, I continued, "We would like to walk you down the aisle. The two of us have talked about it." The room was utterly silent. It was apparent that I had to say it again, for him to grasp how firm both Sheldon and I were in our resolve, our support, and our love. "Daddy and I want to walk down with you, together."

Andrew's eyes were moist and wide. Otherwise his face was a blank slate. He looked to his father, and then to me.

Finally he asked—betraying a trace of surprise—"You do?"

PART THREE

The Wedding

Marriage has long been recognized as one of the vital personal rights essential to the orderly pursuit of happiness by free men.

—*Loving v. Virginia,* 1967

CHAPTER 9

The Invitations Are Out.
And So Are We.

SHELDON, ROSLYN, ANDREW, AND DOUG

May 1996–July 1996

SHELDON Besides all the work we were doing to communicate with each other, there was something else that helped ease us into the upcoming event. Because there were so many people expected from out of town, the invitations were sent out a little earlier than normal. With a ceremony scheduled for September 1, you might typically mail them in July, but we did it in early June.

At that particular moment, when the envelopes went in the mailbox, I said, *That's it. It's too late now. They're gone, for better or worse.* The instant those invitations were dropped off, it was right on the table. Everybody *knew.*

And the fact that there was such a lengthy period of time between the invitations being sent and the event itself was good not only for me, but for the guests themselves. They could talk to each other. They could condition themselves as I had had to condition myself. They could see it on paper, in black and white.

ROSLYN   It's like we were coming out of the closet. We were saying to everyone, *"This is what the reality is in our family. And we don't have to hide it anymore."*

Hiding takes a lot of energy. It takes energy away from relationships. And it's stifling.

SHELDON   That's all true, but you could come out by putting an ad in the paper, too. And I didn't want this event to be equated with something like that.

ROSLYN   We had handled the invitations with great care, with an eye toward keeping everybody at ease. We were in our third meeting with Dennis, in May, when we worked out the wording. There was one crucial point we had to resolve.

ANDREW   What's in a name? Plenty.

One month my mother was calling it a "wedding," the next month, a "commitment ceremony." She had been a yo-yo when it came to giving this event a title.

ROSLYN   But so was everybody else. There's no language for this yet. Other people would twist into linguistic pretzels trying to ask us a simple question. "How's the . . . *plans* going?" "What's going on with your . . . *thing?*" So what were we supposed to call this?

SHELDON   Since my professional background is in law, I think about marriage in legal terms. I understand that it'll make Andrew and Doug feel better when they walk down the aisle, but I asked myself, and I asked Andrew and Doug as well, *will they be any different after they walk down that aisle?*

From a legal point of view, the answer is no. So until gay marriage is legally recognized, which I honestly imagine will be a long time from today, I wish a new terminology could be created.

ROSLYN Meanwhile we were aware that Andrew and Doug were calling it a wedding. *So what were the invitations going to say?*

With Dennis moderating, I asked how the boys planned on handling the wording. It wasn't a surprise when Andrew recited, "Sheldon and Rosyln Merling invite you to attend the wedding of their son Andrew Neil to Douglas Alan, son of Fred and Estelle Wythe."

I was prepared with an answer. "Daddy and I have discussed it, and our friends and family wouldn't be comfortable with the word *wedding.* We'd like it to say *commitment ceremony.*"

Doug responded, "But if it's our ceremony, and we're calling it a wedding, and it's got every element of a wedding, wouldn't *commitment ceremony* be false advertising?"

"I'm just telling you what we're comfortable with," I answered. Is there a way we can compromise?"

ANDREW "Can we do two sets of invitations?"

ROSLYN "I don't see why not. Who would get the ones that said *wedding?*"

DOUG "Well, correct me if I'm wrong, but the friends and family you're concerned about are the older generation, aren't they? Over forty, or maybe fifty? Andrew's cousins aren't the ones you're worried about. Or our friends. So why don't we make age the determining factor?"

ROSLYN And that's how we did it, more or less. Everybody from the younger crowd, including all of Andrew and Doug's friends, got an invitation that said "wedding," and our set got the "commitment ceremony" invitations.

SHELDON   Speaking of the older set, the patriarch of the family, my Uncle Rudolph, is ninety-two years old. He was eighty-eight at the time of the ceremony. He's the only one left from my father's family; there were nine children. He was one of the younger ones, so you can imagine the generation he grew up in. We felt we'd better go and speak to him before the invitations went out. He took the news with surprising good humor. He said, "Listen, we're very proud of you to stand behind your children. What do you think, just because I'm eighty-eight, I don't know what's going on? I watch television. I see all about this."

Still, I knew he was the most religious of our family, so I gave him an out: "Listen, I'll understand perfectly well if you're not comfortable coming. I'll love you just as much. Please don't get nervous about not being there. Do whatever you feel."

He didn't answer whether he was coming or not, but said, "You're great parents." For the time being, that was it.

This was an even bigger expression of support from him than it might sound like. He's a very shy guy who hardly expresses himself. So it meant a lot.

ANDREW   We were with Dennis when my father conveyed my Uncle Rudolph's wish, "Whatever makes him happy . . . as long as he's happy." I was pleasantly surprised. He's very old-world. Uncle Rudolph is the brother of my late grandfather. My grandfather was known by all us kids as "Zadie," which is Yiddish for "Grandpa," and my grandmother as "Bubby," Yiddish for "Grandma." Zadie died in 1992. When he was alive, it was assumed we wouldn't tell him, or Bubby, that I was gay, presumably because they wouldn't even understand the concept. Or if they did, we figured they would be intolerant of the notion. They both carried other prejudices that they were very open about, so you might expect an antigay remark from them, though I'd never actually heard one, other than the occasional "fairy" or *"faigeleh"* being tossed out in casual conversation.

I had always wondered what his reaction might be if we had told him I was gay. So when my uncle Rudolph responded so warmly, it made me wonder if Zadie would have done the same. And now I weighed whether we should tell Bubby. She was the only family member we hadn't informed about the wedding. She's eighty-nine now, and she's—as I call it at work—"pleasantly demented." In fact, she's the happiest I've ever seen her. She's still as critical as when I was a kid, but now in a less mean-spirited kind of way.

There were moments when I thought she might already know. A couple of years before the wedding, before she became confused and disoriented, and prior to living in a nursing home, she was sitting in my parents' backyard with my other grandmother. My mother's mother already knew my story. I was on the way to giving each of them a hug. Then as she saw Doug step out onto the patio following me, Bubby called out real loud to Grandma, "Oh, here comes the boyfriend!"

Did she say "boy friend" or "boyfriend?" we all wondered. Everybody giggled, but nobody came out and asked what she meant.

ROSLYN I always thought it was Andrew who didn't want his Bubby to know he was gay. Anyway, I'm sure none of us wanted to be the one to tell her. And now that she's got a tenuous grip on reality, it doesn't make much sense to do it any longer. As for my mother, I had told her back in 1992. You'd think my work with parents of gays would help me at times like this, but sometimes it worked the other way around. After you've heard a couple dozen parents say, "I'm afraid to tell Grandma—what if she has a heart attack from the shock?" you almost believe the news could kill. I didn't have any nitro tablets, or even smelling salts, handy. But I did have a great big lump in my throat. Once I said it, she answered right away, "I thought something was different, because he always comes to Montreal with Doug. I'm still shocked, though. I can't believe it. I can't believe Andrew's like that."

"You understand he has an attaction to a man?"

"Yes, I know, I watch television. I know they like the same sex."

"That's right."

"I like Doug, but . . . well, I'm shocked." That was all she said.

About a week later we came back to the topic. My mother said, "I've been very sad, because every time I think about Andrew not marrying a girl . . . oh, I even cry."

"If you feel sad, imagine how I must feel."

"I know it must be awful for you," she said.

"Not awful. Difficult. We're used to the idea. You'll get used to it, too. With time."

A year later, I was doing another workshop at Yachdav with Mark, when he suggested, "You should bring your mother." The group is open to parents and extended families as well, so I figured, why not? I explained what the group was about, and she agreed to come.

We had sixty people that night, so we broke up into smaller subgroups. I put her in a group with another grandmother. After an hour or so all sixty came together again to discuss what happened. One of the lesbians from my mother's group came over and said, "Your mother is the cutest, she is too much. I just love her."

Oh, boy. "What happened?"

As she told it, the other grandmother was very upset about her grandson's sexuality, but had never expressed it to her daughter, or anyone in the family, grandson included. Tonight she took this opportunity to say out loud just how hard it was for her, after keeping it inside for so long. And my mother countered, "You know, my daughter did the best thing. She gave me books to read. I read them all, because at first I didn't understand. But then I did. And I think you should do that too. Because that's really the best way to learn about homos."

Homos. Exactly which book did she read that one in?

Anyway, it turns out she was a great help with the other grandmother.

When I told her in March that Andrew was getting married, she said, "Oh my God, what do you mean?"

"They're really going to have a wedding."

"Oh . . . I'm so happy for Andrew. And I like Doug so much . . . but it makes me want to cry." And she did. "I always dreamed he'd marry a beautiful girl."

"He's marrying a beautiful boy," I told her.

"I know," she said, while I supplied her the next tissue.

I tried to warm her up. "It's going to be a beautiful wedding, just like the girls'."

This elicited a curious response. "Do you think I have to wear one of my long dresses?"

She had two long dresses, from my two daughters' weddings. "Of course you do."

And she tossed back, "My short black cocktail dress is good enough for this one."

Hurt, I shot out, "No, it isn't. Why is it good enough for this one? It's going to be the same type of wedding. It's formal. The men are wearing tuxedos."

Her previous reactions were more expected. Now she was as much as saying, *This isn't as important, it's not a real wedding.* So I followed coolly with, "It's your decision." After some thought, I realized that I'd broadsided her with this news. The rest of us had had time to adjust. And we were still adjusting, really. She'd never had any chance to take it in. So I added, "It's OK, wear whatever you're comfortable with, but I want you to know, I'm wearing a long dress."

Over the summer I tried to keep her more up-to-date about the wedding plans. Six weeks before the wedding, in July, I'd told her it would be held at Eaton's.

"Oh, I remember I used to go there as a little girl . . ." She drifted away in reverie. Then she switched gears at breakneck speed.

"Do you think I could fit into the dress I wore to Debbie's wedding?"

What brought this on? I wondered.

"If I can't zip it up," she thought out loud, "I'll have to work and exercise until I can get all the way in." We dug out the dress, and sure enough, it was too tight. So she started an exercise regimen as promised, walking furiously every morning. My mother marched up and down the hallway of her apartment building, working up a sweat, until finally, after five weeks, she fit.

She could have showed up in a ratty sweatsuit at that point, as far as I was concerned. My mother's effort was all the reminder I needed about the immensity of her heart.

(OK, so sue me for dramatic license: we did let the dress out a *tiny* bit.)

SHELDON By the time the invitations were going out, most of the community knew the event was imminent. However, the rabbi of our own Orthodox synagogue hadn't been told, and I wanted him to find out from me, not another member. He is a serious-looking man for his thirty-seven years. And don't forget he leads an Orthodox congregation. So when I set up the appointment I didn't expect him to lead any cheers over my announcement.

I had a second reason for wanting to meet with him. On one hand, he's a rabbi, with the obvious background in religious teaching. And I know the basic premise of that. He also has a doctorate in psychology from Tulane University. What I wanted to learn was how he reconciled the religious reservations about homosexuality with modern psychological thinking. I figured maybe he could help me acquire a new understanding.

After services, I went up to his office. Without trying to lecture him, I started things off with, "I'd like you to allow me to speak for ten or fifteen minutes about my family. In preface, I'm not here to be confrontational. Also, I'm not a baby. If you want to be harsh, I can take it like a man. Of course, I don't have to agree. So please speak freely." This rabbi had never officiated in our family affairs, because he'd just come to the synagogue a couple of years before. So I spent a minute giving him some background on our family. Then I explained our current situation at length. After he knew all the details, I said, "I don't want to know if it's the right thing or the wrong thing. We're doing it. I've come here with the hope that your reaction will be helpful to me. So go ahead, and don't treat me like I'm tender."

Surprisingly, his first words were comforting. "I'm honored you would share these thoughts with me." Then he cut right to the ending: "Not only did you make the right decision, you made the only decision. This theory we used to have in European communities that the only way you could get a child to fall in line was to threaten, with the ultimate threat being 'sitting shiva,' doesn't work in modern-day society, to the extent that it ever worked. Now you must keep the communication open."

He didn't, however, attempt to reconcile the differences between religious and psychological thought. The closest he came was when he observed, "Wearing my psychologist's hat, I recognize the importance of family relationships. But with my rabbi's hat on, I must acknowledge that we must continue the cycle if we are to carry on the faith." I had prepared myself for a lecture, invited it even. And though I didn't get an answer to my question, the rabbi had been very sympathetic.

ROSLYN Everyone in New York and California must have received the invitations by the last week of June. They arrived even sooner in Montreal, probably by the end of the third week. We had included response cards with the mailing; guests could send back a note on the card with a personal greeting. The responses were just as positive. I can't recall one that didn't have something warm and congratulatory to say.

SHELDON Of course, I wouldn't expect anybody to be so impolite as to formally reply in a negative way. The surprise, if you want to call it that, was that when I asked my closest confidants if they'd heard any unfavorable comment behind our backs, they all said, "Truthfully, no." These same friends had been very forthright about their reservations all along, so I knew they were being up front now.

ROSLYN   The response to the invitations was terrific, but we were still hearing the occasional comment from acquaintances, like "Why does it have to be so big?" Soon after the invitations were in the mail, I asked Sheldon, "What do you say to friends when they bring it up now? Because if you're still saying, 'I'm uncomfortable,' it reinforces their negativity." I was only too aware that some of the negative reactions we'd heard for months had been fueled by Sheldon's own ambivalence.

About a month before the ceremony, we were on our way to dinner when I asked Sheldon again if any of his friends had mentioned the wedding recently. He said that as a matter of fact, two of the guys had commented to him, and not for the first time, "Why did it have to be pushed in people's faces?" and "Why couldn't it have been in New York?"

I asked how he had responded. He said he replied forcefully, "Listen, Andrew is *my* son and I will do whatever I think is right for him. I love him and I'm not ashamed."

I breathed a sigh of relief. At last the truth was spoken.

DOUG   I felt there was a basic irony underlying the settlement reached on the invitations, and in fact, the entire wedding. Much of the apprehension from Sheldon and the wider Jewish community was about the fact that the wedding was so *large*. Sheldon himself had asked at one point much earlier, "Why can't this be held in a rabbi's study, like a second marriage?" Forget for a moment that most of the weddings in their circle are bigger than ours; size, it turned out, really did matter.

The strange thing was, neither Andrew or I was married to the idea, pardon the expression, that we should host a party for 175 people. The list we'd prepared of our friends and close family came to 130. It was Sheldon and Roslyn's list of *their* friends that pushed the number up by sixty more. Andrew and I were happy to have his parents' friends. There were two good reasons, however, for not issuing invitations to their list: First, Sheldon wanted a smaller affair. Second, the all-important concern over the comfort of his friends. I was aware of how many (if not which exact people) had expressed either disapproval or dismay over our plans. Of course, Andrew was happy to have his parents' friends at our wedding. He'd grown up with their children, and knew each of them all his life. But I asked Sheldon several times, if he wanted to keep the list smaller, why we couldn't kill two birds, and shorten the list by cutting the very people whose displeasure he worried about?

ANDREW I tried to explain wedding etiquette to Doug, but he didn't get the concept. He kept trying to apply logic, but anyone who's had a couple of family weddings under their belt knows logic has nothing to do with it. My parents had been invited to the weddings of all of their friends' children. How could they not reciprocate, even if our nuptials were as welcome in Montreal as the mumps?

SHELDON Despite all the criticism we'd received along the way, Roslyn and I found that almost every single friend from our invitation list had confirmed their attendance, and would be sitting in the hall for the commitment ceremony.

A few weeks before the event, I referred to it as a "celebration." Did I really see it as a celebration? I was asked. And what was I celebrating? After some thought, I replied, "I'm thrilled that Andrew has a companion, a partner. And I'm thrilled with his choice of partner. Mostly, though, I'm celebrating the fact that any shackles that I felt were binding me from being open about my son are being pried loose, even though it wasn't my doing. I won't have to explain that I have a gay son anymore. I won't have to decide how, or even if, I should say it. We're out in the open now. And the chains are off."

I thought this was as far out of the closet as we could get. Once again, I was in for a surprise.

CHAPTER 10

Show and Tell

DOUG, ANDREW, SHELDON, AND ROSLYN

July–August 1996

DOUG   A couple of weeks after the invitations went out, I was in Chicago producing a tape for my friend Louie's nonprofit company. Since the whole project was done on donated equipment and time, including my own, Louie found a place for me to stay with an acquaintance of his, an older, respected doctor with an eccentric air. He invited me to dinner with his significant other. He and his nearly silent, much younger partner had, I gathered, a rather open relationship. Or at least the doctor seemed to. His leering, lecherous behavior may have only been an act, but it gave them, as a couple, the air of another world of gay relationships. They seemed a throwback to another time. Maybe this old-fashioned arrangement is the sort that right-wing activists refer to with the term *gay lifestyle*.

Couple number one invited another pair of partners along as well. I was the fifth wheel. Referring to my missing half, I mentioned our impending nuptials. Since most of our friends are heterosexual couples, this was the only time during the year and a half of wedding planning that I heard reaction from a group of gay men. It was an education.

The first question was from the other couple. One was sweet; his slightly older partner was cool and aloof. Mr. Cool said, "So, are you *registering*?" When I said, yes, as a matter of fact, we're going to Bloomingdale's next weekend, he made a pronouncement: "Oh. So that's what it's about."

Well. I barely stopped myself from firing back, "Bitter, aren't we?" His boyfriend broke the awkward pause with a question about the ceremony. Then my host, the doctor, interrupted my answer to announce, "Oh I must come and see it. Are either of you going to wear a gown? No? Tuxedos, how boring! Well somebody must wear a gown. Oh, let me!" Even if it was his third drink doing the talking, the liquor was a loosener, not a hallucinogen. He meant to be catty. Since I knew I'd never see him after this weekend, I played along, in my best approximation of bitchy camp. "Oh, please, you must have some old taffeta number from a debutante ball where you didn't scuff the knees too badly. Pull it out of mothballs. I'm sure it'll do just fine."

Unbowed, he went back to ribbing our plans. He probably meant no insult, but this wasn't a response I ever anticipated. As far as I could tell, those at the table with the loudest voices were behaving as if I'd attacked them. By implying that Andrew and I were playing house, they acted like our decision to marry was devaluing them and their relationships.

Finally I noticed that the cynical reactions were coming from the two oldest people present. Old dogs who, perhaps, saw new tricks as a threat.

ROSLYN   There was a kind of backlash in Montreal's gay community as well. The word was, as I heard it, that if this affair didn't turn out well, or wasn't received well, it would reflect badly on the entire gay community. I already felt like the heterosexual end of a bridge between the gay and the straight Jewish camps. So the expectations placed on this event were added pressure I didn't need and couldn't bear.

ANDREW   In mid-July Doug and I went to Montreal to work out the last details of the big weekend, and we had one last group therapy session with my parents. We hashed out the kind of minutiae that I'm sure every couple faces with their family.

It was during that trip that my sister Debbie stopped by my parents' house, and I reminded her it was less than two months to the wedding. Would she and Abraham be walking down the aisle with my niece Rachel? Debbie looked away, pained, and said, "You'll have to talk to my husband."

SHELDON   I knew Abraham had been troubled because of Rachel. "It would be OK if she'd experienced fifteen, twenty heterosexual ones, maybe," he said once. He meant, I think, that he'd have to tell his daughter she was going to a wedding, and now this was going to be her first impression of what a wedding *is*.

My other son-in-law was more pragmatic about it. "What are you going to do about the commitment ceremony?" David asked me. This was back in the previous fall. "It's a year away," I said. "Plenty of time to worry about it."

"What are you fooling yourself for?" he chided. "I know you. You're going to support your son, if that's what he wants. You're going to suffer through it, it's going to be over, and that's going to be it."

DOUG   Long after the fact, I asked Abraham if he could reflect back on the root of his inner turmoil. He said: "The first thing I thought about when I heard about the wedding: Two human beings, they love each other, but they're males, they can't procreate. The feelings they have for each other, that's great. But two people being together, that means continuity of the people.

"You see, I have the basics of my education, then I have more recent information that's telling me what's going on now. I grew up one way, but I'm getting information that's completely different. It's all contradictory with the rules I grew up with. The world, it changes around you so slowly. You don't feel it happening. It's like the sun sending rays to the earth. You don't feel it, but it's happening.

"It's not enough for me to listen to Bible verse, I need an intellectual answer that speaks to me. I have a mind to think about this. I'm not an extremist. So I spend time working it out."

While I can't say I know Abraham extremely well, I can say I know something of the depth of his search for truth.

ANDREW   Abraham was forthright in his objections. My sisters weren't quite as bold. To some extent, I had to read between the lines of their disapproval. Some of Debbie's best friends are gay. *Really*. She's an interior decorator, so that's part of the explanation. Anyway, she's very comfortable with gay men. That's why her subtle uneasiness and withholding caught me off guard. She never said anything outright unsupportive, though.

About a year before the ceremony, my other sister, Bonnie, told me she was fine with the wedding, as long as my father was comfortable. That, she said, was her major concern. She knew my father would go through with it, but she just wanted to make sure he was as comfortable as possible. She wasn't as concerned about my mother, because at the time she was under the same impression I was—that my mother had no qualms about the wedding.

A couple of months later, Bonnie made another statement, and this one had long-lasting repercussions. It was about nine months before the wedding, during the time when it seemed possible there might not be any ceremony after all. Bonnie asked my mother, "Why is Andrew doing this to Daddy?" Either my mother forgot the context of Bonnie's comment or I didn't hear it, because Bonnie now says she was referring not to the wedding, but to the therapy we were going through.

DOUG I think I was the one who reacted most strongly to Bonnie's reported comment. Of course, I didn't know that I was hearing her taken out of context. But it disturbed me that an expression of love between two people could be judged an act of aggression against a third party. Over the years, Bonnie had shown me nothing but kindness. Now I yearned to tell her how I felt she'd contorted our intent and confused the issue. Worst of all, I feared such a third-party accusation could set a tone: *This wasn't our wedding. This was Sheldon's cross to bear.*

ANDREW Obviously both of my sisters faced an unenviable challenge. They were both confronted with my decision, and had to deal with it, plain and simple. It wasn't as if they had an outlet, like my parents, who at least were engaged with Doug and me in a dialogue, contentious as it may have been at times. Bonnie and Debbie were merely bystanders. And any feelings they might have had—positive or negative—were obviously complicated by our sibling relationships.

DOUG After I got back from Chicago, Andrew and I headed over to Bloomingdale's. We knew we wouldn't be the first same-sex couple to cross their threshold. It was a busy day in the registry when we stepped into the appointment line. When our turn came, we sat down with a fortyish matron with a big, if slightly frozen, smile. She looked at me. Then her head pivoted to Andrew. Soon it swung back hesitantly to me, like a rusty lawn sprinkler. She started to check a box on our application when the death grip she had on the pencil snapped the lead, and the pencil flew from her hand. I looked over to Andrew, and we both straightened our smiles while she fumbled for it on the floor. Once she recovered from the initial shock, she was nice as pie. And she only dropped one more pencil.

To be fair, once we got past the flying-pencil welcome, everyone we met was totally unfazed and very helpful. Andrew and I spent the afternoon arguing over flatware and dishes alongside straight couples without raising anybody's eyebrows.

The next morning we were one foot out the door when the phone rang.

"Good morning. This is Bloomingdale's Registry," a nice lady announced brightly. Then she added, gingerly, "Could I *double-check* some information?"

"Sure." What was there to double-check? We hadn't chosen any items yet. All we'd done was put our names in the computer.

"The groom is listed as Andrew Merling. M-e-r-l-i-n-g?"

"That's right."

"And the, um, other name . . . Let's see if I spelled all this right: W-y-t-h-e? And the first name, is that, um . . . D-o-u-g?"

"Yes. You've got it."

The tiniest pause, and then she chirped, "OK, great! Thanks a lot! Sorry to bother you!"

"No problem! Thanks!" I chirped back. Andrew stood by the door waiting for me. We were on our way to register at ABC Carpet and Home, a store full of unique household items. While we walked to the elevator, I wondered out loud if ABC would have a more nineties setup than Bloomie's. Sure, it was kind of cute to flip a coin and see which one of us would go into the computer as a bride. It was also annoying, as if they felt we were playing dress-up in Mommy and Daddy's clothes. ABC was near Union Square, so maybe their attitude would be more downtown too. Then Andrew asked what was going on with the phone call. I laughed out loud, because it finally hit me what the conversation was really about.

"Oh my God, they weren't just checking the spelling of our names! She had me spell my *first* name. How else did they think I could spell D-o-u-g? D-a-r-l-e-n-e maybe?" Somebody must have taken a look at our printout that morning, seen D-o-u-g under "bride," and figured it had to be one heckuva typo.

I know the staff at Bloomie's didn't mean that as a put-down, it was just a little confusing for them.

Then, on Monday, I was walking down the street from the gym to get a cup of coffee when I ran into Wendy Roth, one of the senior producers of *Turning Point.* The show had been on the air only sporadically since it had been taken off the network schedule a year before. Now, in September, it was being resurrected with a weekly time slot, even if it was in the suicide position opposite *ER.* Though I'd never been told an exact start date, I knew it would be on by mid-September. This was the first time I'd seen Wendy since they'd called me in May to see if I was available. After hug, kiss, and howyadoin', I asked if she knew when I should start work. When she suggested the second week of August, I told her I'd need to be away for the first week of September.

"What's going on?"

"I'm getting married."

"Oh, really?" Smiling, she lowered her sunglasses and deadpanned, "We'll talk." Later that day I got a call. Sure enough, *Turning Point* had a show in the works on gay marriage. They were looking for couples with ceremonies sometime between now (early July) and October. I told her it had been so stressful just getting to this point, I couldn't imagine adding any more pressure to our wedding. But I said I'd talk to Andrew. As expected . . .

ANDREW   I said, "What, are you crazy?" First of all, there was the added pressure. Second, I had no idea what they wanted to do. Neither did Doug. And as far as I was concerned, I wanted to leave it that way. A few days later, Doug got another call, this time from the woman who'd be producing the program. Her name was Denise Schreiner, and according to Doug, she was a great producer. After talking to her on the phone, he thought it might be worth our time to just sit down and meet with her.

DOUG   Again he said forget it. And that was that.

The next morning, as Andrew got out of bed, he said, "If you want to talk to her, fine. We can sit down and talk."

When Andrew decided to sit down with Denise, he didn't just

open Pandora's box, he jumped in. Denise is many things, among them canny, whip-smart, compassionate, and intuitive. Above all, she is persistent. Not that she needed to convince Andrew and me, because once we'd all sat down together in her office along with associate producer Rebecca Wharton, Andrew and I were enthusiastic about her approach to the subject. Nevertheless, Andrew warned her, "Good luck with my father. We'd do the show, but if you need to talk to my parents, I can't believe they'd do it."

ROSLYN   The first time Denise called, I said I didn't want to do it, and I was sure Sheldon didn't want to either. I also felt it would be an intrusion, and God knows we didn't need any more stress.

I was curious, though, as to what her approach would be. I asked her what she planned to focus on, and when she explained that it was her intention to leave out the politics and zero in on the intended couples and their families, I was impressed. So often people forget that gays and lesbians are born into heterosexual families. Knowing what our family had been through to date, I was happy to hear that the viewers would get an insight into the emotional turmoil that is created when one has a gay child, much less a gay child who wants to get publicly married. As our conversation progressed, I found myself responding easily to Denise's engaging and sensitive manner.

After her second call, I felt I had a relationship with her. Of course, that's part of her job, bonding with people on a deadline. Even knowing that, I responded to her warmth. On this call she invited us to New York, to stay in a hotel, where we'd do the interview. She asked me to speak to Sheldon again. He'd already said it was out of the question after Denise's first call, and he's a consistent man. Once again, "Forget it." By the third call, Denise was wearing me down. "I have another idea. How would it be if we came to Montreal with our crew, and did the taping there?" I said, "Maybe if we have some reassurances . . ." She offered the chance to immediately retract anything in the interview we didn't like the sound of. This escape hatch was appealing, so I considered her offer. But Sheldon remained firmly opposed.

SHELDON I thought I'd heard the last of it until Andrew called. "Denise wants to fly up to Montreal and take the two of you out to dinner."

"If we go, it's a tacit acknowledgment," I said, "that I'm interested in doing it. And I'm not."

"What are you worried about?" Andrew said. "You get a free meal out of it!" We both laughed, and I said OK. "Just be sure to say she shouldn't interpret this as evidence that I'm giving it serious thought." *At least it should be an interesting meal,* I figured.

When Denise and her associate producer, Rebecca Wharton, flew into town, we suggested a warm, intimate French restaurant, Le Mas Des Oliviers. What impressed me about Denise, aside from the fact that she was obviously no fool, was her approach to the program she was producing. I'm always offended by the kooks they show on television in gay pride parades. She wanted to portray the norm—illustrating to the rest of the world that plenty of gays and lesbians come from normal, well-adjusted, middle class families. People could watch the show and see that this isn't an aberration, that you don't have to be crazy to face a situation like this.

So I liked everything she had to say, but I still felt I couldn't be a part of it. After all, I'd look like a hypocrite. First I'm so distressed by having a large public affair. Then I'm willing to go on national television? People would say, "This guy's an act!" Denise was clever, though. She never asked during the course of the evening if I would participate in the show. After dinner I gave her a tour, and tried to give her and Rebecca a feeling for our city, its character and its contrasts. We drove for miles, taking in the views. As we got out of the car, she asked me to give it more thought. When she got back to New York, she started calling me directly. And sure enough, she started to wear me down, too. She had one stipulation, though, that I couldn't reconcile. *She wanted to interview us before the affair.*

"The purpose," she explained, "is to see you with all the anxieties, and let you express them. If I show that, people will see how you felt before, versus how it actually turns out." I had to admit it made sense, but I just couldn't do it.

DOUG   I heard about this last roadblock. I had had no burning desire to be part of the show at first, but the more I thought about it, the more I'd grown passionate about what this program could mean to a broad audience, and how perfect Sheldon and Roslyn could be for it. And the way the wedding was shaping up, I imagined how much it would have meant to me, a kid in Van Nuys, to see that such a thing was possible. Now that I'd fully pictured the scene, I was frustrated that we could be so close to being a part of it, yet have it fall apart over a tiny detail.

I called my friend Sue Pomerantz, the assistant director who had been my partner in creating the short segments I'd written and produced for *Turning Point*. She'd been at ABC for many years, and I'd confided to her each twist of the negotiation process over the wedding, and now over the program. She listened to this deal-breaking dilemma, and after a moment's thought, came up with an idea. "What if Sheldon and Roslyn did the interview before the wedding, but could wait until *after* the wedding to decide if the footage could be used? If they could pull out of the show, if they weren't happy with the wedding, or the reaction to it, how would they feel about doing the interview?"

As soon as we got off the phone, I left a message for Denise, repeating Sue's idea. I don't know if Denise had already gone down this road with Sheldon and Roslyn, but the next evening we got the word. They were in.

ANDREW   In my family's weddings, there was always a litany of different celebrations, from engagement party to shower. I looked forward to some of that too. Many of these are typically given by friends, but my friends weren't talking about planning anything. I know it was hard for them, since there's no protocol for this situation. Still, I found it hurtful. I'm nervy though. So I suggested to my old friend Diane that maybe we could have a brunch or a small party at her house. She seemed open to it, at first. A few weeks later I asked her about it again, and she put me off. Finally she said her mother didn't want to do it. And her tone suggested Diane herself thought it was a serious imposition to do anything for our wedding. I told Doug about it, and he egged me on, asking why Diane was reacting so coolly.

So I called her up, and said I was hurt. "It's not just about the wedding planning, but about the wedding itself. You've been saying things that echo my father's reactions. It's stuff I expect your mother to say."

"This is new and different," she explained. "It isn't the norm. You can't expect everyone to treat it like any other wedding. So you can't expect this to go by the rules you're used to." Still, she apologized if I'd felt hurt. For the time being, we left it at that. Soon, though, I noticed a turnaround in her response. About a week later, Diane offered to help put together an engagement party for us, in our apartment. She got together with Doug's friends Debbie and Anita to organize the guest list and the food. And even more important, she told me, with sincere enthusiasm, how "wonderful and courageous" it was that we stuck with our plans. Though I'd never looked at myself, or anything we'd done, in that light, her change of heart moved me tremendously. I waited so long to tell her how pained I'd been by her trepidation, and now I wished I'd done it months earlier. It seemed that by being honest with her, I opened up a door between us that had been shut for far too long.

Before this, I'd been weighing whether to ask her to sing at our reception. You see, Maxine and I always made jokes about Diane singing at family celebrations. Prior to one of her sister's weddings, when Diane and I were traveling in Europe, she spent the whole summer with headphones on, singing the Barbra Streisand favorite "Evergreen," prepping for her big moment. It always seemed natural to ask her to sing at our wedding. Now it finally seemed right.

She agreed, sounding genuinely excited. With one caveat, however. If Doug would play the piano.

DOUG It was a sentimental request that made me misty. OK, so I cry at Hallmark ads. Ever since Diane moved to New York three years before, we'd sit together at the piano. I'd play, we'd both sing, and Andrew would cringe. I'm more of a classical guy, and my pop folio is pretty thin, so we'd do the same two or three dozen songs, as the old saying goes, until we got 'em right. Anyway, our favorite duet was "Your Song," the old Elton John standard. It was the first pop song I ever played, back when I was too young to know why growing up to be just like Elton wasn't every parent's dream for their son. Diane's request that I play backup for her was too perfect to pass up.

Her turnaround set into stark relief exactly where the rest of our crowd stood. While most of our friends were wholly accepting of our wedding, some were less enthusiastic than I would have imagined. It seemed that our plans were pushing all sorts of different buttons. Several of our gay friends aren't open about their orientation. Other friends, who fit loosely into the category of *bisexual* (although, as somebody once said, labels are for food, not people), were currently in heterosexual relationships. Among some in each group, I noticed a vague reticence.

And when I told them all about the *Turning Point* episode, that reticence got hiked up a notch. "Will I be on camera?" was the question I heard most often. I explained time and again that we'd already hired a videographer to shoot and edit our wedding video, and that his cameras would be the only ones at the ceremony. Still, I could tell that many of our friends imagined blazing lights and on-camera correspondents shoving microphones at them, asking how it felt to be at a real live gay wedding. So I can just imagine how Andrew's sister Debbie felt when she heard about *Turning Point*.

ANDREW I was sitting on the balcony, in prewedding tanning mode, when Debbie called, saying they'd heard about the show. *How could they have found out?* I wondered. We'd tried to keep this totally secret from everyone in Canada. The only people in Montreal who knew were my parents. And my siblings were the *last* people they would have told. I'd told Diane in confidence. Even though she's good friends with Debbie, she wouldn't have told . . . *would she?*

As expected, Debbie said they didn't want to be on television. "Are you just doing this for the Hollywood aspects of it?"

"Hardly. For a long time I didn't want to do it at all. But we finally saw how we could help other people." I said I respected her wish not to be a part of it, if that was the case.

She said, "I don't know if Abraham will even come to the wedding if I tell him about it."

I tried hard to compose myself, feeling pissed off at my sister and even her husband for this underlying threat of a family feud. Again we were being forced to accommodate other people's fears and misgivings about an event that should have been about us. But rather than lash out at my sister with anger, I internalized it all, continually trying to reassure her that neither she nor any other guests at the wedding would be on television unless they consented. When I got off the phone, my ambivalence about doing *Turning Point* began to surface. I was ready to pull out of the show, but that was the last I heard from Debbie, so it was forgotten . . . for the moment.

DOUG Forget *Turning Point,* just the wedding video itself was causing consternation. No, not among the guests—between me and Andrew. And, as usual, comfort level was the issue. (Have you noticed yet that "comfort level" is a nearly universal all-purpose euphemism for "homophobia"?) After all the discussion about whether we'd have a wedding, we'd made a down payment and signed a contract. I wondered, though, what we would do about the traditional "couple walks hand in hand through the woods" section. You didn't know there was such a tradition in the world of wedding videos? Neither did I, until I'd looked through several others while researching our own. And it turns out, nearly every video out there has a section in which the happy couple pose in schmaltzy romantic tableaux, making goo-goo eyes on a beach or in a park. This section of the video usually comes before the actual wedding footage, and is often shot during the weekend of the wedding.

Though I didn't want ours to look so sappy, I did like the idea, from a producer's point of view, of getting to see the betrothed (in this case, us) together before the wedding, in street clothes. Theoretically I would have liked to horse around with Andrew for the video, with the occasional casual display of affection. But I figured there was no way I'd get Andrew to loosen up enough to do it, because he'd never even been willing to hold hands in Manhattan (except on gay pride day in the Village, where you're surrounded by a million other like-minded partyers). So I suggested to Andrew we have our closest friends go out with us for the shoot, with the hope we could get fun group footage of our gang traipsing around Montreal. He said it would be too stressful trying to assemble a group on the afternoon of the wedding. And he wanted to do the shoot with just the two of us.

"Will you be able to kiss me?" I asked suspiciously. "Or even hold my hand?"

"Don't worry about it," was all he had to say. We left it at that. But I worried: *Will the shoot be a waste of time?*

Don't get me wrong, I'm not saying Andrew's the only one of us dogged by residual "coming-out" issues. I've got my own internalized homophobia. And plenty of it. I'm shadowed, during all my waking hours, with the fear that nothing I ever do is good enough, because I worry, if I'm going to be "out," I'd better be a good representative—a proper delegate to the world at large. But where Andrew and I, as a couple, are concerned, I haven't got much concern about public perception. The pride I take in our relationship trumps my anxieties.

One afternoon in July, I attended a meeting of gay and lesbian journalists. There was much progress to celebrate, from increased representation on newspaper staffs across the country to domestic partner benefits being offered at several companies. On the subject of where the envelope still needed pushing, a staff member from the *New York Times* mentioned rumblings about the paper's wedding announcements. Some staffers, he said, were pushing for the inclusion of same-sex couples. And though it would be an uphill battle, he wondered if the change might come sooner than later. When I got home I asked Andrew, half kidding, if he'd like to send our announcement in to the *Times*.

"They don't list gay weddings," he answered.

"They might. You want to be one of the first?"

"I'm not interested," he said.

I dropped the subject. Andrew's answer was evidence that we've all got our own boundaries, and they don't always follow a logical path. He'd agreed to appear on national television, but a wedding announcement in the nation's paper of record (which still hasn't come to pass at the time of this writing, three years later) might mean a sort of historical notoriety. And that seemed too much for Andrew. Though politics was never on my mind when I proposed, the challenges we faced along the way continually underscored that when you're gay, and not expending energy on hiding the fact, every moment is potentially political.

ANDREW   Doug's closet door swings both ways, believe me. I'm not the one who broke into flop sweat when we went *ketubah* shopping. A *ketubah* is the traditional Jewish document that provides official record of a marriage. (The original language, by the way, betrays the time-honored degradation of women. One phrase states that the man is "buying" the woman for ten *zuzim*. I don't know what ten *zuzim* will get you today, but I'll bet it was a great deal even then.) After five minutes in our first Judaica store (a shop that carries Jewish religious wares), I noticed Doug's forehead and upper lip densely dotted with beads of perspiration. I figured it was the July heat and the cramped aisles we were rummaging through. Then I suggested Doug ask somebody for help. He cautiously stalked a bearded, *kipa*-topped salesman, then just before getting his attention, doubled back toward me in a beeline and demanded, obviously intimidated, "Let's just go, this place gives me the creeps."

It was better that we didn't buy one that day. Instead, we decided to create our own, with wording that would be more appropriate for us. That decision added one complication. We would have to scare up a calligrapher who could render a *ketubah* in Hebrew and English in less than two months.

DOUG   I got the job of finding a calligrapher, and again I felt hemmed in by my own internalized homophobia. I called Jewish organizations, and each time I needed to announce to a stranger, in a religious context, that I was marrying a man. Obviously, religious figures, be they rabbis, salesmen, or artists, represented a kind of authority that stirred up fear for me. Eventually Andrew found a calligrapher in Montreal, and we faxed her our new, self-written, inclusive *ketubah*, in English. We still needed someone to translate the unorthodox language into Hebrew.

ROSLYN   It was only a few weeks before the wedding when we agreed to do the *Turning Point* interview. The following Saturday, Sheldon and I drove to a downtown Montreal hotel to meet Denise. As we got out of the car, we were almost giddy. Laughing, we each said to the other, "Can you believe we're doing this?" From a year and a half ago, when we could barely cope with the news of their engagement, to sitting down in front of a camera to talk about a wedding two weeks away . . . How did we get from there to here? It was tough to fathom.

Denise was waiting with a small crew. We sat down to talk, only to find Sheldon was too tall and I was too short. So I sat on a pillow for two hours. They juggled us, and the camera, until the positions were OK. I was uptight, and the only thing I could think to ask at that point was, "Are you using the Barbara Walters lens that softens the image?" Everyone sort of snickered. As vain as I am, I hoped that reaction meant yes.

My nerves dissipated once I got interested in the process of shooting an interview. I started to watch the action, almost detaching myself from the scene.

SHELDON   Denise hadn't given us any instructions beforehand, except "Don't wear a white shirt." No more details. On the way to the interview, Roslyn asked me, "Are you thinking about the kind of questions they'll ask, and your answers?"

"On the contrary," I told her, "I don't want to think about anything at all. I want it to be off the cuff. She'll ask honest questions, I'll give honest answers. If I anticipate it, I'll sound rehearsed." As it was, I felt stiff when we started. But after a while, I started answering the way it was.

ROSLYN   It felt good to hear Sheldon say, with a camera rolling, and—theoretically, anyway—millions of people listening: *"Andrew is entitled to experience all of life's joys in the same ways as anybody else."* Though he would never think of it in these terms, he'd taken a controversial stand. Remember, this is the same husband who had told me privately—and on several occasions—that he wasn't interested in "helping society." We'd had that argument many times. It usually started when I would mention that supporting Andrew would help other parents of gays and lesbians in our community. And when we'd talked about whether to do this interview, I pointed out that we could help parents far outside our own sphere. At the time Sheldon shot back, "I like Denise. If doing this will help her, I'll do it." I answered, "But if one of the by-products of this could be that it would help other people, is there anything wrong with that?"

Anyway, now that the lights were on, and the tape was in the camera, Sheldon came through. And so, too, did his real feelings.

"Here is our child," he said to Denise, "who needs our support, and needs our love. And we have to help him."

Well. Good thing I had on my heavy-duty, cry-proof mascara. (Actually, as silly as it sounds, if there was just one thing I could go back and change about the interview—I'd wear less makeup! Live and learn.)

When Denise asked why we decided to speak on-camera after all our trepidation, Sheldon stuck to his guns about Denise herself being his motivation. I think we all knew *that* wasn't going to end up in the show. Then I gave my reason:

"I'm here because I hope that I can help make the world a better place for my gay kids. By being visible. Legislators and others who make decisions affecting our lives have to see that there are families behind these people."

After hours of talking, the catharsis was followed by a letdown, a sad realization. You know the old Peggy Lee song, "Is That All There Is?"

SHELDON   When the camera and the lights were turned off, the sound man came over to me and said, *"Mazel tov.* I want you to know, I bonded with you." Now, maybe he says that to every interview subject, but the sentiment seemed genuine. So I guessed the interview went OK. We all went out to lunch afterward and said good-bye. Then Roslyn and I put it out of our minds. When we'd decided to do the interview, we agreed not to tell anyone about it.

ROSLYN   We couldn't go through more comments from friends, judgments about our actions, defending ourselves. And now it was only two weeks until the wedding.

ANDREW   While my parents were being interviewed, Doug and I were shopping for wedding clothes. As we stood in front of a mirror at Barney's, struggling together to tie our first bow ties, there was a spark between us. We both knew the other was thinking, *icantbelieveitsreallyhappening!*

DOUG   We bounced between stores on Madison Avenue, splurging unconscionably, opening our wallets to the wind. A special cologne, just for the occasion. Decadent suspenders. Then we both fell in love with the same tuxedo. And neither one of us wanted to give up wearing it just because we'd look alike. Of course, we'd never really look like twins, since Andrew's half a foot taller.

We straggled home like looting conquerers, laden with bags.

We ripped open the spoils and had a frenzied fashion show, trying on all the goodies for the first time. The simple shirts, no studs or buttons cluttering up their clean lines, the socks, then the pants. We dressed in the same order, as if it were an ancient ritual. We clipped the simple black cummerbunds in place, hooking on our classic suspenders, Andrew's with a fin de siècle French beach scene, adorned with bathing beauties in blue swimsuits sheltered by red umbrellas in a sea of white sand, and mine laden with frolicking nymphs, in blue and gray, cascading down from shoulder to waist. It was such a little thing, but you couldn't possibly strap on those suspenders without having their halo cover you too, making you a little lighter, a little more unearthly, for just as long as you wore them. And maybe a little longer.

ANDREW Then we worked on our bow ties, and after fifteen minutes of practice, I was pretty sure I'd stick with the prefab version I'd bought as a backup. Doug was adamant about learning to do it for real. Finally, we put on the jackets and stood in front of a nearly full-length mirror. It was a spine-tingling preview of coming attractions, now only two weeks away.

When we'd stripped out of our Cinderella ball gowns and slipped back into our scullery-girl rags, the phone rang. When I picked it up, the caller identified himself as a distant relative from out of town. I had to take him on faith since we had different surnames and we had never met, or even spoken, before. He'd found me through a series of coincidences that prove truth is absolutely stranger than fiction. I have to resist the temptation to tell some of the juiciest details of the conversation, and soon you'll see why.

He said he was a Hasidic Jew and had called to get some information on our family tree. He asked what I did for a living, if I was married or had children . . . that sort of ordinarily innocuous background information. I'm not in the habit of hiding my life, but this was somebody I would never meet. I didn't see the point in shocking him. Besides, since Hasids are among the most orthodox of all Jewish groups, I knew he wasn't going to be thrilled to hear I was in the abomination business. So I said I wasn't married, and left it at that. Because this was only two weeks before the wedding, I considered that statement accurate in fact, if not in spirit. I didn't have all the family history he wanted, so I gave him the phone number of the family patriarch, my great-uncle Rudolph, wished him luck, and said good-bye, severing the momentary tie to a distant genetic connection.

I explained to Doug the bizarre coincidence that led this long-lost relative to find me. He listened, mouth wide open, catching flies. I'd almost finished the story when the phone rang again. We both stared at it as if an alien spacecraft had landed in the living room. Finally I answered, and sure enough, it was the long-lost relative.

This time his tone was different. No attempts at warm familial bonding. He had something to say, and he delivered it with hushed import, like a state secret to a foreign agent. "I talked to Rudolph. He said you were a . . . *homosexual. A shame to the family.*" What was more surprising? Uncle Rudolph contradicting his warm response to my father, or having this total stranger reveal it to me? Before I could think twice, he dropped the real bombshell.

"There's something I have to tell you."

For God's sake, what next?

"I, too, am a homosexual."

Until then, I'd pictured him with his flowing beard and *kipa* covering his crown, sitting at the head of a huge table with the usual Hasidic brood of a dozen or so offspring. So what would a Hasidic homosexual household look like? My imagination reeled.

Our chat wasn't over yet. He saved the best for last.

"I've been with the same man for ten years. And my first relationship was over twenty years ago. With a black man."

A relative I'd never met had just come out to me. Getting married was like knocking over the first domino and watching the crazy-quilt pattern of falling tiles spill out in all directions. For a moment I asked myself, was this some elaborate practical joke? As his tale continued, it was clear you couldn't make this stuff up. And even if

I could tell you more details of his story (which, to preserve his anonymity, I can't), you wouldn't believe me.

SHELDON   Just over a week before the ceremony, Uncle Rudolph came into my office. Typically, when he stops by, it's to say hello and use my fax, copier, or stamp machine. This time he looked sheepish, and said, "I want to talk to you. I hope you won't be offended . . . My wife —" Rudolph is married for the third time "— she's sick and depressed, doesn't go out of the house. She can't come to the wedding, and I don't want to go by myself."

I reminded him, "I told you, we'll love you just as much if you can't make it. Please don't worry about it." And I assumed that was the end of that.

DOUG   Andrew and I hadn't heard the latest details on his Uncle Rudolph. Instead, we were wondering how the youngest generation was being prepped for the upcoming event.

Long afterward, Bonnie's husband, David, told me how they handled the subject of our wedding with their children. "Our initial thoughts were that we would say nothing unless they asked. Bonnie and I have always worked with the theory that children ask what they need to know, that they are their own best gauge of what information is necessary. That's been our policy of talking about birds and bees in general. We'd been waiting for our oldest to ask us some specifics. We didn't make an issue of it. Of course, they knew we were going to a wedding, since they were walking down the aisle all dressed up. But it was quite a while before we got a direct question. It was fairly close to the date of the ceremony. Bonnie and I had decided to explain it this way: there are different types of families; some families where there's only one mommy, some with one daddy, others where grandparents take care of their grandchildren, and some with a man and a man, or with two women. And that, in fact, is how we presented it to our oldest daughter. She asked if this was called a wedding, or a marriage, and I said, 'It doesn't matter what you call it. Andrew and Doug call it a wedding.

Some people call it a commitment ceremony. What's important is, they're starting a family.' *Family* was the key word in several respects. Being there for the ceremony was a matter of family. Andrew is Bonnie's family. So he's my family.

We don't have to agree about everything. The rule is, if it's for the family you do it. That's what family's all about."

ANDREW   Exactly one week before the wedding, Doug and I were scheduled for our *Turning Point* shoot. Denise was set to arrive with the crew at noon. We were just about ready to go when the phone rang. It was Doug's brother, Jerry.

DOUG   My parents' plans to attend the wedding were sidelined in July when health problems intervened. It became increasingly doubtful that they would make it, and finally my father asked me, with great regret, to take them off the guest list. The depth of my disappointment caught me by surprise.

When I first proposed to Andrew and we started planning the wedding, I told him I didn't expect my parents would be able to make the trip. And in a way, that felt OK at the time. I hadn't seen them in a social situation since my college graduation fifteen years before. And I feared that they'd be proverbial fishes out of water, struggling with their own discomfort in a crowd of strangers. Selfishly perhaps, I wanted my wedding to be a celebration, unsullied by concern over my parents' social limitations, three thousand miles away from their home in a room of strangers. Or perhaps those feelings were an elaborate self-deception. Maybe I feared they wouldn't make the effort to come. And I knew, given their respective health issues, it would be a significant effort.

Then, when both my mother and father showed enthusiastic interest in making the trip, I realigned my image of the event. By the time my father called to put the kibosh on their attendance, I almost couldn't imagine having the wedding without them. I'd talked a good game to everyone else, saying for months, "Well, it looks like they're coming! But you never know. They haven't traveled together on a plane in God knows how many years." But deep down, I'd figured once they made the decision to do it, they'd pull it off.

When he heard the bottom fall out of my voice, my father held out a glimmer of hope, saying that if things changed, he'd call me as soon as possible. Of course, I responded that we'd juggle hotel rooms and other specifics to include them.

Now, as Jerry called so close to the date, I thought perhaps the purpose was to give me the news that they'd be at our wedding after all. As it was, the only family I'd have present would be my sister, Lynn, my niece Michelle, Jerry, his wife, Roslyn, and my nephew Natan.

So his call came as a sharp blow. Due to health problems within his branch of the family, none of them would be able to attend, either. He apologized profusely, and with obvious sincerity. And though the depth of his regret certainly eased my pain a bit, I was devastated to realize that while Lynn and Michelle would walk me down the aisle, not one member of my family would be present in the hall. Of course, this was about more than my parents, brother, and his family bowing out. As I noted before, the physical distance between my nuclear family and the rest of our relatives had left me a wayward twig in the family tree. Now I felt very much alone.

ANDREW Some of Doug's sadness over this news might have been alleviated if he had invited some of his more extended family. While I was aware that he had only met most of them a couple of times in his life, I always thought he would at least invite the contingent from Florida: Uncle George, Aunt Verona, his cousin Pookie, and her husband, Tom.

DOUG My Aunt Verona and Uncle George spent the winter in the same condo where my parents have an apartment. The unit remains empty except when Andrew and I stay there a few weekends each winter. The proximity of the two apartments allowed us to see each other over the last few years, and during that period I'd grown very close to both of them. And we'd also gotten to know my cousin Pookie and her family.

ANDREW   I began to view them as part of my extended family as well, and wanted them to be present at the wedding. I think it would have been especially meaningful to Doug. I kept telling him to get his aunt and uncle's address in the Hamptons where they spent the summer with their son, Barnet, and his family. But he procrastinated until finally he told me, with a tone of regret, that he was not going to invite any of his Florida relatives. We never got into the exact reasons. He gave several plausible explanations, but I still wonder if his hesitation was driven by a fear of what their responses may have been.

DOUG   I did have additional concerns, but not about their responses. Aunt Verona's health had deteriorated, and just as we mailed the invitations, I changed my mind and decided, with conflicting emotions, not to invite them to the wedding, or even to tell them about it. I knew Aunt Verona's health would prevent her from attending, so I worried that offering an invitation might sound like I was just begging for a gift. More significantly, I worried that sending them an invitation could open up a bigger can of family worms. How could I come out to the rest of my enormous extended family—people I hardly knew, and had only met a handful of times in my life? So rather than invite a select few, I chose instead to invite none.

Further, Sheldon, Roslyn, Andrew, and I had all bickered about the size of the guest list on many occasions. We'd all heard Sheldon say a hundred times that he wanted to restrict the scope of the affair. I knew it wasn't primarily a monetary concern for him, but I was also sensitive about the fact that he and Roslyn were footing the vast majority of the bill.

There were lots of good reasons for not inviting the family I'd long been separated from by time and distance. And yet somehow, none of them was a good excuse. And with my brother's phone call, I now felt the full weight of my decision.

Thankfully, the imminent video shoot didn't give me time to dwell on the negative for long. Once they all arrived, our apartment was a hive of activity, Denise and crew buzzing about for the best spots for a shot. Like Sheldon, I hadn't given thought to anything I might say, or that they might ask. Preoccupied with the fear of sounding canned, I hoped spontaneity might make up for lack of eloquence.

ANDREW   After the interviews at home, the crew followed us as we finished our wedding shopping. We'd purposely waited an extra week to pick out some last key items, so they could tape the interview and the shopping all in one day. Our first stop was the Judaica store (not the same one we tried in July—this shop was on the street, so it was less claustrophobic). Rebecca, the associate producer, went in to ask if a television crew could shoot inside for a few minutes. She returned with an OK, and I asked what she'd told them the shoot was for.

"A show on marriage," she explained simply.

True. They hooked on our wireless mikes, and we walked to the storefront. We looked in the window, not knowing if they'd started taping yet, when one of us, who will remain nameless, got a little attack of nerves. Let's just say the sound man got his microphone tested like I'm sure he never had before.

DOUG   I wasn't the one who sprung a gas leak. I swear.

ANDREW   Whatever. We both looked over at the crew, and I asked, "Are we rolling?"

They nodded yes, so we'd just have to move on. Faced with the task at hand, Doug and I looked in the store window.

"Are we going to tell them it's for two men?" Doug asked.

"I'm sure they'll figure it out," I stalled. Inspecting Doug's forehead and upper lip, I nudged, "Are we starting to sweat yet?"

DOUG   We laughed and headed in. The camera was behind us, but stayed at a discreet distance, and either the light was off or low. They were relatively unobtrusive, for a television crew wedged into a little Upper West Side shop. The salesman who approached us wore a *kipa* on his head, and had a trimmed beard. *Very Conservative, or mildly Orthodox*, I figured.

"Can I help you?"

"Well," I answered, "we're looking for a large tallis." We'd decided we would use a large prayer shawl, or tallis, for the tent of our *chuppah*. The first one he showed us was too small, so I added the crucial detail. "It has to be big enough to use for a *chuppah*."

"When's the day?" he asked, smiling.

"Next Sunday," I answered. *Well, that was no big deal!*

The surprisingly cool Judaica salesman nodded, knowingly. "Women, always waiting till the last minute!" *Whoops. So he didn't get it yet.* Andrew and I suppressed nervous smiles and dug through the selection. We found a simple white-on-white pattern, and asked the salesman to hold up two corners while I held up the other two. Andrew stood underneath to judge whether we'd have enough room for everybody.

ANDREW   We'd shared moments of excitement before this, but standing under the billowing tallis, I was transported a week forward. For the first time it was as if I stood in front of Rabbi Bolton pledging my love to Doug.

DOUG   I picked up on the faraway look in Andrew's eyes. Then I caught the eye of the salesman, who looked from me to Andrew. Then he turned back to me again. Andrew stepped out from under the *chuppah,* and we folded it up. The salesman carried it as we picked out woven black and white *kipas* and went to check out. Once I'd signed the credit card receipt, the salesman handed me the bag. He looked from me to Andrew, saying, "I hope the two of you have many happy years together."

Andrew and I glanced at each other, both relieved and surprised.

You never know, huh? It was just another lesson I'd learn in this crash course on *never assume anything*.

ANDREW   Outside the store, I asked the crew, "When we started that shoot, did you hear anything . . . funny?" The audio man leaned forward, sharing a confidence: "You hear everything in this job. Don't worry, it's just between us. And the answer to your next question is no, the tape wasn't rolling yet."

We moved on to buying our wedding bands in the Diamond District. We didn't actually want diamonds, just white gold or platinum bands to go with our yellow gold engagement bands. Since nearly all the gold and diamond stores in the midtown area are owned by devout Jews, we figured we might draw a few stares. With a camera crew tagging along, it was a safe bet we'd attract attention. But again, nobody seemed perturbed. You could say they all treated us like our money was just as green as anybody else's. It was more than that, though. We were treated with respect. And looking back at the entire process from a consumer's point of view, we were extraordinarily lucky. Or maybe something else was going on. We never actually encountered a cool response, let alone hostility, from any merchant along the way. And there were many meetings, rentals, and purchases we haven't recounted, from party suppliers (where we rented tablecloths and other odds and ends) to our sexagenarian invitation designer. Every one of them was a pleasure.

There was more shooting to be done later that afternoon, back at our apartment. Diane was out of town for the weekend, but was rushing back to New York to meet us at home so she could rehearse her song with Doug, on-camera. Before that, Doug and I had plans to visit Orna, a friend from graduate school, and her then-boyfriend and later, husband, Nigel. When we arrived at their apartment, they had a typically international group of friends gathered. Orna is Israeli, so we had asked her help in translating our *ketubah* into Hebrew. A few of the friends sitting around the living room also spoke Hebrew fluently. We'd brought along a typed copy, in English naturally, and read it for the group.

> On the first day of September, 1996, Douglas, son of Fred and Estelle, says to Andrew, "With this ring, I pledge to honor and treasure you, sweetening your days as you sweeten mine. I shall share myself, trying ever to hear your heart, just as my heart will always be open to you. And I shall strive to provide you comfort, sustain your will, and support your dreams. I give you my faith, my respect, and my undying love."
>
> Andrew, son of Sheldon and Roslyn, says to Douglas, "With this ring, I promise to lift your spirits as you lift mine, as we spend each day celebrating our love and commitment. I pledge to be honest and faithful, to support and protect you, and to be a source of strength in your life."
>
> We will always cherish each other's uniqueness. We promise both to comfort and challenge each other through life's sorrow and joy; to share our intuition and insight with one another; help one another achieve our full potential; and most of all, to listen, always trying to truly hear. And we pledge to create a home filled with reverence for learning, loving, generosity, and justice; a home where diversity and creativity are honored, where we endeavor to touch the lives of others, sharing our many blessings; where we remember wrongs from the past, and work together for a greater future.

DOUG   For half an hour we hashed out the challenges of translating idiomatic language. Even though many present were strangers, the act of working together as a group, and maneuvering through the interpretation of Hebrew that would be written on our *ketubah* and read aloud at our wedding, gave me a rush. It was a tangible connection to a tradition I wasn't even aware I'd felt estranged from all my life. And it was different from trying on our tuxedos. That was a visceral thrill. This moved me right down to my genes.

CHAPTER 11

Bells Are Ringing

Time: August 28–September 1, 1996

ANDREW   The task of packing for the trip fell to me, as usual. Whenever it comes time to organize bags for travel, Doug will be running around from edit to edit, and ask if I'll take care of it. Then he'll complain I've overstuffed them, and packed only the clothes that I like to see him wearing. Only five days until we stomp on the glass, and I wondered, *Am I ready for a lifetime of bickering over baggage?*

Once I arrived in Montreal, my parents wanted to get together for dinner on Thursday night, when Doug was set to fly in.

DOUG   My last stop before the airport was the *Turning Point* office, where I finished up some work, then I stuck my head in to say good-bye to Janice Tomlin, one of the show's senior producers. She offered firsthand advice that stayed in the back of my mind all weekend: "Don't sweat details at this point. You've done all that already. Now just try to have a good time. Do you have somebody else who can do the worrying for you?" The party planner's assistant, Shelley, was the point person for all the minutiae. "Good. Now forget about it and enjoy yourself." She gave me a hug and sent me off. As I zipped through the office to the elevator, a few coworkers called out their good-byes and congratulations. By the time I'd hit the ground floor and headed through the network lobby, the sun was blazing onto the street outside. Suddenly all the work was behind me, and stepping onto the pavement, I broke into a gigantic grin, wondering about the weekend that lay ahead. *Finally, after so many times when we'd nearly given up, finally . . . it's about to begin.*

In Montreal, Andrew was at the airport to pick me up, with my friend George in tow. We'd all exchanged big hugs and kisses at the curb and popped into the car when George cried out from the backseat.

"Ohhhhh! You won't believe who Terry, Monica, and I ran into last night on the street!" Terry is an old mutual friend, Monica her new flame; for Terry, the first of the female variety. I couldn't think of anyone else George knew who was in town yet.

"Lynn and Michelle?" I asked, remembering my sister and niece had come in early.

"No, I got together with Lynn and Michelle today. Last night Terry, Monica, and I are all standing on some downtown street, no idea where in heaven's name we are, huge map unfolded like *turistas,* and a charming woman asks if we're lost. With both of my hands wrapped around this enormous map, I cackled, 'How could you tell?' We all had a good laugh, and she asked what brought us to Montreal. We said our friend was getting married, and she cocked her head when she asked the names of the wedding party. When I told her Wythe and Merling, she said, 'You're looking at the mother of one of the grooms!' "

You can always count on George for a good story, but this was above and beyond the call of duty. What a lovely way to start things off, with a serendipitous brush with his new extended family, there on a street corner three thousand miles from home.

"Thank God that's what brought you together, not a fender bender in the parking lot! I can see it now—you lock bumpers, get out of your cars hollering at each other, exchange driver's licenses, and you see the Merling family name staring back at you!"

ROSLYN   I was most anxious about Thursday night's informal dinner with Lynn, Michelle, and Doug's friends George, Geri, and her husband, Steve. I was looking foward to meeting everyone, but I worried that Sheldon might retract into his shell. But after only a few minutes at the restaurant, I knew the evening would go just fine. He was obviously enjoying himself. Later that night, Sheldon said, "Everybody's very nice, they're terrific people." It was a signal that the rest of the weekend might get easier.

ANDREW   By the time dessert rolled around, my father loosened up completely. Doug's niece Michelle has a picky palate, and Doug and I always try cajoling her into trying a new dish. My father loves showing off the city, its culture, its food, whatever. Michelle was skittish about ordering any of the strange desserts we recommended. "You oughta try the crème brûlée. It's great here, I'm telling you," my father teased. Then George jumped in, "Oh, absolutely. You must. And if you twist my arm *verrry* hard, I'll give you a hand with it." Michelle squirmed, unconvinced. But neither Daddy nor George would let her off the hook until she bit.

It was a microcosm of the weekend, with my sixty-something Jewish father from Quebec and George, the thirty-something gay WASP, introducing Michelle, the teenage Jewish girl from California, to her first French dessert. She wasn't the only one who'd get a taste of something new before the weekend was up. That night's dinner started the weekend off like a pebble dropped in a pond. Each event after that was a new, wider ripple, creating an expanding—and ever more diverse—circle. And Michelle managed to polish off her dessert—with a little help from her new extended family.

The next morning, Doug and I had our last meeting with Rabbi Bolton. She wisely asked for copies of our vows, so she could prompt us if we blanked. After a few rabbinical words of wisdom, Doug and I squeezed in an hour of sunbathing and then hurried over to Eaton's for the wedding rehearsal. My father, Mr. Punctual, was already there, foot tapping, visibly irritated.

DOUG I didn't want to spend all weekend running fifteen minutes late to everything. But to Andrew, fifteen minutes late means on time. Just one of the many quirks I'd soon be saddled with for a lifetime. Did I wonder if it was too late to back out? Well, just a wee bit. But after all, we'd put up with each other's quirks for five years already. What's another fifty?

We both knew Sheldon was going to be there early—if anything, in hopes an early start would mean an early end. But we weren't the only ones who were late. Almost everyone else we expected was even more delinquent than Andrew and I. No one looked at the rehearsal as a big deal, but it seemed like a good idea for the *chuppah* holders and other key people to get their bearings. I suppose I was particularly keen on having a rehearsal since I was the one who'd pushed the idea of a rehearsal dinner. And we couldn't really have a rehearsal dinner without a rehearsal, now could we? The rehearsal was half-baked by design, since we knew the restaurant serves all day. So we had to wend our way between the few scattered tables of late lunchers while we mimed our walks up and down the imaginary aisle. The run-through was pretty aimless until Louie showed up. He commandeered the rehearsal and we wrapped up in a few minutes.

From there we moved on to Mitchell's apartment. Andrew's brother had generously offered to throw us a cocktail party that evening, before the rehearsal dinner.

Everyone from the rehearsal, except Sheldon and Roslyn,

walked through downtown from Eaton's to Mitchell's apartment a mile or so away. We stopped along the way to clown around for a few pictures with a life-size sculpture of a crowd scene on McGill College Street. (I didn't find out until we got the pictures developed that Louie had been standing in front with his zipper down and a finger protruding from his fly.) Soon after, on the walk to Mitchell's, I heard Louie make a crack about "all the cameras they're having at the wedding. So when do the crews pull up?" From that point on, I was determined to make the wedding my sole focus, and forget about *Turning Point*.

ANDREW   Next up was the rehearsal dinner at my parents' house, after a pit stop at the hotel. Like us, most of our friends were staying at the Loews Hotel Vogue, a half mile from Eaton's. We could have stayed with my parents, as we usually do when visiting Montreal. This weekend, though, I knew we'd need our own space, physically and emotionally. Just one more ledger line to add to our magically expanding budget, but it was worth it. When we got back to the room, we found a tray laid out with a bottle of Cristal, two champagne flutes, a goblet with strawberries, and a silver ladle filled with what appeared to be crème fraîche. The note was from the *Turning Point* staff, wishing us a wonderful wedding. So much for Doug's forgetting about *Turning Point*. But it was a charming gesture that lent our room a little extra elegance.

The bathroom came equipped with a double Jacuzzi, and we made the most of it, taking a fifteen-minute sanity break in the bubble-filled whirlpool. Looking like a kid with foam dripping from my chin, I got an idea. "When the crew comes to shoot us on Sunday, let's ask the photographer to take some shots while we have another bubble bath, and we'll use the champagne and strawberries as props. We can give a copy of the photo to your friends at *Turning Point—after* the show airs."

"You mean we'll keep the video cameras outside, right?" Doug got his I'm-a-producer-listen-to-the-expert look. "Because if they get that shot on tape, you know it'll end up in the show."

"Of course!" I was starting to look forward to the shoot on Sunday. Our photographer, David Sternfeld, would follow us around, along with Enrique, who was taping our wedding video, which *Turning Point* would get a copy of. Rebecca Wharton, Denise's associate producer, would come along too, and probably ask a few questions at some point during the day. Though it promised to be fun, I was still battling with my anxiety over public displays of affection.

After our fingers had puckered like prunes, we went to my parents', and before Doug tells you, I'll just say, we were fifteen minutes late. What were they going to do, start without us? Just about everybody was already there, including most of our friends in the wedding party.

We had appetizers in the backyard while my sister Debbie, her husband, Abraham, Doug's sister Lynn, his niece Michelle, my parents, and our friends all did the getting-to-know-you waltz. Later I passed Louie and Abraham chatting on the patio. Doug was introducing them, and he pointed out to Louie that Abraham is Brazilian. One of Louie's many nicknames is Mr. International. He's fluent in Spanish, and speaks several other languages more than passably.

"Oh!" Louie exclaimed, then said something in Portuguese to Abraham, to show he knew the lingo. Then, in English, he threw in, "My old lover was Brazilian!"

You might think that would give them something in common, but it didn't look that way.

DOUG After an uneventful dinner, we sat around the living room. I'd asked several of our friends to prepare a few things to say. When I was at Geri's rehearsal dinner five years before, I loved how that part of the evening allowed everyone to share a common bond, days before the ceremony. You know how, when you go to a big party, and you meet a stranger, often you'll initiate a conversation by referring to your host? "So, how do you know Bob?" Well, I found that the speeches at Geri's rehearsal dinner gave everyone an opportunity to do just that, but in a much more formalized way.

"How do you know . . ." took on a more significant meaning, as if to say, "What history do you share?" I'd hoped that this evening might offer us the same opportunity. In trying to dig out the subtext here, I'm making it all sound very heavy. In essence, if the evening was done right, it would be a lot of laughs, like a roast. Of course, the risk with any roast is that someone will stick the fork in too deep and draw blood. The people most likely to skewer me were George and Louie. Andrew wasn't likely to get poked or prodded much, because a couple of his oldest friends, Maxine and Lorne, hadn't come. I knew nobody would say anything too risqué, since everyone was well behaved at Mitchell's party. But I wondered how Sheldon would hold up if the stories got in the least bit racy. We weren't driving in his car anymore, and he couldn't just turn up the stereo if he wanted to tune out.

SHELDON   Before the party that night, Roslyn asked me, "Are you nervous about tonight?" and I said, "At this stage in the game, to tell you the truth, I'm nothing." I'd taken my tranquilizer, so to speak. For a year, I'd been adjusting to the idea that this was going to happen. And recently I'd been hearing a new refrain from various corners—Roslyn, Denise Schreiner, some of our friends: *Sure, you're anxious now. You'll feel different after this is over.* And I knew it was probably true, I'd feel better later. Would it be relief or joy? That, I couldn't tell.

DOUG   I don't think I was the only one glancing over at Sheldon to gauge his response. George went first. As he told sanitized stories of our bawdier days, I waited for a truly embarrassing pearl to drop. But George was the model of charm and etiquette, as always. He closed by reminiscing about the night we were out dancing and the club closed by playing the "Blue Danube" just before 2:00 A.M: "I don't know if I'm the only one here to have waltzed with Doug, but I can say he does it *well*."

Sheldon's foot tapped unconsciously, with alarming rapidity, but that was as bad as it got.

ROSLYN   Actually, we both thought all the stories we heard that
night were wonderful. Louie spoke movingly; other friends told anecdotes as well. Sheldon and I got to see Andrew and Doug through
new sets of eyes, through their friends. That night was one more
step up the ladder on the way to the top.

ANDREW   It was a good warm-up for Saturday night's out-of-
towners' party, when the house was jammed with over seventy
guests. And once again, we were late. This time it was Doug's doing.
Whatever. No one seemed to mind, except my father, of course. The
evening was in full swing as we made our way from room to room.
There was a hum of excitement in the house like I'd never felt,
though we'd had plenty of parties over the years. And it wasn't just
because I was one of the guests of honor. Well, I'm sure that was
a big part of it, but there was a buzz in the air, as if someone had
piped in extra oxygen. Everything felt brighter, clearer, moving in
a vivid swirl of color and light. We kissed and hugged everybody
we could get our hands on. It was a kick getting to see all of our
friends spiffed up. Everywhere you could hear the sounds of eating,
drinking, laughing. The weather was ideal, and most of us were
trying to squeeze into our backyard. Doug and I were standing on
the grass when Diane asked if anyone was home next door. I told
her they had gone away until Sunday, and I went inside for a minute. When I stepped back out, Diane, Doug, and a dozen friends
had set up camp in our neighbor's backyard, commandeering their
lawn chairs, tables, and deck. Fitting, considering the whole wedding
had started with the same philosophy behind that maneuver: *Work
with what you've got; and if you haven't got it, appropriate it.*

DOUG   I sat on the neighbor's porch with our friends, drinking
in the night. Terry was sitting next to me, and I put my arm around
her and whispered in her ear, "When you go, you go all the way."
She laughed, since she'd heard that line before. As far as I knew,
until a year ago Terry wasn't just heterosexual, she'd dated practically every man I ever introduced her to. Back in the old days when

we were inseparable, I practically felt guilty that I wasn't straight, so I could be another notch in her garter. Now, well over ten years later, and in her first lesbian relationship, she nabs Lauren. Terry's great-looking, don't get me wrong, but Lauren is a *babe*, with legs for days.

"First time out of the gate, Terry, really, I'm impressed." I raised a glass. "To you and Lauren." "To you and Andrew." She tipped hers right back at me. Her late arrival in the land of Sappho was just one more in a series of lessons I've long been learning about the fluid nature of sexuality in many women. A few of those who attended our wedding had crossed from dating men to women, or the other way around. Others crossed one way, then back the other. These friends helped me see that women are often less caught up in superficial differences than men. They weren't looking for blondes, or bodybuilders. Or even men, necessarily. Or women. That's not to say they don't appreciate beauty. One more look at Lauren reminded me of that.

My sister Lynn approached me, concern furrowing her brow. "Michelle thinks you've forgotten her birthday." Since I'd been at the party, I hadn't thought about it. But we'd already arranged with Roslyn to have a birthday cake decorated that I would present later on. "She said, Uncle Doug hasn't even wished me a happy birthday!" Ouch. I wanted the cake to be a surprise, but I certainly could have said "happy birthday" without tipping her off.

I picked up Andrew on the way to the Merlings' patio door, and told him I wanted to get everybody inside. We passed Roslyn's sister, Helen. With their hair done alike, they could pass for twins. Her husband, Andrew's uncle Gary, sat sullenly on the edge of the patio, wearing a disapproving scowl. I shot Andrew a look, and he said, "Forget about it. What can you do?"

SHELDON My friend Nookie, who'd ridden this whole roller coaster with me, giving me advice all along the way, had agreed to say the traditional prayer over the bread, which follows soon after the ceremony. He offered to prepare a few words to say over the blessing. It's a job that usually goes to the family patriarch, but I knew Uncle Rudolph wouldn't be coming. Then, that Friday, Nookie called me at the office and said, "Would you mind? I want to call Rudolph and tell him that I'm representing you." "Sure," I said, "why not?" Later he called me back and said, "I called him, and everything's great."

Now it was Sunday morning, and just a couple hours until I'd put on my tuxedo. Bonnie, her husband, David, and our granddaughters were in from Toronto, and staying with us. David's a sporty kind of guy, and I like to beat up young kids, so we went to play tennis in the park a couple of blocks away. Roslyn was out at the hairdresser when we got home. The housekeeper gave me a frantic message. "URGENT—call Miriam Friedman." Why would my cousin make a call like that today? *God, someone's sick. Or worse.*

"Sheldon, you'll never guess who called me this morning."

"Is everybody OK. Is everybody coming?"

"Uncle Rudolph called. He can't live with himself. He has to come. By himself. I'll pick him up. I had to call you, because he's ashamed to call you himself. He wants to know, can you fit him in?"

"What do you mean? Of course! I'll call him. You'll take him to Eaton's?"

"Yeah, I'll take him."

ANDREW   Noon on Sunday, the crew was at our door.

Ready or not, here I come out. On the streets of Montreal.

We all drove to a park at the base of Mount Royal, and there wasn't any dipping of toes into the water—we jumped right in. I guess it's like the fear of the unknown that my father was feeling about the ceremony. I'd built this up in my head, and now that we were actually doing it, now that I was holding Doug's hand walking up the street to the park, now that we were embracing, now that I was kissing him under the trees with still camera snapping and video camera circling us, now that our lips touched in the open air, the fear evaporated.

DOUG We sprinted all around town shooting stills and video in silly vignettes. We played on the railroad tracks, hid in bushes with our heads sticking up, popped out from behind grand columns of the Old City. It felt like we were making our own little *Hard Day's Night,* minus the music and the adoring fans. It was lots of fun. And I was thrilled with how comfortable we both were in the mushy shots.

ANDREW We stopped for a shot wherever the mood struck us. Driving through downtown, we spotted two Italian sailors in skin-tight navy outfits right out of a New York City Ballet ad. We pulled over and got a "Hey, sailor" picture with all of us in the shot. Back at the hotel, after two hours of action, we stumbled through the lobby, ready to take a break, when I saw the pièce de résistance. A bride who'd gotten married earlier was sitting with her husband, and her gown was draped over a chair. I asked if we could borrow it, and David, our photographer, snapped a handful of choice poses. In the best one, I'm holding the dress just under my neck, the frilly lace tickling my chin, and Doug is standing right next to me, holding the veil behind both our heads like a medieval halo framing us together in a drag tableau.

DOUG If *Turning Point* were on a more conservative network instead of ABC, this shot would have been the publicity photo . . . *Fags in drag getting married: How to keep your family safe! We Distort, You Decide.* And even though I trust and admire the gang at *Turning Point,* I made Enrique turn off the video camera for the wedding-gown shtick. *This one's for our photo album only, thank you.*

ANDREW Back up in the room, we relaxed in the Jacuzzi bubble bath as planned, for a precious fifteen minutes of privacy and quiet. The crew came over just before we got out, so we could get a couple of silly snapshots, and from then on, as far as we knew, the cameras were running. George came over to do the best-man-type duties, like helping us into our tuxes and hosing Doug down as he obsessed over our tardiness.

DOUG Well, guess what. We were half an hour late. Supposed to arrive for group photos at 4:00 P.M., we didn't get there until 4:30. And the wedding was scheduled for 5:30.

ANDREW What he's not telling you is that everyone else was late too. Whatever. We took as many pictures as we could. It was a flurry of direction: stand here, scoot over, move in, step back, where's Grandma, smile, turn, do it all over again. And throughout all the groupings, my auntie Helen, my mother's sister, was coming over to Doug, tugging on his jacket. "It keeps doing this . . ." And she'd gesture like the lapels were floating away from him. Doug would tug it down. By the time we took the next photo, Auntie Helen would step back in and they did the whole dance over again. Doug was getting frustrated, so I whispered, "Never mind, she's always been fussy."

When time came for the full family photo, David Sternfeld gathered everybody, all my aunts, uncles, and cousins, and rather than "cheese," he said he'd call out, "One-two-three-*yes!*" As we all stood ready to smile, he called it out for real: "OK, everybody, get ready, one-two-three—" And just as the rest of us zestfully countered back one enormous "YES!" my uncle Gary called out a resounding "NO."

Well, he made his point. His disapproval was hardly news. So we made a point of ignoring it.

After a few more chaotic group pictures, Doug went off to practice with Diane for their song.

DOUG It was all happening too fast. We went through the song a couple of times, and Diane sounded good. I was unaccountably nervous. I'd only been playing "Your Song" since I was *twelve*. Just as we were about to sign the *ketubah*, Roslyn stopped by with the news that Andrew's uncle Rudolph would be coming after all, and what's more, he'd be sitting at the head table. Heck, I'd never met him, and all I knew was that he'd said Andrew was a shame on the family. I bristled at the notion he'd sit on the dais with us, but I knew instinctively to drop it. *This is the way it's going to be, and even if I could change it, what would be the point? So now he wants to sit alongside us?*

Next we moved into a large storage room where we were set up to sign the *ketubah*. Geri adjusted the boutonniere in my lapel. Then more pictures as we signed. People whizzed around me. It was like one of those nighttime picture postcards taken on a long expo-sure. You know, the ones with the head and taillights from cars drawing garish streaks of light across the road. For a minute I was as lead-footed as a monument in the middle of one of those photos, with everything, everyone, every moment, skidding by, just out of reach. Dizzy, I sat down and listened to the hum of activity coming from the next room. The click of high heels and just-shined shoes on the tile traced a path from the hall to the chairs where they'd sit and watch . . .

Our Wedding.

I stood up, and before I knew it, the string quartet was playing the theme from *Out of Africa,* which was the cue for the procession to begin. I gave Andrew a kiss, then stood between Lynn and Mi-chelle, and gripped their hands.

ROSLYN   I said to Sheldon, are you nervous?

"No, not really," he told me.

I didn't believe him. "*I* am," I said.

"I'm not," he countered. "Really. I just want the ceremony to be over."

The music was playing. And as I watched our family, our daughters, their children, my mother, and Mitchell all take their turns going down the aisle, passing all our family, our friends, I had a strange sensation.

Defiance. Laced with a twinge of pride. *We've done it,* I thought. *In spite of all your petty cruelties, the thoughtless snubs. And I'm so proud. Proud of myself. Proud of my son. Proud of my husband. And proud of my family that we would do this. So many of you out here tonight said, "This shouldn't be." And here it is. Whether you like it or not.*

And it felt great.

ANDREW   Ready to go. As I stood between my parents, the meaning of it all hit me full force. My mother grabbed my hand tightly, then my father and I joined hands. It was a powerful kind of togetherness. Stepping slowly together down the aisle . . . *This is so weird . . . After all this struggle, here we are, standing together. In front of everyone.* And when they released my hands and let me ascend the stairs by myself to join Doug, I stepped up quickly to be beside him, to bask in that moment together with him.

We did it, I said to myself. *We did it!*

And as the music stopped, I took Doug's hand in mine.

He looked shocked. He certainly never expected it. Neither did I. But I was so emotional walking down the aisle, I wanted to experience this with him as close as we possibly could be. We were so connected in that moment. I needed to connect physically, to sense him feeling the same thing, hand in hand, together.

ROSLYN   As Sheldon and I took our place under the *chuppah*, to the right side, I looked back over the room. We'd climbed to the mountaintop. We could share that instant, all of us. With the stunning view back down the steep slope came a new clarity. And with it, the rush, the dizziness of breathing in thin air. You can't live in a moment like that for long. But what a moment it was.

DOUG   Still settling in after the surprise of feeling Andrew's touch, I gazed down to see the evidence, his fingers wrapped around mine. As I looked back up at Rabbi Bolton, she began:

Welcome to this holy moment, this sanctuary in time and space. In this time and place, we are gathered to celebrate a union, a match of souls, the moment when Andrew and Doug publicly declare their love for each other. Though this full and precise a gathering may never again take place with all of you, friends, family, witnesses, chuppah holders, you will perpetually be a presence in their lives. May you always bear with you the blessings of this moment and this joyous celebration. This moment, although unique in its particularity, also represents the power and potential of the Jewish tradition.

Like all Jewish weddings, it takes place under a chuppah, *a canopy. And for their* chuppah *Andrew and Doug chose a tallith, a fringed prayer garment important not so much for the color or design but for the knotted fringes. The* chuppah *itself is open on four sides, and supported by friends. The tallith, with its fringed edges and corners, shows us a blurring of boundaries, soft edges, a smooth transition from garment into space. It's a model for Andrew and Doug's partnership and this ceremony: Centered. A little bit on the edge. Solid. Yet . . . fringy. Bordered. Yet open. We cherish this moment when two individuals and two families are brought together.*

Then she instructed us to taste from the first of two cups of wine that we would drink during the ceremony. This cup would be, as she called it,

. . . a cup of promise and hope. It is a transformed substance. And what happens after the wine is blessed and drunk makes this space and time different than the moment before.

Next it came time to read the vows we each had written and kept secret from each other, until this moment.

ANDREW I was choked up as I took in the meaning of the words I was saying to Doug, and thinking, as I spoke, *What a wonderful moment. Try and remember this feeling:*

From this day forward, I, Andrew, promise to envelop you with the warmth of my heart as you struggle to conquer life's challenges.

I will always be by your side, with never-ending support and encouragement, patience and understanding. I vow to be faithful and to never leave your side in sickness or in health.

You are the dearest and most special person in my life. And I will always love you.

DOUG   As I listened, I thought . . . *How strange. How disorienting. Hearing such a pure expression of love in front of a throng of onlookers.* At the same time, this was a unique intimacy. When Andrew finished, the soft glow in his eyes invited me to let loose the stream of tears I was a hairsbreadth from unleashing. I held on. I know exactly how unattractive I look when I blubber. I gathered up a last scrap of calm, and spoke to Andrew, haltingly, barely maintaining my equilibrium.

> *I, Douglas, vow to share my heart with you, my mind and my soul, to listen, to hear, to hold you, to care for you in times of need.*
> *To love you sweetly, fondly, dearly.*
> *To try to keep the kitchen sink clean.*
> *And to cherish every silly loving rhyme you make up for me.*
> *I will be your confidant, your cheerleader, your partner, lover, friend.*
> *Your home.*

ANDREW   *How moving—and how funny,* I thought. Especially because no one knew that I almost included one extra vow: . . . *And I'll try not to complain when you don't clean the kitchen sink.*

But I couldn't do it. Not because it wouldn't be fitting. Because I couldn't give him that escape clause in front of all these witnesses!

Next it was time to read the *ketubah.*

Only one problem. *No ketubah.*

We'd produced this event meticulously, as if it were a movie, yet somehow none of us ever figured out that the *ketubah* had to get from the room where it had been signed to under the *chuppah.* Lucky thing our rabbi is good on her feet. She cued Shelley to bring her the document, and in the meantime, she covered:

> *Andrew, Doug, I have something very important to tell you. In all our meetings and meals together and discussions, I neglected to tell you: Surprise! You don't really need a rabbi to get married. The*

Mishnah says you need three things. And those have become trans-
lated into: witnesses, vows with an exchange of rings, and the signing
of a ketubah. But you sought out a rabbi to say this is a wedding.
We want a chuppah and we want to ground it, root it with the
resonance of Jewish meaning, Jewish history. It means we want to
underscore both how very special and how very ordinary this mo-
ment is.

. . . Andrew, when I asked you what was special for you about
Doug, you said he's generous, warm, kind, loving, and sensitive. And
also the subject of some silly rhymes. Doug, you talked about your
shared love of culture, and the comfort you get from Andrew, and
your shared love of talk shows.

DOUG   *Thank God the crowd is laughing,* I thought. If they thought
we were serious when we said it to her all those months ago, I'd
crawl right under the rabbi and die.

After the *ketubah* was located and rushed to the *chuppah* and the
rabbi read it for the gathering, our friends came forward to a microphone placed next to the *chuppah* and recited the seven blessings in
English. Rabbi Bolton sang each in Hebrew. Then she read a special
"eighth blessing" which she had brought to our attention months before.
This was as overtly political as the ceremony was likely to get:

Blessed are you, Adonai, our God, source of life, Who enables
us to strive for the devotion of Jonathan and David, the honor of
Ruth and Naomi. May the time soon come when the voices of all
lovers, the music of all friendships, rise up and be heard and be
celebrated in the gates of all our cities, and may we all soon drink
from a full cup of joy. Blessed are You, source of love.

Now it was time for Geri to do her stuff. For the first time, I
worried what someone would think of the ceremony. Would Sheldon
approve? I didn't lack faith in Geri, but I grew anxious because
the decision whether to have the speech had come under so much

consternation. And it occurred to me in that moment that I hadn't the faintest clue what she was going to say.

She set up the speech around a series of talk-show promo parodies, in honor of my daytime television experience. She said, in part:

> *George Bernard Shaw said, "There is no subject on which more dangerous nonsense is talked and thought than marriage."*
>
> *Author Ellen Key wrote in 1911, "Love is moral even without legal marriage, but marriage is immoral without love."*
>
> *And in 1969 John Lennon observed, "We've got this gift of love, but love is like a precious plant. You can't just accept it and leave it in the cupboard. You've got to keep watering it. You've got to really look after it and nurture it."*
>
> *But where do you put it? Planter boxes, greenhouse windows, and wainscoting are the hot topics Wednesday on* This Old Condo, *with Merling and Wythe. Then, on* Douglas and Andrew, *"I MARRIED A FOREIGNER—Men Who Cross the Line for Love!" One's Canadian, one's American! The Expos versus the Dodgers! Mounties versus the L.A.P.D. "Like, totally" versus "What's it aboot, eh?" Can it work? Find out Thursday!*

She closed with a parody of Kahlil Gibran's oft-quoted *The Prophet*, which read, in part:

> *Attend together the Broadway show, but do not hum the identical tune.*
>
> *Give your hearts, but not into each other's keeping. For they may be put somewhere you can't find them, or accidentally go through the wash.*
>
> *Stand together, yet not too near together; for the pillars of the temple stand apart. And the palm tree and the maple grow not in each other's shadow.*

As she finished, I was brimming with tears. And pride. Pride in Geri's accomplishment of meeting a tough challenge with wit and warmth. And pride that I could return the privilege she'd given me four years earlier. Speaking at her wedding was one of the greatest honors of my life. Now I could only hope that her marvelous speech was as meaningful for her as it was for me.

ANDREW   The audience response was clear: she had been a hit.

Next, the rabbi, back at the helm, cued Doug and me to give each other the second cup to drink. Once we each sipped, she said,

> *It's been a privilege and a blessing to stand here before you. As of now, what was before will have been changed, through your willing it, and through your love for each other. I'm going to give you one final blessing before you break the glasses. This is the blessing of the Davka, from an eighth-century ritual, recited before two men, in another time and place, invoking God's blessing:*
>
> *"For peace we beseech You, O God. For the peace of the entire world, we beseech You. For this holy place, we beseech You, O God. That these servants Andrew and Douglas be showered with Your spiritual benediction, that they be granted all that they need the rest of their lives."*
>
> *Andrew and Doug, may you remain nourished by all of the roots beneath you, and sheltered eternally by the power and broche of this chuppah.*

She indicated that it was time to step on the glasses that had been placed on the floor wrapped in cloth napkins. Some Jewish couples step on lightbulbs because they're easier to break and make a more dramatic *pop!* But we wanted the real thing.

So here goes—

We both stomped down with gusto, but I needed a second try to finish the job. And with this last smash, we drew close together for a sweet, brief kiss and threw our arms around each other, in an embrace I can only call the deepest union. For a moment, we were truly one in our love, in our purpose, and our accomplishment.

Standing at the center of this enormous gathering, for that endless instant we were totally alone. I never wanted to let go.

ROSLYN   On the left side of the room, where the younger people sat, the clapping began. On the other side, the older friends and family were sitting stock-still. After a few seconds, a smattering of applause could be heard among them. As Sheldon and I walked back down the aisle, we saw heads turn as couples murmured, conferring some as-yet-undelivered judgment. Sheldon and I waited out of sight behind a divider, where we'd sectioned off the room for the dinner tables. Once all the guests had retreated into the lobby for cocktails, we made our move to face them. Although the response during the ceremony was warm, it was also tempered. As if half the audience was waiting for the other shoe to drop. Now it was over, and after all the months of hostile remarks and furrowed brows, we would get to hear what they thought. We opened the swinging door, and the crowd that stood nearby turned and descended on us.

CHAPTER 12

Quite a Reception

September 1, 1996

SHELDON In the swarm of guests reaching to shake our hands, embrace us, one friend said, "I'm proud to call you my friend." Even now, when I remember the kind tributes, I still get emotional. Some were congratulatory, others were sympathetic, saying, "We're proud you were able to go through it," and "We know how tough it was for you." Gay couples and singles came up and said things like, "I only wish my parents could be here to see this. It would have made it so much easier for us." As wonderful as all this praise and gratitude felt, it also taught me something. At most weddings, the attention is on the couple getting married, particularly the bride, maybe because of the trappings, the gown, etc. The parents are far in the background. There's no spotlight on them. Now I realized that Roslyn and I were sharing the focus with Andrew and Doug. As far as our friends were concerned, anyway.

DOUG   Andrew and I had planned to share a few moments of privacy after the ceremony, back in the storage room where we had signed the *ketubah*. Bonnie had set up a breast-feeding station back there for Eden, her four-month-old, so our seclusion consisted, more or less, of a quick kiss and "How ya feeling?" Then we opened the doors from the main hall into the lobby where cocktails were being served. It was a Fellini-esque fish-eye-lens view of the world. Face after distorted face pressed in for a kiss, hug, or handshake. The first dozen to press our flesh were friends of Roslyn and Sheldon. After each one offered sincere congratulations and hearty well-wishes, I said something like, "I'm so glad you could be here," *and actually meant it*. I knew much of what Roslyn had suffered, but every face I saw was beaming, and all the dissension, quarrels, and controversy seemed aeons away.

Incredibly, it took nearly an hour for us to travel the seven or eight feet to the bar, with the crush of the crowd, all the smooching and backslapping. I floated through that hour.

ROSLYN   Andrew and Doug had asked their best men to offer toasts that would close out the cocktails and announce the beginning of dinner. Lorne offered a few quick words which seemed surprisingly off the cuff. (We learned later that he'd written a speech in the style of a roast, but decided to scrap it after he saw the tone wasn't right for the event.) Then George stepped up to make his toast to the couple of honor. And as George spoke just the first few words, it was clear he had captured the aura of the evening, and spoke a blessing from the heart. And the tears he barely held back, I shed for him.

I have a lot of wishes for their relationship. The service was so beautiful and so moving. And they all spoke many of the things that I've been feeling. In my family my grandmother spoke a great deal about cherishing. It's a very big word in our family. And tonight, Doug, Andrew, I say to you that anytime two people fall in love and have the courage to stake out a little strip of territory and make a home together, it is something to be cherished.

May being together multiply life's joys and minimize life's obstacles. May you always remember a dream we all wish for has enfolded you. Protect that, cherish each other. May there always be a little patience. You have never been closer together. May you never be farther apart. I wish you a lifetime of joy. Mazel tov.

DOUG   As the crowd applauded, I rushed up to throw my arms around him. I'd barely held back tears during the ceremony, determined not to blubber in front of everybody. But damned if George didn't turn my waterworks on full force. Andrew rushed up too, and we all embraced. Once I had my composure back, I reminded him of his one remaining duty.

"Now," George called out, "the most important thing I have to say this evening: ladies and gentlemen, dinner is served!"

Once everyone else was inside, those of us at the head table had a moment to settle in. Then I heard Louie announce the head table's arrival, and the band started the hora. It was Andrew's idea to have us enter and go right into the hora. Traditionally the family enters first, and the couple of honor have a first dance, which may be followed by a hora. Or the hora might come much later.

Having the hora right at the top, it turned out, was ideal. Usually it starts out with ten or twenty people, then widens to include more. But this night a huge crowd rushed the dance floor. The hall was instantly transformed into a kaleidoscope of kinetic energy, hands clapping, bodies whirling and turning in concentric chains that trapped the intensity and kicked it up to some exponential power.

ANDREW   Everything was moving at lightning speed when somebody brought out the chairs. And before we knew it, we were hoisted up, bouncing in midair. Or should I say, I was bouncing, and Doug was flailing.

DOUG   Whoever was holding the front of my chair wasn't pushing as high as the people in back, so I was tipped on a steep downhill slope. Andrew held the napkin in his hand, and was waving for me to grab the other end, but I clutched it for just a second before I went down with my chair. Everyone was laughing, and though I was mortified, I knew the sight of my goggle-eyed fright just a few feet in the air was pretty funny. In an instant we were back in a chair, kicking like crazy. Then, one by one, Roslyn and Sheldon were pulled out in the middle, and it was their turn to bob four feet off the dance floor. After my rapid dethroning, I was both impressed and depressed over how long they stayed aloft.

ROSLYN   The hora was the perfect antidote. It was an outlet for the incredible tension that had built up prior to and during the ceremony. It was also an outpouring of joy and support for the family and for the couple. Suddenly a movement began to take place and it seemed as though all of Andrew and Doug's friends had embraced a mission, to get Sheldon and me on chairs and hold us aloft, a tradition I thought was reserved for the newlywed couple.

While I was precariously perched on that chair above the crowd, I was sure that either one of us or both would end up sliding off. I was shrieking, my mouth so wide open that I was sure my tonsils were on display for all to see. At the time I believed the terror was just about falling off the chair. In retrospect, I realize it was in part because everything at this point in the evening had gone so well that I was concerned about the high that had been reached. I wanted to remain at this level, supported at last. Could this exhilarating moment be sustained?

DOUG   We all cheered as if Sheldon, then Roslyn, had been shot into space, and when they returned to earth, the hora broke into the usual subcircles so everyone could dance with their nearest and dearest. In a jubilant blur we joined hands, leapt, bobbed, and swirled. Every couple must feel enveloped by love at their own wedding. But it was so profoundly moving for me, having always felt such an outsider, to find myself invited—at long last—to the inside of the circle, at the center of this uproarious celebration. As the tempo shifted into high gear, signaling the end of the song was near, Andrew and I clasped hands and whirled in a dizzying ring, my feet toe to toe with his, our bodies leaning back and the centrifugal force of all our weight linked in our fingertips. With the music hitting a breakneck pace, we spun like children, without a thought in the world but the music and each other. As the band played its last ecstatic notes, we slowed back down at last, and had one more deep, long embrace.

This embrace, this instant, this place with these people, is the single happiest moment of my life.

ANDREW   As we stumbled to the head table, I stopped and hugged Doug again. Filled with the love I felt in the room, all the support and enthusiasm, I told Doug, "We should have had a first dance after all."

It was hard to believe that only a few days ago, when I first arrived in Montreal, I was still fighting my own discomfort over the photo shoot, and even aspects of the wedding itself. Doug smiled up at me, and I told him again, as I stopped to give him one more hug, "I would have loved to have a first dance with you tonight."

ROSLYN   Friends came up after the hora, "It's so funny—you know what I just realized? I didn't even miss the bride." And neither did I. For at that moment the image I'd carried with me so long of that woman at the other end of the procession had finally been put to rest. I was confronted with the happiness and joy of Andrew and Doug. At that moment and forever after I knew it was right, and gender lines were simply obliterated.

DOUG   Louie took the podium to introduce Sheldon's Uncle Rudolph, who rose slowly, took a long knife in his hand, and ever so carefully cut the bread and said the prayer that traditionally accompanies the ritual. Suddenly my objection to his being at the head table seemed awfully petty. This task accomplished, Louie introduced my sister, Lynn, who read a brief letter from my parents:

> *Because we are unable to make the trip to Montreal, we have asked our daughter, Lynn, to speak for us, as proud parents of our son, Douglas Alan. While it would have afforded us a wonderful opportunity to meet with Andrew's family and friends, we regret that health concerns prevented us from attending these festivities. Estelle and I take great joy and pleasure in this day and have asked our daughter, Lynn, and granddaughter, Michelle, to let everyone in attendance on this special day know that we are with them in our hearts and in spirit. Mazel tov to Andrew and Douglas, and shalom to all, Fred and Estelle Wythe.*

ROSLYN Louie took the podium once again and introduced the next speaker, my husband. "The prime minister is coming, Elizabeth Taylor is on her way, Ross Perot's plane is late. But in the meantime, I want to introduce the man I happen to call my favorite Canadian, Sheldon Merling."

SHELDON As Louie introduced me, I could almost feel in the air all the tension that had built up over the question: *What's this guy going to say? What words is he going to use? Is he going to gloss over it, is he going to express platitudes that could apply to any situation, like "Thank you very much, I hope you had a good time"? Or is he going to give a political speech?* I began:

> *Rabbi Bolton, Family, and Friends,*
>
>   *On behalf of both the Merling and Wythe familes, I welcome you to this unique celebration.*
>
>   *We have just experienced a "first" for most of us—which, I hope, has been both meaningful and rewarding.*
>
>   *My son-in-law David has suggested that this experience is like*

an examination. *You worry about it for many months, you work on it, study and prepare for the big event—and then, suddenly, it's all over in about four hours. I think I will elaborate and expand on that thought. True, it is an exam in one sense; that is,* a test, *which we all hope to pass. But it is much more than that. Like an exam, it is not only a* test, *but a* learning experience. *Personally I have learnt many things along the route culminating with tonight. I should like to comment on two of them.*

Firstly, I have learnt that it is right and proper that two individuals with a strong bond of love and affection for each other should be allowed to enjoy all of life's beautiful experiences, freely and openly with their family and friends. We value the relationship of Andrew and Doug—two wonderful people whom we love dearly—and we would never want to suppress this.

ANDREW Applause broke out in the hall. And while Doug's waterworks were going full force once again, I was dry-eyed, smiling a huge, appreciative grin. My father's words, spoken in a measured, thoughtful cadence, felt like a gift he was giving to me, to Doug, to my mother, to everybody who'd worked so hard to make this happen. Yet it was much more than that, too. Until this moment, I had seen the evening as a celebration of my union with Doug. And that was all. But those last few words took this event, this experience, to another level. The impact he made was enormous. This wasn't just about us anymore. Now everyone, including me, could see the broader importance of what we had all achieved, as a family.

DOUG This pillar of the status quo, a kind, generous, and conservative man who never met a boat he wanted to rock, had taken a public stand on the side of the revolutionaries. Certainly he'd never see it that way. But what else can I call it, when Sheldon said, in effect, these men are gay, and they deserve the same as anyone else, the right to experience all of life's joys—*"freely and openly"*? Sheldon had, whether he knew it or not, taken a profoundly political point of view.

And the room burst into applause. What greater wedding gift could we have asked for?

Once the applause subsided, he went on:

SHELDON *And so, tonight, we wish Doug and Andrew a lenghty, healthy, and happy life together with many more celebrations to follow.*

Secondly, I have learnt through this test or exam that my concern and hesitation were not well founded. That there was much more love and support out there than I could have ever imagined.

Beginning with my wife, Roslyn—who perhaps began this journey at a different starting point than myself—whose counseling, understanding, and patience, and above all, her love for Andrew, Doug, and myself, have allowed me to catch up to her and be addressing you this evening.

To my family—Mitchell, Debbie and Abraham, Bonnie and David, and even my grandchildren, all of whom, when it was time to be counted, were there to support us.

A special sense of gratitude to my dear mother-in-law, Grandma Esther Briskin—from another generation, but well ahead of most of us—whose immediate acceptance of the reality was very positive and most meaningful . . .

I have had many "heroes" or people that I have admired and respected over the years. They have changed and evolved over time. They may have started with comic-book characters in my youth (remember, there was no television then), progressed to people in sports during my adolescent years (such as Maurice Richard, Jackie Robinson, etc.), but today I have a clearer picture of the people I truly respect and appreciate—my "heros of today," if you like.

I am referring to you, my friends—*not compelled to be here, with plenty of available excuses, Labor Day weekend, etc.—not related or obliged to attend and with my full awareness that if* we *had some worry and concern for the unknown, certainly they must have existed in your minds as well. But despite all of this, and the accepted rule of* thumb to expect that approximately ten percent of invited guests will be absent, we are batting almost a thousand tonight.

Andrew, Doug, Roslyn, and myself receive this outpouring of your love and support with great humility and appreciation and consider it as a tribute to us, and we are greatly honored by your presence.

Once again, we wish Doug and Andrew a hearty mazel tov and tell them that they are amongst true friends. So let us party and celebrate for the rest of the evening.

To conclude—from the bottom of my heart—I thank you most sincerely.

ANDREW   At that, every person in the hall rose up as one body and stood, applauding my father for his courage and his honesty.

I wasn't surprised that my father directed much of his admiration to other people in the room, and their ultimate support. Yet when he spoke to them, I sensed he was also trying to talk to us as a family, to me, to Doug, and to my mother. As if he were saying, I *didn't have to be here. I could have been somewhere else. I didn't have to be supportive and loving, but I'm here tonight, doing this for you.*

DOUG   As Sheldon walked behind the dais to take his seat, I threw my arms around him and said into his ear, over the still thundering applause, "That was the greatest speech I ever heard." And it was.

SHELDON   I think the reaction to the speech was not so much because of any great words or inspiring message. I was only telling the truth the way it was. And the audience was heaving a sigh of relief, almost. Their applause said, *He's facing it. He's going to make it through the evening. It's going to be OK.* Now they knew nobody was going to collapse and break down in tears. So they could all relax and have a good time.

I had done just what I set out to do. Not to ignore the reality of how different this event was and not to give a political speech, either. I just faced the situation honestly, without taking a stand.

ROSLYN   How interesting that Sheldon still believes he hadn't taken a stand. How much more of a stand could anyone take? His stand was related to many facets of the process, both familial and societal. Firstly, he had become 100 percent supportive in terms of both money and paternal approval. Then he let the world know he'd done it because it was the right thing to do. His message came out strong and clear, though unspoken: *My friends, I put aside my fear of what you would think of my support for gay marriage. I followed my heart.*

ANDREW   A very different set of expectations surrounded my mother's speech. No one had sweaty palms waiting to see if she'd survived the evening. If anything, they just expected her to make us laugh and cry a little. And she did both, rising to the occasion with stories that gave me the roasting I hadn't gotten on Friday night. Toward the end, she turned her attention elsewhere:

> *There is someone sitting here tonight who deserves honorable mention. That is my mom, fondly referred to by her great-grandkids as Grandma Esther. We are truly blessed to have you here tonight. You are so special. You have always been there for all of us. You are so loving and accepting.*
>
> *Now I want to pay tribute to my best friend and wonderful husband, Sheldon. I love you with all my heart. I respect you highly for the wonderful person that you are. You are fair, open-minded, and loving.*
>
> *You are a special person and I feel blessed to be your partner in life.*
>
> *Thank all of you here for sharing in our joy.*

Then my old friend Diane gave a short speech that started with a perfectly ironic anecdote:

> *Most of you think this is Andrew's first wedding. Fourteen years ago he was my groom, and I was his bride, at my masquerade sweet*

sixteen party. Since then we've both gone through many boyfriends. But who thought he'd be the first one to get married?

Once Diane wrapped up, it was time for her big song.

DOUG The way we'd rehearsed it, Diane and I were dedicating the song together, to Andrew. But when she got the microphone in her hand, she said, "This is for my dear friends, Andrew and Doug." It may seem like a tiny, perhaps subconscious gesture, but to me it was dear.

Once our song was over, the band jumped back in and played the tune that signals a conga line is about to be formed. Before you can say Carmen Miranda, a dozen people were behind me, gyrating frantically to a Latin beat. I'd just been in the spotlight during "Your Song," and I didn't want to be in front again, so I grabbed the first person I could get my hands on and thrust her ahead of me in the lead spot. She's not the type to jump in front of a writhing conga line, and though all her friends know she's a lesbian who had lived with her partner for years, she and her family had been complicit in the "don't ask, don't tell" game. Later on, when I realized the implications of what I'd done, I recognized her deer-in-the-headlights look may not have been about garden variety shyness. For all any of us knew, that conga line could have ended up on *Turning Point*, with my friend wiggling away in the starting position, like "Hey, Mom, I'm not just a lesbian, but I play one on national TV!"

ANDREW When the conga was over, we kept on dancing till we were sopping wet. Doug, in particular, was all over the dance floor. We even danced when the band played "YMCA," even though we'd specifically told them, NO VILLAGE PEOPLE. I guess they couldn't resist the temptation to play the painfully obvious. When the band took a break, I went out to the lobby, where cocktails had been held. My Uncle Gary was hanging out with a few other people, and he came over to shake my hand.

"Andrew, I'm an ultraconservative right-wing dinosaur. I came here with great fear and trepidation, feeling very negative. I thought, why is my nephew being such a spoiled brat, and putting on such a party for himself, and shoving it in everybody's face? Now I'm going home feeling wonderful that I was here. Now that I've seen how much you two love each other, I have to say, why shouldn't you celebrate this and have everybody participate in it? I've learned a lot tonight, and I'm delighted I came. And I wish you both a very happy life together."

DOUG   Andrew tapped me on the shoulder and repeated his uncle Gary's startling about-face. Then he reminded me we'd planned to call my parents. We went into the hallway and piled into the tiny wooden phone booth. By the time we got them on the phone, Roslyn stopped by. We went for the Eaton's record, three in a booth, while Roslyn told my parents not only what they'd missed, but how much we'd missed them.

ROSLYN   Soon after, the video crew asked Sheldon and me to say a few words for the camera. It was hard to know who our words were intended for, Andrew and Doug and their wedding tape, or *Turning Point* and a national audience. At first it sounded like Sheldon was speaking more privately: "It was beyond our wildest expectations. We feel very, very good inside that the evening was so successful." Then it was clear he was talking to a wider group: "And I'm sure we'll be seeing more celebrations of this nature in the future." That was the broadest statement yet from my husband. I kept my comments short and sweet. "This whole weekend has been absolutely magical. I've enjoyed every single minute. I don't want it to end!"

And in a few minutes my mother paid her on-camera regards as well: "My dear Andrew and Doug, I was very happy to attend your beautiful affair. And when I look at you both, I know you're going to be happy together. I am very happy to see you with that kind of a look. Because—" she paused, wistfully, her eyes welling up "—it makes me feel . . . very, very good. I want to wish you both a long and happy life together. With lots of love, Grandma."

DOUG Andrew and I went back to the dance floor for what must have been half an hour. Eventually we peeled ourselves away and headed for the north end of the room, where we'd said our vows just six hours before and the sweet table had just been laid out. We stopped for a picture, embracing, drenched and overjoyed.

Standing on the spot where the glasses had been crushed beneath our feet, we looked down together on this magical scene, the rich colors, the spiral centerpieces shedding their glow, tiny dots of flame scattered in midair, the sound of laughter syncopating amid the beat of disco tunes, all reverberating in the majestic hall. It's the moment I'll remember most vividly: the raw, fresh hope of beginning. The hall was filled with forty- and fifty-something couples dancing gleefully together with gay couples in the same room that only hours before had been rife with fear.

ANDREW A little after midnight, when people were starting to leave, we gathered all our friends out in the lobby for one huge group picture. The next generation. The people who had come here with less baggage than my parents' crowd. But most of us, I think, myself included, left a few of our bags behind there that night, too.

ROSLYN It was well after midnight when I lay down in bed next to Sheldon and said, "You know, we've done a good job."

"It went well," he answered. "And I'm amazed by the support, the outpouring of love. I knew it was going to be all right, but I didn't expect this kind of reaction, the depth of it, or the acceptance."

As for myself, I was particularly surprised by the friends who'd given me so much trouble, and hurt us all in the process. They'd been so effusive in their praise tonight. Every one of them had come, saw something new, and applauded us for how it turned out.

It was a total metamorphosis. Really, it was unbelievable.

ANDREW   Back in the hotel, we headed for the action in Debbie and Louie's room. Louie was off painting the town thirteen shades of red, but Debbie was hanging out with Geri and Steve, George, Nancy, and Bennett.

After we drank a few toasts, Geri asked, "And what was with Sandra and the video? Whenever your cameraman came anywhere close, she hid like a vampire with a cross stuck in its face."

Enrique had been asking our friends and family if they would say a few words for the wedding video. Sandra's a mutual friend of ours and Louie's, and she could be described in personals-speak as "straight but curious." Apparently she'd gotten an earful on the subject of *Turning Point*.

"I asked her what the problem was, and she said, 'The camera steals your soul.'"

"I thought she was a TV executive, not a medicine woman," Doug cracked.

I told everyone what had happened with my Uncle Gary.

"What did you say when he told you that?" Debbie asked me.

I quoted myself verbatim: "Could you say that again on camera?" Everybody gathered in the hotel room laughed. "No, really, that's what I asked him. And he agreed. No problem. I ran and got the crew, and he was terrific." I knew his speech would go into our wedding video, but I wondered if they would use it in the show.

"Oh my God," Debbie gasped. "Speaking of cameras, can you believe what Terry said?"

Apparently Doug and I were the only ones in the dark, because everyone else laughed. We looked to Debbie for answers.

"Oh, you guys missed some of the best stuff!" Debbie explained. "Your cameraman asked her if she'd say a few words, and she says, 'Sure!' She obviously had a lot to drink—I know, I'm one to talk tonight—but anyway, when the camera's rolling, and Lauren's standing right next to her, she says, 'This is so wonderful, and it's such an eye-opener for straight people, and this just shows why it's so important that everyone come out.' And that's why she's 'thrilled' she can be here with her 'girlfriend.' Well, Lauren just stood there with her jaw down around her knees. You could read her mind: 'Oh my God, you just outed both of us on national television. We're going to have to call our parents before this airs. Somebody beam me out of here.' Anyway, Terry was brilliant. It was a really heartfelt speech, but I wonder if she'll remember any of it tomorrow. I wouldn't want to be the one to break it to her."

"But what she said was so right," Steve added. "A night like this shows exactly why it's so important that people come out. Because it *does* create change."

George broke in, "Oh, God, don't you just love sensitive straight men!" As we all laughed, he lifted a glass. "To Steve and Bennett, the coolest straight men in the house tonight!"

Oh, that George, any excuse for a toast. He was right, though. There's nothing cooler than a straight guy who's secure enough with his own sexuality that he's not threatened by gay men.

DOUG   We did a little more catty gossiping, laughed and drank, until Andrew and I went back to our room around two in the morning. Totally drained, and light as air, we kicked off our shoes and slid out of our jackets. It was the first quiet moment we'd shared since we'd gone downstairs for breakfast sixteen hours before. As I struggled to unhook my suspenders, I saw Andrew staring dumbfounded at the tuxedo jacket he'd just taken off.

"Let me see your jacket," Andrew ordered, intensely. I handed mine to him, and he thrust toward me the jacket he'd been wearing. "Put this on."

After all the treacherous hairpin curves we'd negotiated in the year and a half since we announced our engagement, now, as we stood in our hotel room at two in the morning exchanging jackets, we finally discovered the great hidden hazard of same-sex marriage. Andrew's six foot four. I'm five foot ten. Clothes that fit him hang on me like drapes. And clothes that fit me are snug as spandex on him.

And yet somehow we'd managed to wear each other's jackets all night long.

AFTERWORD

DOUG At just seven days, our honeymoon was more like a minimoon, or maybe a half-moon, but who's counting? Since we were starting our trip in San Francisco, we'd arranged to join Geri and Steve on their flight home. And though Andrew had upgraded his seat to business class, I didn't have enough frequent-flier miles to do the same. So Andrew, the amateur travel agent, had a plan. On the first leg of the trip, the quick flight from Montreal to Toronto, I sat with Geri and Steve. Then, in Toronto, Andrew played the honeymoon trump card. As Geri, Steve, and I sat in the departure lounge, we watched Andrew approach the flight attendant working the desk. Geri turned to me and asked, "Where's your husband going?" I did a slow take, and cocked my head back at Geri as if to say, "My *what*?" The words had an unfamiliar, odd, yet cozy sound, and I knew I'd warm to them.

Andrew likes to work alone, but I wanted to hear how he'd handle this, so I snuck up to the desk.

ANDREW   I told the gate agent, "I'm on my honeymoon, but we're not sitting in the same section. I'm in business class. Can we get one upgrade so we can sit together?"

Aghast, she exclaimed, "That's awful! Where's your wife?"

"Ummmmm . . . he's right over there," I laughed, and pointed to Doug, who was walking toward us.

She looked over to Doug, then back to me, and winced.

"Well, that's even worse!" she cried, then clacked away at the keyboard. "Let's see what we can do about this . . ." In a minute she looked up, self-satisfied, and extended the new boarding pass to Doug. "Here you go." Then, reprovingly tongue in cheek, she glared over her glasses at me. "How *could* you?"

DOUG   Maybe we've just been lucky, yet I can hardly recall a single hotel clerk, on any trip we've taken, looking at us askance when we asked for one king-size bed. Thankfully our honeymoon was no exception.

Midway through the week, I rang Wendy Roth at *Turning Point*. When I left for the wedding, there were a few loose ends at work, and I needed to know what to be prepared for when I returned.

"Wendy Roth."

"It's Doug calling, from Santa Barbara."

"Hey! You should know, we all want your wedding."

"*What?*"

"It looks fabulous."

"You've *seeeeen* it?"

"*Yeeees*. It's terrific! Your wedding videographer sent us the tapes. We dubbed them and shipped them back."

Dumbstruck by my own naïveté, all I could do was laugh. Wendy and I talked briefly about work, she wished us a great rest of our trip, and we signed off. I was left to ponder the decidedly unromantic frieze: a dozen people huddled around a monitor in the office, the first audience for our wedding video.

ROSLYN   Sheldon and I had our own honeymoon. Not that we went anywhere. This was one dividend I never expected could come from the wedding. I'd grown closer to my husband than ever before. We were stronger as a couple, having survived the struggle, and had learned more about each other than we'd ever known. I discovered a side of Sheldon that he had never allowed me to see before: his sensitivity, his feelings. It's not that I ever doubted that he had feelings, or that he was sensitive. It's just that prior to seeing our therapist, Dennis, Sheldon had never allowed me to see him as being vulnerable, and now for the first time we were on common ground. We were able to share our hurts and support one another in a manner that felt safe and comfortable. It seemed so natural that I wondered why this special understanding of each other, which we had recently developed, had taken so long to come about . . . forty years to be exact!

DOUG   Early one evening shortly after the honeymoon, Louie dropped in for a visit. Before we went out to the balcony, he set down his usual "New Yorker on the go and I'm goin' with everything I've got" complement of bags and backpacks. Following a brief exchange of "who do you have to sleep with to get some food in this place" pleasantries, he welled up and poured out directly from his soul. After all the months of bearing the sting of Louie's ambivalence about my betrothal to Andrew, I realized I'd never come right out and told him how I felt. Now here he was, displaying a strength I hadn't tapped for him, the capacity to be truly vulnerable. He confided in me the depth of what it meant for him to have attended our wedding. Certainly I was aware that Louie had had a good time, but I hadn't a clue as to the sentiment it had stirred in him. We embraced, and he told me that he had decided to come out to his mother. And it brought the two of us closer together as well. "Thank you again for letting me be a part of your wedding," Louie said as we embraced one more time. Forget for a moment the joy it brought me, the ordeal of getting all of us down the aisle was worth it, if only for the inspiration it brought him.

ANDREW   While we're getting a little emotional, let me point out that in the months between our wedding and the *Turning Point* episode going on the air, I got an unexpected, slow-dawning surprise. I never realized the impact the wedding would have on my feelings toward Doug. That public expression reinforced in my mind the strength of our relationship. And now that we had made this statement before all our friends and family, it intensified the commitment to being together through the rest of our lives. The old subconscious escape clause had to get dropped. Instead, I was forced to say to myself, *You've got to get through the tough times, and get through them quickly, because you're going to be together forever. So why be in pain longer than necessary? Just deal with it.*

It brought our relationship to a whole different level. The ceremony and celebration made us much, much closer. I started asking friends who had tied the knot recently, like Nancy and Bennett, *"Don't you feel the difference now?"* And most friends answered," *Yeah, isn't that strange?"*

ROSLYN The promos for the *Turning Point* show began airing about one week before the show was on. It was at this point that we began to tell a wider group of people that we would be on the program. Most people were flabbergasted, all of them wanted to know how it had come about, and everyone wanted explanations as to why we had finally decided to go ahead with it. Word spread like wildfire. People made comments like, "I knew there were too many video cameras at the wedding . . . I knew it was being recorded by ABC . . ." I tried to explain that this wasn't true, but I don't think the skeptics believed it when I told them that we had refused to allow the ABC cameras and crew to be at the wedding. For the record, both the cameras and crew were our videographer's. It was true, however, that ABC subsidized the cost of the second camera.

Regardless of what they believed about the details, no one, it seemed, was going to miss this episode of *Turning Point*.

DOUG Just a week before the show was set to air, my Aunt Verona passed away. Since I had grown to feel closer to her than any of my extended family, news of her death hit me hard.

It also put me in an awkward position. Aunt Verona's shiva fell just a few days before *Turning Point*'s airdate. Only two months after my wedding, I was seeing the family I'd seen at only two family get-togethers in the past ten years. Both parties, not incidentally, had been in honor of my Uncle George, one for his eightieth birthday, the other celebrating his fiftieth anniversary to my aunt Verona.

Andrew couldn't get out of work, so I attended the shiva alone. Throughout the day, I reconnected with much of the family from whom I'd long felt so distanced. Two of Aunt Verona's last surviving siblings, my Aunts Sylvia and Ruth, were there. I'd only met my aunt Ruth once before, many years ago. For the past several years she's lived in a nursing home on Long Island. My father often spoke of her with a warmth he reserved just for Aunt Sylvia and her. Because she's confined to a wheelchair, I knelt down to introduce myself. "Aunt Ruth, it's Doug Wythe, Fred Wythe's son."

"Where do you live now?" she asked in the salty rasp that oral surgery had branded her with.

"New York."

"How long?"

"Six years," I answered, pleading guilty, though the charges were still pending.

She leveled a lethal stare. And after a beat for dramatic intimidation, she growled, "You're full of crrrrrrrap!"

It's hard to argue with the facts. And it's funny how she managed to let me know, in so few choice words, that I had a hell of a nerve living in New York six years without ever visiting her in Long Beach. After I'd been cut down to size, with only my nervous laugh distinguishing me from a mound of quivering jelly, I moved on to my Aunt Sylvia. Other than my Aunt Verona and Uncle George, my Aunt Sylvia and her family were the people whom I felt most conflicted about not having invited to the wedding. Granted, I'd only seen them a half dozen times in my life, yet that was twice the contact I'd had with almost anyone else in the room.

Now, standing here at Aunt Verona's shiva, I wondered what Miss Manners would say about announcing that your gay wedding would be playing on national television in seventy-two hours, to the very relatives you hadn't invited to your nuptials in the first place. Somehow, I wasn't quite sure this was the appropriate time.

I weighed the options: would I step up and tell them all, boldly, what to expect, or was I going to simply lie back and let fate determine if they'd catch it on the tube by chance?

I snapped back into recline, lay flat down, and let destiny ride roughshod over me.

ANDREW I had my own decisions to make. After the wedding, and the completion of my internship, I was fortunate enough to find a job fairly quickly at a substance-abuse treatment center in Manhattan. As it happened, Denise Schreiner wanted some footage of me at work, and I knew permission from hospital administrators was required. And until now, few of the staff knew about either the wedding, the upcoming program, or even my sexual orientation.

As the *Turning Point* airdate neared (it was scheduled to air the Thursday of election week, November 7), I shared my excitement with some of the treatment-center support staff. Some reacted to my disclosure with genuine surprise, and seemed curious. Others smiled nervously and examined their shoes. It made for some strained conversation, from which I quickly excused myself.

I hoped that once they saw the show, the reactions would improve.

ROSLYN The day that the program was to air, I awoke at 5:30 A.M. I couldn't sleep, so I figured that I might as well plunge into my exercise routine. Today it was especially important to get rid of the tension I was feeling. I was stressed because I didn't know what to expect. We didn't know if we'd like how we came across, or what the general tone would be. We hoped that Andrew and Doug would do us proud and that they would be pleased with us. Simply, I was scared.

SHELDON Would we appear sincere, truly concerned, but also truly supportive parents—or idealistic, self-righteous, self-proclaimed heroes? (God forbid!)

At ten that night we sat down to watch, just the two of us. As the program progressed, I must say that both Roslyn and I were pleased with the presentation (even-handed without preaching or taking sides) and the choice of couples (just as Denise promised, from all categories of the population—older women, younger women, intelligent professionals), all from good, normal, middle-of-the-road families (perhaps with the exception of the one villain—if you saw the show, you know which one I'm referring to—who actually, I think, made a positive contribution by making outlandish remarks and behaving so inappropriately as to show up at her sister's wedding with a card denouncing the proceedings). But frankly, the reason I was so happy about the program was that I felt all of the participants (including Roslyn and myself) came across not as play-acting and giving the answers they thought the interviewer wanted, but as genuine and natural.

ANDREW   Only once did I find fault with the show—and you might say I'm too close to the material—but I wish they had included the moment when the salesman in the Judaica store had said, "I hope you have many happy years together." It was the surprise twist that provided the punch line to the entire encounter. I didn't want it included just for dramatic purposes, but because it showed how unfair all stereotypes are: We pegged him before we walked in the store, without even meeting him. And he proved us dead wrong.

DOUG   When it came to Sheldon's big speech, he appeared calm and self-possessed. Cut to me, blubbering. Cut back to Sheldon finishing the speech to rapturous applause. When he left the podium to take his seat, Denise added an inspired touch. While Andrew and I hugged Sheldon, the audience heard a piece of what must have been Sheldon's earlier interview. The quote was (and it soon became the most misquoted line I've heard since "Play it again, Sam"); "In twenty years from now, we'll look back at this and say, 'What was all the fuss about?'"

SHELDON   As soon as the program was over, we received a call. It was Lona, who catered our wedding, expressing her admiration for us. The conversation lasted two or three minutes, no longer. After it ended, our telephone indicated that we had some messages on the machine. Would you believe *nine* (9!) in number? Remember, it was now after 11:00 P.M. We just let them wait until the next day. I leave early for work every day, about 7:00 A.M. As I pulled out of the garage driveway, a passing jogger whom I knew stopped to tell me how great the show was and how well we came across. Needless to say, after I arrived at my office, the phone started to ring off the hook all day. All the calls were very flattering, some quite revealing (for example, one disclosed having a gay son, one a gay brother, etc., and they all thought this program would help—both their relatives as well as themselves).

DOUG   The next morning, back in the *Turning Point* office, computers were humming. The E-mail flurry had begun.

It goes without saying that the thousands of E-mails were directed to Denise Schriener and the rest of the producers, from executive to associate, and everyone else on the production staff. Yet being in a profiled family and seeing the massive computer file that was building up, it felt like the story we were part of had taken on a life of its own. And America was writing it a collective letter.

A disk of the latest mail was copied off a main computer, and I scrolled through it on my laptop. Of the thousands that would eventually arrive, several hundred were already in the system. I saw only a fraction of those.

I set aside a few key pages and faxed them to Sheldon's office. He and Roslyn could see the response once he went into the office on Monday. I knew Roslyn would be gratified. I hoped Sheldon would be shocked.

When I got home from work there was a message on my machine from Uncle George's son, my cousin Barnet. "I'm here at the house with my dad, and Aunt Sylvia. We saw the show last night. *Mazel tov!* Give us a call."

It turns out another cousin, Barry, was watching television on Thursday morning while he was on the treadmill, and saw a promo for the show. He'd just seen me a couple of days before at Aunt Verona's shiva, so he was pretty sure the image on TV was me. He called Barnet, and they all tuned in that night.

I tried to excuse my way out of how I handled it all, and Barnet seemed understanding. Aunt Sylvia, however, wasn't letting me off the hook. I squirmed while she stuck me with a couple of sharp questions.

A few weeks later, I saw Barnet and his family at their home in Los Angeles, where he told me the story behind the story. "When the show was over, Sylvia turned to my father and said, 'I don't know if I approve . . . and why wasn't I invited?' " It reminded me of the old joke about the two Jewish ladies going out for dinner. One says, "Such terrible food!" and the other answers, "And such small portions!"

Anyway, Barnet then reminded me of a story that put a memorable spin on Aunt Sylvia's response. Her late husband was Greek. A non-Jew. When they married some fifty years ago, it split the family. Everyone had to choose sides. Isn't it funny how the great stories stay the same, and only the players change places? Marriage cleaving a rift through a family has been one of humanity's favorite plot lines since long before *Romeo and Juliet*. By today, the Montagues and the Capulets would have hung up their swords, unless, that is, Juliet was a Julius. And the travails of Bridget and Birney probably wouldn't warrant a sitcom today. So what's next in fifty years? Maybe that's what scares people. We've come so far, it's hard to imagine what the next frontier could possibly be.

Not long after that, I got a call from my Aunt Ruth.

Though her trademark gravel was tougher to make out over the phone, I heard her ask, "So when you come out to see me, you're going to bring your better half? Don't you think it's about time?"

It's tough to answer Aunt Ruth without sounding like a yammering dope by comparison, so I stuck to short statements. "Yep," I answered.

"Loveyabunch," she signed off.

ANDREW The weekend after the show aired, Doug and I were invited to a friend's wedding in Florida. I flew down first on Friday morning, and Doug met me that evening. I picked him up at the curb at the airport, so when we went upstairs in the condo elevator, it was the first time we'd been in public since the show aired. One of the building's countless septuagenarian busybodies got in with us on the ground floor. As the cab rose slowly, she glanced back and forth between me and Doug. When I caught her squinting our way, she looked down. When the elevator stopped at her floor, she stepped out, then turned back, propping the door open with a bony, perilously tanned arm. "Did I see the two of you on television the other night?"

Doug and I gaped at each other, flabbergasted that anyone would recognize us, let alone a little old lady from Miami Beach. "Ummm, yes . . . What did you think?" I genuinely wondered over her response.

She screwed her face up tight, like a Cabbage Patch doll in a vise, composed her thoughts carefully, and looked me squarely in the eye. "The parents they interviewed were yours, right?" I nodded as brightly as possible. Her face uncrinkled, then she deadpanned, "They are *incrrrrrrredible* people." The delivery could have been subtitled, "Wild horses couldn't have dragged me up to that *chuppah*! Either your parents are *meshugge,* or they're the first Jewish saints! *Feh!*"

Then the elevator closed again, and it was just me and Doug. We stared slack-jawed at each other, then laughed out loud. "What the hell was that?"

Just the beginning.

After we dropped off Doug's bags at his parents' apartment in Miami, we took a walk down Ocean Drive. As soon as we hit the main drag, a few Roller Bladers traveling toward us hit their brakes and asked, "Were you the guys on TV the other night? Is this your honeymoon?" We told them the show had been shot two months ago, and one of them said, "Good going! Great job!" and before we knew it, a couple of cars slowed to a creep, and people started

calling out of their windows, "Hey, that was great! Good for you!"
For the rest of the afternoon and evening, wherever we went, shopping, walking, you name it, people stopped us—straight couples, gay
couples, singles, men, women, whatever—to tell us how much they
liked the show, how they admired all of us, and my parents in
particular. It sounds like an ego trip, and in a way it was. But the
thrill wasn't merely in being recognized. The real thrill was in being
recognized for doing something we cared about, sticking with it,
making it happen, and in doing so, making an impression, a dent,
being a part of change.

Time and again gay couples told us they had taped the show
and were going to send it to their families, or watch it together with
them. Time and again we heard how my parents' acceptance and
support was an inspiration. And time and again people would say
things like, "Your parents were so comfortable with the whole
thing!"

Finally we said out loud to each other, "If only it was as easy
as it looked!" Once we spoke the truth to each other, we started
telling people who approached us that our journey was infinitely
more challenging than it appeared on television. The reality of our
ceremony was portrayed on TV, but somehow a truth or two about
the *wedding* got lost along the way.

And I'd like a dollar for every person who asked me what
happened in the end with the *chuppah* salesman.*

DOUG   The wedding was over, long ago. Yet suddenly it wasn't
over. Not anymore. Thanks to *Turning Point*, that climax in our lives
was taking on a new, wider life. And this new wave of response
was having a remarkable effect on all of us.

Though the E-mails were often more dramatic in their content,
meeting affected viewers face-to-face was a stirring, intimate experi-

---

*When ABC reran the program a year later (on Valentine's Day, by the way), they
cut the entire Judaica store segment.

ence. For all my worrying about whether the show would reach people, and if so, with what message, the response I got back loud and clear was that Roslyn and Sheldon had had a choice, and they'd made the right one. And for that, they were heroes.

I couldn't wait to talk about it, and the next morning we called them. "You're big news here! When people stop us to talk about the show, it's like Andrew and I are chopped liver. It's you two they want to meet. What's it been like up there?"

"It's just . . . well, it's all been one incredible experience," Roslyn told me. "The wedding, the show, then all this . . . It's so unbelievable how it's all turned out. It's so gratifying to know we've been a part of this."

"I know what you mean. It's a high, you don't want it to stop."

"You know, I asked Sheldon, 'Isn't it a great feeling, knowing you've affected people like this?' and still he insists, 'That's fine, but I'm not out to change the world.' No, but isn't it great to have made some impact? I should write a book . . . or get a ghost writer!"

How many times have you said, "I oughta write a book!" or suggested it to someone else? This one time it sounded an echoing alarm. And I answered it.

"Well, you know I'm a writer, Roslyn. Maybe we should work on something together." No response. "To keep the feeling going . . . of being a part of something."

Then Roslyn said, in the offhand manner that might signal a perceived lack of seriousness in my intent, "That sounds good." Then she paused, and asked, a little more interested, "How would we do it? Would it be just you and me, or shouldn't it be all four of us?"

"You think Sheldon would do it?"

"He's come this far. Why not?"

Down at the beach, I told Andrew about my conversation with Roslyn. "Would you want to do it?"

"Sure."

"But do you think your mother's right about your father?"

"Maybe. Who would have thought he'd go on national television?"

Andrew and I ruminated together over the events of the last couple of years, and the past few months in particular. "Think about how much of this was hard—not just for your parents, but for us," I said. "You holding hands with me in public, me going into Judaica stores . . . I mean, in the beginning you didn't even want to have the ceremony in front of people . . . Me officially coming out to my parents, starting to deal with my wider family . . ."

ANDREW The topic turned from the personal distance the two of us had traveled to the political boundaries that still confined us: specifically my Canadian citizenship and lack of permanent residency in the United States.

"I'm still considered a temporary resident. And what happens if one day immigration rules change, and I can't live and work in the States? I'd be forced to move back to Canada. And what would you do? Move to Canada with me?" I didn't wait for an answer. "If I was a woman, I'd have a green card, and that would be the end of the discussion. It pisses me off. Maybe I should call LAMBDA and see if they would represent me in this."

"What if it was a test case, with all the publicity?"

"I'd still do it."

DOUG This, from the same man who just four months ago said he didn't want us to be, theoretically anyway, the first gay couple in the *New York Times* announcement section.

ANDREW It's so corny, but I can't think of any better way to say it: I'd begun to think I could make a difference in people's lives. And if challenging my immigration status could help not only me, but others as well, suddenly the concept of being the first seemed an honor, not a burden. With no specific plan of attack, my real growth wasn't in action, but intent. Before, I'd been more concerned about keeping my privacy than making a mark.

No question, this journey has been as liberating and empowering for me as for anybody else. And educational. Much of what I learned came in the form of the E-mails that I read through when we got back from Florida. Once we started thumbing through the stacks of mail Doug printed out from the *Turning Point* disk, there was no stopping.

DOUG   And just to state the obvious, we know the mail that the program generated was aimed at Denise and her crew above all, and to ABC for the courage to present such a groundbreakingly honest depiction of gays, lesbians, and their families. The remainder of the praise was directed toward *all* the families who participated in the program. Since we haven't told the stories of those other families in this book, we've stuck mainly to the E-mails that pertained to our story. But I'm proud to say that my in-laws were singled out for their courage by many respondents.

. . . I am going to save this show and show it to my entire family, who are not dealing with my sexuality well at all. You will be helping so many people in their personal lives. You should be very proud of yourselves, as we all are proud of you. —URBANA, IL

As a gay man, I cried twice during the show. Once when the parents of one of the men said they would walk the aisle with him and once when they did. My parents definitely do not support me and I can only hope that they would send a gift. —INGLESIDE, TX

I stumbled across your program tonite and was moved to tears. I had no idea I had such strong feelings about marriage . . . Now suddenly, I realize how deeply I long for my family to accept me, to support me in such an essential way . . . Thank you for airing this show tonite. You opened up a part of me I didn't know was there. —NEW YORK CITY

This reminds me of what African Americans had to go thru in the 60's. Hopefully, 20 years from now, we will look back and wonder what all the commotion was about . . .

The Queer community is finally getting the media to portray us as the average couple next door instead of some depraved lunatics bent on destroying the world . . . My partner and I have set a tentative date of our own wedding after watching your show . . . —(LOCATION UNKNOWN)

My husband and I have been married for over 10 years. I watched your report last night with interest and with regret. Chuck and I went through the same feelings and emotions that were represented last night in your story. I cried during the ceremonies and laughed at the anxiety that they all had, knowing that it would all be right as soon as the ceremony began. I also cried because my family chose not to attend our marriage. That part still hurts. And will always be there. —MINNEAPOLIS

One quote has summed up what we have been saying since this issue began: "Twenty years from now we'll look back on this and wonder what all the fuss was about." With positive shows like yours, this future will come sooner. —HAWAII

. . . You now have my mother asking my partner and I, on an almost daily basis, about when we will be able to legally marry. She is looking forward to a "real" wedding, as our commitment ceremony was not official enough for her. —NORTHERN ILLINOIS

THANKS FOR SENSITIVE REPORT stop
FATHER WAS RIGHT stop
WILL LAUGH 20 YEARS FROM NOW stop —SAN FRANCISCO

You showed the love that comes thru when people face their fear and simply love each other. What Andrew's parents said was pure love for their son and I thank them for their support . . . —(LOCATION UNKNOWN)

. . . Tears were rolling down my face throughout the hour . . . I've been wondering why I found it so touching. I think it was the triumph of love over the prejudice and misunderstanding those individuals must have endured for much of their lives. —VANCOUVER, BC

Thank you, thank you, thank you! My parents watched your show last night on same sex marriages and have completely changed their minds about attending the ceremony that my partner and I are having next month . . . —(LOCATION UNKNOWN)

At one point during the show, I became very emotional. It was during the wedding cermeony for the two men from New York. When one man's parents walked him down the aisle, I began to cry. If and when I find someone to share my life with, I plan to get married also. I know my parents will do the same for me, and I know I will cry then as well. —ROCHESTER, NY

SHELDON   As I read the E-mail when it arrived in November, it started to sink in. Maybe what Roslyn and I did isn't what everybody would have done. I don't understand how some people can think any other way, because it never would have entered my mind that I would have done anything different. Even if someone's not happy walking down the aisle, how could any parent do anything else? It's an education to me that this simple action is touching to some people:

I was so impressed with the very articulate, caring and so very supportive parents you interviewed from Montreal. I wish and hope that more of our supposed caring nation could understand the quality of love that these parents show toward the son whom they raised and his choice for his future happiness. —LAGUNA BEACH, CA

ANDREW   Believe me, my parents' support is appreciated. After reading E-mails like those, now more than ever.

DOUG   That certainly goes for both of us. By the way, there were a few respondents who weren't quite so flattering. Here's a sampling:

Don't you realize how patently offensive it is to show gays getting "married" in a traditional religious setting? I especially like the con job that the two Jewish men pulled off on the hapless seller of chuppas—nice touch there ABC . . . —(LOCATION UNKNOWN)

You wonder how deep the ABC sewer is . . . Women marrying women. Soon the only people watching television will be perverts and morons. —KALAMAZOO, MI

They are rotten people to the core and they violate God's law. What you should show on TV is how to rehabilitate those assholes; whoever had the brainstorm for this show should consider a lobotomy for themselves. This trash is abhored by God and spoken of in the Bible as an abomination. The parents of those involved are as much to be shamed as those who think they were married in the eyes of God. GIVE GOD EQUAL AIR TIME. —WALDORF, MD

. . . These people are violating all the laws of God and nature. They are extremely sick people. They should be confined to separate areas. They are a burden to society and should be put in hospitals for mental treatment. Those Jewish people ought to be ashamed of themselves. —SOUTHEASTERN PENNSYLVANIA

DOUG We were riveted by what we read, positive, negative, or in between. Many of the specific stories they contained were extraordinarily moving. They illustrated the pain that so many people have experienced. And they put in perspective the rather tame struggle we had all survived.*

Weeks after the show aired, I would come home and find Andrew poking through them. It took over a month for us to go through all of the stacks, and as I found particular letters that I knew would give Sheldon *nachas* (that's Yiddish for joy), I'd fax them to his office.

---

*(Many of these E-mails were so enlightening that we have added an appendix to this story, which contains several of the most remarkable.)

SHELDON   As time passed, and I re-read the E-mail, and heard compliments from friends and acquaintances about how we made things easier and paved the way for many people, including friends of ours who have gay children, of course I was pleased. But I said to Roslyn, "That's all well and good. I'll tell you what, though. If there is one more ceremony like this in one year, then I'll be happy that I did something worthwhile. Never mind a handful, never mind a dozen, just *one* in the Jewish community in Montreal. On half this scale even. Then I would say that I really accomplished something."

ROSLYN   Sheldon said that *more* than once. And I chastised him for it each time. It was a self-defeating, trivial goal. I could never be sure if he was trying to dodge his responsibility, as if to say to his friends, "See, I wasn't part of this 'movement' after all?" Or did he really believe such an arbitrary measure could determine the extent of our contribution? For me, the best measure came a few weeks after *Turning Point* aired. Together with my friend and colleague, Mark, I showed the program to our psychoeducational group. We had a long discussion about it, and when the meeting was almost over, someone asked Mark, "Were you at the wedding?"

And he said, "I sure was. The wedding changed my life."

I was shocked because he never said anything like that to me, even three months after the wedding. I wondered over his comment: Mark's not struggling through Coming Out 101. He's a proud gay man, a social worker, a therapist. He's a leader. *How could that one night have changed his life?*

"Until this wedding, I thought only in terms of the present," he said, answering my unspoken question. "Now I see a future."

CONCLUSION

ROSLYN Remember Sheldon's dare, cast heavenward, that there
be one more wedding, one year from now, and then—only then—
would he believe our efforts had amounted to something in the
broader community? Well, just over a year from Andrew and Doug's
wedding, there was, in fact, another large same-sex wedding in Montreal. And by all accounts, it was marvelous.

ANDREW Remember my butterflies over taking part in a public
display of affection with Doug for our photographer? The last photo
in our wedding album is a full-page, panoramic picture of me plant-
ing a kiss on Doug, in the shade of an enormous elm in a public
park on a busy street in downtown Montreal.

Remember my concerns over Diane's tepid reaction to our engagement and impending nuptials? Doug and I spent our first anniversary together with Diane and her new husband, Steven, at their
splendid wedding in Stowe, Vermont. We were gathered together
with a crowd of Montrealers who'd trekked a hundred miles south

from home. And in front of some of the same community who attended our wedding, Diane made special mention of several family members and friends, including: "My good friends Andrew and Doug, who are celebrating their first anniversary, here with us, this weekend."

DOUG   And remember Roslyn's vacillating over what to call our "thing"? I'm relieved to report that by the time of the big day, our "celebration" was not even a "commitment ceremony" as far as she was concerned.

ROSLYN   It was a wedding. In every sense of the word.

Of course, I couldn't use the word *wedding* for a while. It got stuck in my throat. If *wedding* did pop out, my friends would recoil, because they couldn't see this event as a wedding. And for a while, neither could I. Then, closer to the event, all of a sudden people started using the word *wedding*. So I was very confused. A few friends said, "How are the wedding plans going?"

There's no language for this. There's no context, no framework. So you borrow, mostly from the heterosexual world. Because there's no precedent.

Once it was over, though, there was no question what we had experienced.

SHELDON   Language *is* important. If one of the key goals of gay marriage is providing equal rights for gays and lesbians, then, though I'm not a legislator, I do have some thoughts on how that can be best achieved. It seems to me that the aspect of a gay relationship that is most difficult for people to accept is the sexual aspect, including the means of having sex. This is based on the underlying belief of many that if it can't lead to procreation, to increasing the population, then it can't be correct. I therefore believe that if we change the semantics, it may be helpful. The word *marriage* to many is equivalent to having children, just as *wedding* to many is between man and woman.

Why not use a word other than *marriage* to describe a lifelong commitment between two people of the same sex? Maybe even create a means of establishing this bond or partnership in a *legal* way. Such as signing a commitment to this effect at the appropriate courthouse, automatically creating legal obligations, one toward the other—and conversely, granting them *rights* similar to a heterosexual couple. What words to use, I leave to others. But create legal obligations and grant legal rights—just don't use the same terminology denoting a heterosexual marriage. (If this sounds similar to "separate but equal," as it was applied to the black population, maybe this could be a *beginning*.)

Funny enough, soon after I penned the previous paragraph—the ink practically drying on the page—I picked up that morning's *Montreal Gazette*. The first article I saw carried the following banner headline:

COURT: GAY BENEFITS CAN'T BE 'SEPARATE BUT EQUAL'

The gist of the article: a federal court judge ruled that the federal government must integrate gays and lesbians into benefit programs by changing the definition of *spouse* to encompass same-sex couples. So maybe Canada is more enlightened than the United States in this field!

ANDREW   Reality check: I would love to report that after our wedding, and once *Turning Point* had aired, the sun blazed, birds chirped, and every gay boy and girl lived happily ever after. In our own little cocoon, reading E-mails and seeing the ripple effects in the lives of our friends, it certainly felt like change was in the air. The reality is, of course, much more complicated. The morning after the program aired, I arrived at work wondering what reactions would be from staff who had previously been aloof. I hung around the front desk, engaged in mindless chatter, expecting someone to finally bring it up. Nothing. No one said a word. Finally I asked, "Did you see the show last night? You know, the one my partner and I were part of?" One person said she had taped it, and thought it was "interesting." The other two said they hadn't, and let it drop. Later in the day, one of the nurses with whom I was friendly approached me. I realized I hadn't told her about the show, but asked if she had seen it.

"No, I didn't."

"We taped it. Would you like me to bring you a copy?"

"No." And with that, she abruptly changed the topic.

Through every awkward exchange, I felt a little like I was on a crusade to change opinions, to open minds. Eventually I had to come to terms with the reality that everyone is at different stages of acceptance. And that's something *I* would have to learn to accept.

DOUG   Reality check redux: if our family had a rough emotional ride over the last couple of years, then the society we live in has been on a moral and ethical roller coaster. While we were planning the wedding, the Family Research Institute called homosexuality an addiction that causes an "octopus of infection stretching across the world." Six months before the ceremony, the Vatican's official newspaper said: "Unions of homosexuals are a moral disorder." The paper declared open for "moral censure" the citizen "who, with his choice, favors the election of the candidate who has formally promised to translate into law the homosexual demand." (Thankfully, our Catholic friends seemed to pay no heed and showed up for our big day anyway.) Around the same time, U.S. Reform rabbis voted to support *civil* gay marriage. But most of our Canadian crowd attends Conservative or Orthodox synagogues, so I fear this news didn't make much difference for them. During the same spring, the U.S. Congress passed new immigration laws. The few provisions that once were interpreted to allow gay partners to stay in the U.S. were eliminated. And on May 31, 1996, Representative Henry Hyde of Illinois said, in support of the Defense of Marriage Act: [A same-sex union] "trivializes marriage and demeans it." Such marriages, Hyde continued, "condone public immorality.*

---

*Two years later, Hyde admitted to committing adultery while in his forties. He called the five-year extramarital sexual relationship a "youthful indiscretion."

And less than a month after our nuptials, the "Defense of Marrige Act," championed by Representative Bob Barr of Georgia (twice divorced and thrice married), was signed into law by President Bill Clinton on September 29, 1996.

While we were working on this book, in June 1998, U.S. Senate Majority Leader Trent Lott compared gays and lesbians to alcoholics and sex addicts: "There are all kinds of problems, addictions, difficulties, experiences of things that are wrong, but you should try to work with that person to learn how to control that problem." And the next month, U.S. House Republicans introduced a proposal to deny federal housing money to communities that provide benefits for unmarried domestic partners.

Despite all that transpired here in the states, on the other side of the forty-second parallel, Canada was on a very different path. In May of 1999 (and not long after the federal court decision Sheldon just mentioned), the Supreme Court in Ottawa announced a landmark 8–1 decision, finding that the definition of common-law spouse should also include same-sex couples.

That same month, Andrew and I saw an off-Broadway play that stripped away the politics and moralizing that surrounds most public discussion of same-sex love. "The Most Fabulous Story Ever Told," Paul Rudnick's gay retelling of the Old Testament, was both hilarious and surprisingly poignant, and it had something to unnerve just about everybody. Given what our family had experienced, one scene struck very close to home. Adam asked Steve (or was it Jane talking to Mabel?) why they should want to get married. The answer: Because *we're entitled.*

One of the most stinging criticisms I received from a member of our family (he was talking not about the wedding, but about his impressions of me after reading this book) was that I sounded like I thought I was *"entitled."* It hurt because it was true. Or close to true. This accusation forced me to a self-examination. Perhaps I did feel entitled; or maybe it was something else, something similar, but essentially different. Perhaps he sensed that throughout this processs,

I'd begun to feel empowered. Because even though so much of the political news I was following had been discouraging, the wedding and its aftermath helped me feel involved and enfranchised, part of some natural discussion.

Or, perhaps, I really *did* feel entitled.

Then I wondered, *What's wrong with behaving entitled, as if I deserve the same as anyone else?* It's a tricky matter for gays and lesbians. If we appear entitled, we seem less likable. But if we behave like we're deserving of less, that's exactly what we'll get.

SHELDON   There are many moments I take away with me after this journey. We've talked about most of them in this book. Others were seen on television. Some, though, don't translate well to video or to paper. For instance, the video that was shot at the ceremony, some of it shown on *Turning Point*, the rest of it on our own video, was very nice, but it didn't capture the feeling of the ceremony. The depth of the emotion between Andrew and Doug was so clear, it changed the minds of many people present that day. They could literally see the love they had for each other, in the vows, and in particular when they hugged at the end of the ceremony. Once the glass was broken, and we were outside having cocktails, most everybody said, *"There's nothing so different about this. The basic underlying theme of the whole thing is love, so why are we so concerned?"*

ROSLYN   The day after my daughter, Bonnie, gave birth to her third daughter, Sheldon and I were on the way to the hospital with Bonnie's older children. I said to the oldest, "This is exciting, isn't it?" And she said, "I can't wait to see my baby sister! Oh, Nana, I love babies!" "That's wonderful," I said, encouraging her enthusiasm. She was revved up now: "I'm going to have lots of babies, Nana!" I said, "That's great. I guess you have to grow up, get married, and then you can have lots of babies. And aren't you lucky, you're going to two weddings coming up. Are you excited?" And she said, "Oh, yeah. My Uncle Daniel's wedding." She paused. I said, "Danny and Tiffany, that's right."

Then she asked, "What's the other wedding?" "You're going to Uncle Andrew and Doug's wedding," I answered.

And she said, "Oh, yeah . . ." And then she pondered, her little forehead creased. "But that's funny," she said. "They're two men. How can that be, how can they be having a wedding?" "When two people love each other," I told her, "they get married. Because they want to be together. It could be two men who love each other, or two women, or a man and a woman who love each other."

She was quiet for a moment. And then she declared proudly, giving birth to an idea, "But they can't have babies!" "I think they could," I suggested. Puzzled, she looked at me, and asked, "How?" "They could adopt," I told her. I knew she understood the concept of adoption, because her mother had explained that her Uncle Mitchell is adopted.

Finally, with all the facts, she added it up. Her face registered that a new way of thinking had taken hold. She struck her head with the palm of her hand, as if it were a V-8 commercial, and exclaimed, "Oh Nana, I'm so silly! Why didn't *I* think of that!"

One of the things I vowed when I found out about each of our sons' sexuality was that I would never hide. They would never disappear from my vocabulary. I've seen it far too often: so many parents stop talking about their gay children. Therefore, above all, I hope I can make the world a better place for my gay kids by being visible myself.

So here's a little unsolicited advice to other parents of a gay child: When acquaintances ask, "Does he have a girlfriend?"—or if you have a daughter, "Is she married yet?"—swallow hard if need be, but answer honestly. Remember that the more *out* you are, the less you have to hide, and the easier it becomes for the people asking you the questions, because they don't have to pussyfoot around, and neither do you. Chances are they already know anyway. Gossip travels fast. Don't waste your energy hiding; use it to enjoy your child and to enhance your relationship.

I often hear people say, *But I can't do that. It's too uncomfortable right now.* No matter how long you wait, starting off will never be anything but uncomfortable. The longer you wait, though, the more firmly ingrained the patterns of avoidance become. And the task becomes monumental. You'd be surprised how quickly the discomfort dissipates once you are actively working on your goal. Where is it written that it had to be easy? Worthwhile endeavors usually aren't.

And before you say, "Easy for her to say, she's a social worker. She does this for a living," I've heard that line before, and nothing has proved more frustrating for me. I'd like to clear up this misconception for two reasons. First, because it's hurtful, since it presupposes that I don't have feelings. Second, people with gay children might become intimidated and say to themselves, "Well, I'm not a professional, so I could never do what she did." One can assist others who are dealing with gay and lesbian issues. One can have all the knowledge and know everything related to this field (and I certainly don't profess to know everything), but that doesn't make things easier when you're dealing with your own family member. Knowing the facts is a good starting point, yet it's only an intellectual exercise. It's not easy for anyone, and you can't do it without emotional upheaval. Despite all that, it's well worth the effort.

Here's another good reason to be visible and stay that way: If we think that legislators and governments are going to simply give our kids their rights, it will never happen without our coming forward, standing up for them. We can't expect society to accept gay and lesbian people if we ourselves don't demonstrate that we accept our children. It's absurd. Politicians and policy makers have to see that there are families behind these people. And that gays and lesbians are just as *"normal"* as anybody else. They get up, they brush their teeth, they go to work, they pay their taxes. They fall in love. They get married.

ANDREW And thanks to my parents, we did just that.

Sure, we could have had a wedding without significant emotional and financial backing from either of them. Instead, the greatest gift they gave us was their involvement and support, exemplifying the commitment they both share for their family. For this, and much more, I will always be grateful.

Hopefully, the courage they summoned to stand by me won't be necessary one day. And because of them, I am certain that day will come just a little sooner.

SHELDON So, am I pleased by the whole experience? Frankly, I am not an observant religious person. I can't even answer the obvious question as to whether I believe there is a God. But I do believe people should act and behave *as if* there is a God—a superior being who might keep a ledger sheet of the good deeds and the not-so-good deeds one performs during his or her lifetime. I am very comfortable with the belief that Roslyn and I did the right thing for ourselves, our son, and his partner, and if it influences society even a teeny bit, all the better.

DOUG As Tony Kushner said in the oft-quoted closing of his classic, *Angels in America,* "The world only spins forward. We will be citizens. The time has come." Well, on that one indelible night, we were given a rare and wonderful opportunity. And in that moment the four of us stood together and gave our world an almost imperceptible nudge. Forward.

APPENDIX

ANDREW Reading the E-mails generated by *Turning Point* opened our eyes to several realities, putting the lie to some stereotypes and reinforcing others. For one, geography was often irrelevant. From Orchard, Texas, one woman wrote:

"We can all learn a lesson from the parents and children of the couples on the program . . . Wouldn't the world be a better place if more of us tried to be as unselfish and non-judgemental?

And this, from a woman in Missoula, Montana:

I am a happily married heterosexual—just for the record—and I was delighted to see your story on same sex marriages. People are people regardless of their gender or sexual orientation.

Evans, Georgia, was the source of a particularly moving note:

My two sons (age 19 and 16) told their father and me that they are gay approximately 3 months ago . . . I watched your show with my 16 year old son. It was my first experience actually seeing men hold hands, kiss, etc., and I had hoped that the show would desensitize me, so that I wouldn't go into shock the first time I saw him doing it with a friend. I am so happy to report that it seemed so natural, so caring, and so loving, that I didn't even flinch. That meant a lot to my son, I can tell you! . . . It also let him know that some of our family values (marriage, commitment, long-lasting love) were available to him even with a gay orientation.

When my daughter got married, I made life-size decorations out of twisted paper of a bride and groom. After seeing the program, I wrote my other gay son that I still had enough black twisted paper left to make two grooms for his ceremony, once he found Mr. Right.

DOUG Significantly, about nine-tenths of the thousands of E-mail responses that *Turning Point* received (most of it in the few days following the broadcast) were positive—often in the extreme. The small amount of regular mail (or snail mail, as I learned it's now called) was also largely laudatory, but the margin was narrower, at around two to one. Of the negative E-mail and letters, virtually all share religion as their central theme. And most imply a direct pipeline from God, i.e.:

"God does not believe . . . God does not want . . . Same sex makes God mad." —INDIANAPOLIS

"These associations are abominations to God." —DETROIT

"God did not intend for men to marry men and women to marry women." —BRADY, TX

It's also notable that many respondents who wrote in *praise* also mentioned a higher power. And like those angered by the program, they also see God in their own image:

While I was a Roman Catholic priest I performed many such ceremonies, and I witnessed countless joys during the celebration of these grace-filled sacraments . . . I pray for the day when the State government affirms what is already happening in our nation: committed, loving families blessed in the sight of God. —MANCHESTER, CT

. . . It seems strange that the Bible is used to justify behavior only when it suits that person's opinion. If we are to use the Bible, then we should use each chapter and book according to what is written and not pick out part of a verse what your opinion is and expect everyone else to agree with you. Thank you once again. I am not homosexual but believe that everyone has the God given right to love whomever they wish and no one should sit in judgement of anyone else. That is God's right . . . —(LOCATION UNKNOWN)

ROSLYN As one E-mail said,

"At least the church's failure to accept [same-sex marriage] is based upon religious belief. What's the state's excuse?" —(LOCATION UNKNOWN)

Of course, I've long been aware of the injustices many governments allow to afflict gays and lesbians, yet many of the letters we read put a personal face on issues that are certainly matters of simple human rights. One such E-mail, from Milwaukee, Wisconsin, read:

My partner died last April from AIDS. His wishes were to be cremated as soon as possible after his death. Unfortunately, his body waited a full three days before the crematorium would cremate him. State law requires the legal next of kin to sign off for cremation . . . I fought with the funeral home and the crematorium about having his father (with whom my partner had little to no relationship from the time he was four years old) come to to sign the papers. All this at a time when no one seemed concerned about my partner's wishes . . . and no one seemed concerned about my grieving. Call it marriage, call it union, call it domestic partnership . . . this country needs to recognize serious, committed same-sex relationships and afford those involved the same rights, and responsibilities, as those involved in heterosexual ones.

While the next E-mail from Clinton, Massachusetts, and many others like it, were less dramatic than the previous one, it shows how every gay and lesbian couple is affected by the inequality they face:

My partner, spouse (or whatever euphemism you care to use), and I have been together for almost 10 years . . . We own a home together . . . [e]verything we own is in both of our names, because legally we are not considered "united." If something were to happen to one of us, the other would have to pay inheritance taxes (presently at 55%) on something we have built together over the time we have spent together, and whether that is 10 years or 50 years, the "punishment" is still the same. At the same time, married couples enjoy the benefit of not having to pay inheritance tax—where is the equity in the legalities surrounding whom you choose to build your life with?

DOUG   A few E-mails, like the next one, made a point that occurs to me every time I see a talk show delve into gay subject matter:

. . . My own study of this issue, though limited, has led me to believe that the bible does not actually contain the condemnations so often cited (see, for example, John Boswell's Christianity, Social Tolerance and Homosexuality) and that homosexuality has not been as universally condemned as many people like to believe . . . Yet I repeatedly hear people on television embrace, without even the hint of a challenge, the supposed condemnations of God, custom and history as though they were facts. Just once, I would like some reporter or interviewer to say to these people, "Have you considered the possibility that you might be wrong?" —(LOCATION UNKNOWN)

The problem, of course, is that biblical debate doesn't make for "good TV," so once a bible thumper has called homosexuality an abomination, the talk show host invariably steers the conversation clear of scripture before the opposite view can be aired.

ANDREW   As a Canadian living in the U.S., mail such as the following came as no shock. Yet I suspect they may surprise a few readers:

> . . .We're a gay couple and have been together for seven years . . . I am American and my partner is from [another country] . . . and has a Master's degree in Architecture, yet is unable to work legally in the U.S. He stayed in the U.S. because of me . . . Just last week he went on an interview to an Architecture firm, they hired him on the spot because of his talent, but they did not ask about his visa status, and he was too scared to tell them . . . (He came here legally on a student visa, which has since expired.) If he were a woman, we could marry, he would become a U.S. citizen, work legally and that would be that. But such is not the case. — (LOCATION WITHHELD)

> My lover is a Ph.D. from Brazil who is working in the U.S. on a work permit. Because we cannot legally marry, we will face expensive, drawn-out proceedings to obtain a Green Card so that he can remain in the U.S. There are no guarantees that he will be able to do so. We are faced with the very real prospect that we might be separated by his having to leave the country. If we were man and woman, we could marry and easily obtain a Green Card for him. Members of the extreme right say that we want "Special Rights." All we want are equal rights. — TEXAS

DOUG   As if things weren't bad enough already, both houses of the U.S. Congress voted overwhelmingly for The Defense of Marriage Act, and it was signed by President Bill Clinton on September 29, 1996, only six weeks before the airdate of "Same-Sex Marriage: For Better or Worse." It was on the minds of many respondents:

Sure, I voted for Clinton; I respect his choice of spouse even though he doesn't respect mine. —IOWA CITY, IA

The insanity of these good, loving couples being denied basic civil rights was brought home at the end of the program when Diane Sawyer did a promo for the upcoming episode of *20/20* featuring a story on Rosalie Martinez, a woman who married a convicted rapist and serial killer. I'm sure glad Congress passed and President Clinton signed DOMA. Now convicted murderers, spouse abusers, deadbeat parents, and tax cheats can rest easy that gay couples will never interfere with their enjoyment of the rights and privileges that go with marriage. —TAMPA, FL

ROSLYN Many E-mails also reflect the many layers of the conflict society faces right now. There are several struggles taking place at once: Governments are grappling with whether to bow to anti-gay extremists, the general public is endeavoring to understand what it is that gays and lesbians want, and gays and lesbians themselves are trying to prioritize where to direct their attention and resources.

DOUG You don't hear many, if any, gay leaders positioning same-sex marriage as *the* top item on their agenda, and for good reason. It's not bound to win any time soon, and it's only one of many important issues facing gays and lesbians. And yet, after all we've been through, I have a vested interest in seeing that change happen someday, and that change certainly won't happen unless many gays and lesbians decide it's an important issue—though not necessarily the only issue— to them. So seeing E-mails like the next one thrilled me:

As a gay man who has always been rather cynical about gay people trying to emulate a straight ritual (and one that, let's face it, bears a huge responsibility for the way women have been kept down through the years) it did my heart good to see these gay couples deeply committed to one another and joyfully embracing the ceremony, each other and yes, even the clichés of modern marriage. It brought tears to my eyes. My mind has been changed. I now say more power to them! —CINCINNATI

DOUG We didn't decide to get married to make any kind of political statement. But once we decided to do it, I felt if we did back out it would be on one level, a political defeat for gays and lesbians in general. And letters like the next two gave me great fulfillment, knowing that sticking with our plans helped us become part of something bigger than any one of us:

. . .I am the mother of a 34 year old homosexual. He is the oldest of my 3 sons and the only one that is gay . . . When he told me, I opened my arms to him and embraced him and we cried together. . . . I cried watching your show tonight, my tears were happy tears, for all 4 couples who seemed truly happy and content, and sad tears, for my son who hasn't found that total peace within himself yet. I love my son from the bottom of my heart and will never give up hope that someday our society will learn to accept homosexuals and realize that they are truly wonderful, intelligent, giving, caring, and loving human beings. Perhaps when that happens, my son will feel comfortable enough to truly come out of the closet and find the true happiness that he deserves . . . —TRENTON, N.J

ROSLYN Being gay and wanting to get married is such a daunting prospect it's not surprising that many gay people can't envision themselves doing so. According to much of the E-mail, *Turning Point* often evoked tears of either sadness or joy. Some gay people may have seen themselves as inadequate, or lesser human beings than heterosexuals (the thought may have even been only subconscious) and therefore not deserving of the honor of being in the spotlight at their own wedding.

Some of the tears were surely shed because of feelings of rejection experienced by gay children because their parents had refused to participate in a celebration of their union with their partner who they wanted to commit to for life. And still others may cry for the family that rejected them completely on finding out they were gay. This is a scenario I've seen so often in working with parents of gay and lesbian children. If the *Turning Point* program and our support of our son, including hosting his wedding, helped one gay person to communicate more directly with their family, and fight for inclusion—resolving not to settle for, "Oh, so you're gay . . . Thank you for sharing that with us, and please pass the ketchup," then all the effort we each expended will have been more than worthwhile.

This last E-mail was both unusual and unusually inspiring. Written in the core of the heartland, it shows the depth of compassion and the expanding boundaries of understanding and acceptance you can find in the most unexpected places:

I am a gay man living in [the Midwest] who has been married to a woman for [many] years. While we are separating soon, my wife and I and our son have a very strong and loving bond and even after we are no longer together, we intend to remain the closest of friends. Eventually I hope to be able to have a "husband" of my own, and my wife, son, parents and siblings all are very supportive of me in this . . . We are a family. We are a good, Christian loving family who realizes that while gays are perhaps not the norm, we can be and are by and large loving, caring people who have the same needs as anyone else. My [young] son watched the program with me and he was also filled with a sense of joy for the couples portrayed. He and I talked a bit and he let me know that when the time came for me to join with a spouse of my own, that he would stand with me in pride and share in my happiness. My parents have intimated that they too would be happy to share such an event with me. Again, thank you for showing what is good in people. I salute you, your entire staff, your producers . . . thanks also to the gay couples and their families for sharing their happiness with the rest of us and bringing a bright ray of hope to the gay community at large.